MANAGING
BEHAVIOUR
PROBLEMS

Diane Montgomery

Hodder & Stoughton

A MEMBER OF THE HODDER HEADLINE GROUP

British Library Cataloguing in Publication Data

Montgomery, Diane
Managing behaviour problems
Treatment
1. Title
371.8′1

ISBN 0 340 40832 4

First published 1989
Impression number 13 12 11 10 9 8 7 6 5 4
Year 1999 1998 1997 1996 1995 1994

Printed in Great Britain for Hodder & Stoughton Educational, a
division of Hodder Headline Plc, 338 Euston Road, London NW1
3BH by Athenæum Press Ltd, Newcastle upon Tyne.

Contents

Glossary vi

Introduction 1

1 Defining Behaviour Problems 3
2 The Teacher as Classroom Manager 16
3 Social and Cognitive Factors in Behaviour Disturbances 28
4 Emotional Origins of Behaviour Problems 42
5 Key Researches for Dealing with Disruption 57
6 Implementing a Behaviour Management Scheme 73
7 How to Identify and Record Behaviour Problems 79
8 Intervention Principles and Practices 89
9 Class Control and Organisation 111
10 Task Management 131

Appendix 1: Case Studies 145
Appendix 2: Analysing Handwriting Errors 159
Appendix 3: Remediating Spelling Problems 160
Bibliography 162
Index 167

To the six-toed person

Acknowledgments

Thank you to all the pupils on whom I practised, the teachers who offered their advice and their case studies and the researchers whose work I have drawn upon. An especial thank you to Jo Foweraker for her most helpful editorial comments.

Glossary

ABA	Applied behaviour analysis
BATPACK	Behavioural approach to teaching pack
BC	Behaviour contract
CBG	Catch them being good
EBD	Emotional and behavioural difficulties
GSR	Galvanic skin responses
HOC	Hindering other children
IPR	Inhibition and positive reinforcement
3Ms	Management, monitoring and maintenance
MPR	Modelling and positive reinforcement
PAD	Preventive approaches to disruption
PAL	Positive attitude to learning
PAT	Positive attitude to teaching
PCI	Positive cognitive interventions
RSPR	Role shift and positive reinforcement
SNAP	Special needs action programme
SPA	Supportive positive attitude
TA	Transactional analysis
TIPS	Teacher information packs
TO	Time out
TOOT	Talking out of turn

Introduction

This book has been written for teachers who are concerned about the seeming increase in the number of behaviour problems of their pupils, and is intended to be a practical guide and handbook to managing and controlling these problems. This guidance extends to ways of working and talking with parents to help support classroom work and improve behaviour generally. It also involves strategies for analysing points at which lessons begin to break down and provides suggestions for changes in lesson planning and tactics which will overcome these problems. It is not intended to be a complete behaviour management programme, but some of the material could be used in this way.

The suggestions for intervention and change are all linked to a particular theory and practice of teaching, so that teachers can not only learn and use the techniques detailed here, but also move on to design their own versions, adapted to their own individual needs. Each technique presented is based upon extensive trials and evaluations by the teachers who attended in-service courses at Kingston Polytechnic, Faculty of Education, or those run by the author across the country.

In addition to a theory and practice of teaching, research has been combed to try to determine useful links between causation, manifestation and behaviour management in classrooms. The strategies found to be successful in the research have similarly been validated in field trials. These techniques have also been validated through the Kingston Polytechnic Learning Difficulties Project on Teacher Appraisal. A system of classroom observation and enhancement has been devised and successfully tested over many years. In this Project teachers experiencing serious difficulty in classrooms have been helped to reach competent and good levels of teaching performance. This system embodies the classroom management principles expanded in this book and is detailed to help coordinators for special needs, support teachers, professional tutors and other senior teaching staff who may be involved in helping other teachers become more effective.

This book is written by a teacher, now teacher trainer, who was once a problem pupil, to help teachers in ordinary schools to understand and deal with those 'nuisances' in their classrooms. It presents

1

a selective review of the literature citing sources which have been helpful in understanding difficulties and devising intervention strategies for use in classrooms and offers a 'bottom-up' approach, viewing interpersonal skills and task relationships as key areas for promoting change. The fundamental focus of attention is teacher attitude. For useful recent reviews of the literature readers should refer to Reid (1986) and Galloway and Goodwin (1987).

1

Defining Behaviour Problems

INTRODUCTION

Parents often complain affectionately about their pre-school children's naughtiness and say that they are 'unmanageable'. This is seldom really true. It is rare to find young children totally beyond their parents' control although the same cannot be said of adolescents. One reason put forward for this by Donaldson (1978) is that parents and teachers of young children tend to be more understanding or more tolerant of their misbehaviour. The misbehaviours and aggression of a small child can be viewed as less provoking and frightening than the same behaviours in a six foot youth in whom they might be considered unexpected for the age group and socially unacceptable. The same child may misbehave with one parent, or one teacher and not with another. Schools may also exert influences and pressures which can predispose to or protect certain children who are at risk from becoming problematic.

In a sense, schools and classrooms are unnatural places in which to keep young people as Booth (1982) pointed out. They are confined there when they are at their most active and it is not surprising that on occasions they 'misbehave'. In fact, if children have any spirit in them, teachers should expect them to misbehave and test out rules and regulations. Most children misbehave at some time or another and this misbehaviour cannot be considered as problem behaviour if it is an isolated event. Pupils' misbehaviours create problems for teachers and themselves when they begin to occur frequently and pervade many areas of activity. These misbehaviours then begin to cause suffering and concern to others and often the pupils themselves.

As pupils move into and through schools certain individuals come to be regarded by particular teachers or the school as having behaviour problems or being disruptive. It is usual for pupils to be regarded as the owners of such problems and for discipline and correction to be directed towards them. Although this is not an entirely surprising response on the part of the teacher, it will be seen in later chapters that an analysis of the origins of the problem can lead to quite different interventions with more success than if the pupil or the behaviour is directly approached.

3

Figure 1   *Sources and interacting factors relevant to behaviour problems in schools*

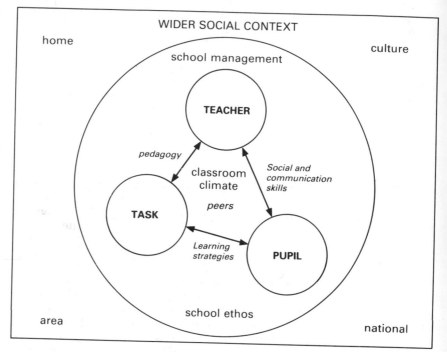

In any learning and behaviour network there are three primary sources, several secondary ones and many ways in which they may interact to provoke an adverse response from particular pupils.

The nature of these interactions will be explored in later sections and a range of different strategies will be discussed to show how behaviour problems of various kinds can be dealt with effectively.

An illustration of the interactions and intervention from the model in Figure 1 might be as follows:

> The teacher is reading from a book to the class of pupils. As she proceeds several of the pupils begin to shuffle and talk to each other quietly. One boy begins to flick paper pellets. The teacher begins to notice the restlessness and looks up. What happens next . . .

This is a typical minor problem scene, but in one teacher's hands it can build to disruption and major confrontation whilst in another's it will recede as quietly as it came. It is likely that the teacher will pause in reading, look pointedly at the talkers, frown at the pellet flicker and resume reading. After a short while the restlessness begins again and the same scene is played until the teacher becomes upset by these interruptions and speaks crossly to her annoyers, snaps the book shut and gives out the paper. The introduction to the next section of the lesson is thus curtailed and some of the children will find it difficult to proceed without individual help, especially those who were not listening, and more inattention and behaviour problems are likely to ensue. Another teacher might at the first instance have reprimanded the 'miscreants' sharply before resuming reading. Sharp public rebukes often

Figure 2   *The main direction of the teacher's attention in the presence of behavioural difficulties*

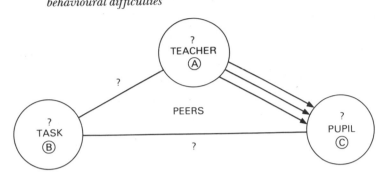

offend and cause an emotional response, after which the pupil attends even less and complains to peers or sulks. This can lead to them seeking opportunities to wreak vengeance throughout the rest of the session.

In each of these cases the teacher ultimately focuses attention on the pupil as the source of the problem which must be tackled. The first teacher's strategy to pause, look and frown was good and temporarily effective but a resumption of noise should clue her to other likely origins of the problem. The text (task variable) may have been *too difficult, too distant* from the pupils' experience or *too dull*. On the other hand her interpretation or reading of it may not have provoked their interest. She may have failed to give it immediacy and audience effect, (teacher variables). If minor inattention persists this is a strong clue that these other situational variables should be considered. Figure 2 illustrates a teacher focusing all attention on the pupil and the problem behaviour (C). However, might the teacher's attitude and explanation (A) be at fault? Was the task set (B) too complex or too easy or did the pupil perceive the question incorrectly? Attention to these variables could prevent the lesson deteriorating as in the example given. However, it is not so easy to switch this attention. It is common to 'treat' the major 'symptom' or the response rather than the 'cause' if we use a medical model. In psychological terms it is common to find us projecting blame for situations upon others rather than upon ourselves.

THE NATURE OF BEHAVIOUR PROBLEMS

One of the main difficulties in defining behaviour problems is that they are *socially disapproved* behaviours and what one person classes as bad behaviour, another might not, hence value judgments are involved. Galloway and Goodwin (1987) suggest that many pupils with behaviour problems have poor social skills. When they engage in socially disapproved behaviour they have insufficient social skills to negotiate themselves out of the trouble this creates, and so this group can easily become labelled as 'disruptive' and 'beyond control'. However, not all teachers' social skills are highly developed and they, too, can become vulnerable as they provoke pupils to further excess.

Some teachers regard much misbehaviour as 'delinquent' but it is wise to avoid this term because it has a specific legal connotation. Delinquent acts are those such as stealing, truancy, arson and vandalism. They were 10:1 more common in boys, according to West (1967), but girls are increasingly to be found engaging in them. To these problems we can now also add drug abuse, but legal sanctions do not apply as yet to solvent abuse. There is no clear-cut psychological distinction between delinquent and non-delinquent behaviour – the difference is a *legal* one. The 'delinquent' is a young person who has been caught and convicted and the term tends to be used in criminology studies rather than in education where it was historically used. The term 'maladjustment' became common for those pupils whose behavioural and emotional problems were so severe as to warrent some form of special provision being made or special schooling. The Underwood Report (1955) was directed entirely to studying the nature of maladjustment and the provision required for such individuals.

In 1955 the Underwood Committee, in presenting its findings, defined the maladjusted child as follows:

> A child may be regarded as maladjusted who is developing in ways that have a bad effect upon himself or his fellows and cannot without help be remedied by his parents, teachers or other adults in ordinary contact with him. It is characteristic of maladjusted children that they are insecure and unhappy and that they fail in their personal relationships.

From this definition it can be seen that the maladjusted child was one who, for whatever reason, could not cope with all or major aspects of his/her life. He/she did not respond to normal discipline in the classroom, participate in classroom routines like most other children, accept affection and concern from the teacher or his/her peers, and was likely to over- or under-respond to normal criticism or blame. Gulliford (1971) described the maladjusted child as behaving more like a younger child in the severity and persistence of his/her symptoms and compared with other children.

The Association of Workers with Maladjusted Children (AWMC, 1984), like others in social services, were still using the old terms. They defined maladjustment as:

> We take maladjusted to include emotionally disturbed, meaning by this last term those children whose fears, guilt, hatred, aggression – and the anxieties caused either by the strength of these emotions or of their effect on others – overwhelm their resources so that their behaviour presents teachers and others with difficult tasks in understanding them and managing them. We also take emotionally disturbed to indicate the presence of intra personal and inter personal conflict which has delayed or prevented children from successfully resolving the psychological and social tasks of maturation and development.

The AWMC perceived 'socially maladjusted' children as:

> ... those who, although they may have suffered deprivations and lack of adequate nurturing experiences, have personalities which are more 'intact' than emotionally disturbed children. They have not been so adversely affected by their experiences.

The AWMC thought that this group were more likely to benefit from rehabilitation programmes in ordinary schools and suggested that severely emotionally disturbed children needed a therapeutic education and stable life style which could be provided in residential schooling. The moves towards integration, the scarcity of resources for residential placement, falling school rolls and community welfare programmes have meant that there has been a tendency to keep families together and to support their members in the community. This has reduced the numbers referred to residential schools (ACE, 1982).

The publication of the Warnock Report (DES, 1978) and the implementation of the 1981 Education Act in April 1983 created major changes in direction in this field. An attempt was made to remove the stigmatising nature of some of these labels and their medical connotations. Pupils' special needs were to be identified and the terms which referred to them were to be made to reflect the pupils' main *educational needs* where possible. The term 'emotional and behavioural difficulties' (EBD) replaced 'maladjusted'. It was always true that there were many pupils with emotional and behavioural difficulties who never posed such severe problems that they needed to be placed in special units or schools. Now these umbrella terms can include the whole range of difficulties without necessarily labelling and stigmatising. Those with transitory problems and difficulties can also be included and may be given temporary support without the damning and seemingly permanent and hopeless condition of 'Malad' being attached to them. Although the 1981 Education Act and the climate of the time encouraged the integration of all pupils into mainstream schools, what seems to have happened is that the special schools for children with moderate learning difficulties which were being emptied, were being refilled with pupils with emotional and behavioural difficulties or more special units were being attached to schools. Referrals were also being delayed wherever possible until the end of infant schooling. This policy also needs to be questioned because it may not be one which meets the real needs of the disturbed pupil or classroom peers. Peers may vicariously learn how to undermine teachers and the school system.

Lisa is an example of an emotionally disturbed little girl for whom the class teacher could obtain no special help and support from the LEA. By the time she reaches the age of eight she could be very disturbed and could create distress and disturbance in any classroom or school. The following report was written by her class teacher:

Lisa   Age 5 years 6 months
            Only child of single parent family. Mother an alcoholic.

Lisa will only settle to a task if she is given continuous individual attention. In story time or in any group or class activity, she roves round the room disrupting other children, singing and shouting and making a general noise. She exhibits severe attention-seeking behaviours.

Using the strategies outlined later in this book the class teacher was able to help Lisa overcome enough of her difficulties to settle her down to learn. Early help and support for teachers in this situation is essential if children are to be helped. Waiting for statements of special need to obtain support or special resources can take up to two years, by which time intervention can have become extremely costly.

Warnock's position on special schooling was:

... we are entirely convinced that special schools will continue to be needed particularly for ... those with severe emotional or behavioural disorders who have difficulty forming relationships with others or whose behaviour is so extreme or unpredictable that it causes severe disruption in an ordinary school or inhibits the emotional progress of other children. (para. 6.10)

The report did not specify day school, unit or residential placement, but stressed that the needs of the child were paramount and should determine the provision.

Determining the best ways in which to meet the needs of pupils with emotional and behavioural difficulties presents a complex picture. Early intervention and support would seem to be essential, but this should be provided for both 'acting out' and withdrawn pupils. Where single problems develop these can often be resolved by the child but a significant number of children identified as emotionally handicapped are not likely to resolve their adjustment problems without help.

Where and how this help can be provided is still a much debated set of issues. The AWMC (1984), for example, argued that many of the most seriously disturbed and deprived children were not the most disruptive, but still needed very special placement. These were often the pupils most likely to be retained in ordinary schools because LEAs tended to seek places for 'acting out' pupils, particularly those who had only a year or two of their school careers to run. At this stage the AWMC reported that it was difficult for schools to provide meaningful and appropriate experiences because these pupils had suffered many years of failure.

Most behaviour problems exhibited by pupils can be catered for in the ordinary school, provided teachers are supported in their efforts with in-service training and help from the LEA and in-school support services. This help should enable them to identify pupils' needs and assess the forms of intervention which might be appropriate, as well as to help them evaluate and redevelop these interventions as this becomes necessary.

The HMI (1986) in *The New Teacher in School* reported on research with probationers showing the issues or problems which were of most concern to them as follows:

1   Class management and discipline.
2   Building good relationships with pupils.
3   Teaching mixed-ability groups.
4   Using unfamiliar equipment and aids.
5   Becoming familiar with pupils' social background.
6   Conditions of work.
7   Personal problems: housing, finance, etc.
8   The functioning of in-school decision-making machinery.
9   Augmenting own knowledge in a curriculum subject.
10 The probationary year assessment.

As can be seen, the probationers' first three major concerns are central to the concerns of this book. When we asked experienced teachers on school-based training days and in-service courses what issues were of most concern to them, they too consistently referred to:

- discipline;
- mixed-ability teaching; *as well as*
- keeping up to date;
- communications.

When teachers came on in-service training courses on behaviour problems and were asked to list the behaviour problems they were concerned about, if any, they gave the following in order of priority:

- attention-seeking;
- disruption;

- short concentration span;
- aggression;
- negativism, disinterest and lack of motivation to work.

The same list was given by many hundreds of teachers in a wide range of LEAs whether they came from nursery, primary or secondary schools.

Attention-seeking and disruption always featured very strongly in the vast majority of their lists, and in their discussions about classroom problems. In descriptions it became clear that disruptive behaviour was also often a form of attention-seeking. At junior school level Croll and Moses (1985) found that teachers classified about two children in a class as having behaviour problems. Only one of the two was usually regarded as disruptive.

Disruptive behaviour was defined by the DES (1979) as '... that which interferes with the learning and opportunities of other pupils and imposes undue stress upon the teacher'.

Behaviour problems which are disruptive seem to include attention-seeking, continuous talking and muttering, making annoying noises, lack of attention, poor concentration, distractibility, shouting out, wandering about, snatching other pupils' property, annoying and distracting other pupils or the teacher, provoking each other by name-calling and unpleasant comments, lack of interest and motivation to work. Although each of these behaviours may be trivial, when they become persistent it is very tiring for the teacher to have to manage them day after day. Other children may also join in with the misbehaviour making the teacher's task more difficult and at times the situation can get out of control. In some classrooms there are no behaviour problems reported; in most, one or two; in some, a handful of children are a continuous nuisance; and in a few classes the teachers report that *all* the pupils are problematic. Although most teachers manage to cope with these difficulties it is as pupils move into the fourth and fifth years of secondary schooling that many more seem to grow disaffected and disruptive (Reid, 1986). This is especially true of the lower attainers in secondary schools and Hargreaves (1984) suggests that this is a product of, for them, an over-academic curriculum and too rigid disciplining techniques. At this level according to the HMI Survey (1988) the successful teachers become more negotiational in their dealings with pupils. HMI saw very few disrupted lessons despite media attention to what is said to be a worsening state of discipline in our schools. This recent survey was based upon the observations of over 15 000 lessons.

In the Kingston Polytechnic Learning Difficulties Project (1984) the less frequently mentioned problems were: swearing, lying, cheating, damaging other pupils' property and work, withdrawal, daydreaming, fire setting, 'bunging up' the lavatories, flooding the sink area, tale-telling, and overt sexual behaviour. Even less frequently mentioned were: glue-sniffing, smoking, drug-taking, alcohol drinking, truancy, although some of these represent considerable problems in the local area.

Within each classroom, school and area there will be different patterns of problem behaviour, but the behaviours which are of the most concern to teachers are naturally the ones which disturb the purpose of their position. Truancy, for example, removes a learner from the presence of the teacher and so teaching processes with other pupils are not interrupted. Similarly, glue-sniffing, drug-taking and smoking take place mostly out of sight and out of lessons, although their effects may be brought back into them. The smell and effects of alcohol may often be noticed at morning registration in tutorial time, as may the effects of glue-sniffing and drug-taking if the pupils actually return to school afterwards, or in the first session after lunch. A careful watch should be kept on those pupils who hang around near the school gates or the outer fence and who make contact with unknown adults during break times or on leaving school. Secluded areas of the school premises attract smokers, drug abusers and alcohol dependents, together with selected spectators and hangers-on.

WHAT THEN CONSTITUTES A CLASSROOM BEHAVIOUR PROBLEM?

Any kind of behaviour which prevents the teacher from teaching and the learner from learning could be classed a behaviour problem. Teachers will tend to centre on those problems which interrupt them and their teaching, but we shall also include those which prevent the pupil from learning because, in the end, they will hamper the teaching process. Behaviour problems also need to be considered from the pupils' point of view. Such problems would include boredom, fear of failure, alienation, and peer oppression. Signs of these should also suggest to the teacher that there is something more than a behaviour problem to correct or a pupil to discipline. Each of them can, in difficult or provoking circumstances, be the precursor to more serious disruptive behaviours. West's (1982) longitudinal research showed that individuals who had been committed for violent and aggressive offences showed a history of minor infringements and misdemeanours, many of them at school. Good management of behaviour problems can protect many such individuals from further difficulties but too often the school response is aversive and a rift develops with opposing positions being taken. When this occurs, schools can mobilise against the 'offender' and reject the individual, either referring him/her for special education, or by suspending and transferring the pupil.

Boredom, fear of failure and alienation also need to be seen as potential causes of *displacement activities* such as attention-seeking and disruption, rather than some children necessarily having an innate predisposition to be a nuisance to teachers. Patterns of behaviour problems will vary from mild – temporarily snatching other pupils' property, to severe – biting beating or stabbing other children, from writing furtively on desks, to spraying offensive graffitti on the school walls. Most children will, at some time, exhibit some form of behaviour problem in their school career but it is usual for teachers and those concerned with education to focus upon the 'acting out' of types of behaviour problems, for these bring themselves to our attention and interfere with the schooling process.

There are, however, a whole sphere of behaviour problems which are, in the long-term, likely to be more serious for the individual (Freud 1958) because they can lead to mental health problems which consist of *withdrawal* behaviours. The pupil becomes subdued, dreamy, apathetic, uninvolved, may be fearful and goes quietly unnoticed. Children have two main responses to emotional distress such as child abuse, anxiety and fear of failure, and these are to 'act out' their emotional distress or to withdraw, becoming subdued and depressed. Thus, a classroom behaviour problem can have an origin in the social context outside school. It may also arise from bullying, harrassment and oppression from peers or teachers within school and it may arise in response to the curriculum task.

THE LINKS BETWEEN LEARNING DIFFICULTIES AND BEHAVIOUR PROBLEMS

Most children in the pre-school years do not show any marked signs of learning difficulties; they mature at different rates. It is only when children enter school that they are found to have learning difficulties. According to Holt (1969) and Donaldson (1978) most pupils in primary schools do well initially and seem eager, lively and happy. Others have shown that the seeds of failure and disruption have already been sown (Laslett 1977, Galloway and Goodwin 1987) and begin to grow as the pupils progress through the age ranges. By the time these pupils reach adolescence the promise of their early years has remained unfulfilled and schools are finding them difficult to manage.

Learning difficulties and behaviour problems seem to become inextricably linked, such that sometimes the term 'remedial' is seen as a synonym for 'disruptive' (Laslett 1985; ACE 1981). In their survey of special needs in junior schools, Croll and Moses (1985) found that teachers regarded four to five pupils in their classes as having learning problems of some kind. Nearly one-third of the children nominated by teachers as having special needs, had both learning and behaviour problems. Two-thirds of the pupils with behaviour problems were described by their teachers as having learning difficulties and a quarter of them had physical or sensory difficulties. Only one-quarter of the children with behaviour problems were seen as having this as their only problem. The group with learning difficulties mainly consisted of children with reading problems, with teachers finding it difficult to distinguish those who were *poor readers* and *slow learners*, from those who were able pupils with reading difficulties, that is, the children with specific learning difficulties.

Booth (1982) suggested that the very structure of our society demands that some children must be regarded as failures. This failure, he argues, is socially defined because we compare one child's performance with another against proposed external standards. As these standards are based upon norms of achievement, by definition, 50 per cent will appear below the mean and 50 per cent above it. Of those below the mean, some 16 per cent at the bottom end are usually regarded as having failed outright. In past decades, measured against the standards of an IQ test, this 16 per cent with an IQ below 85 would be regarded as slow learners and the bottom 2 per cent candidates for special schooling. If they also had severe learning difficulties in the basic skills of reading and writing or had behaviour problems in class, then their referral was almost certain. Since the publication of the Warnock Report (1978) and the implementation of the 1981 Education Act, policies and practices have changed so that it is much more likely that children with learning difficulties will be integrated and maintained in ordinary schools. If teachers teach to the tests, and have an extensive set of syllabuses to cover under the *National Curriculum 5-16* (DES, 1987) and the terms of the 1988 Education Act, it is likely that more children will become at risk from failure in the ordinary school and there could be pressure to rescind the integration policies in LEAs. Integration is important to these pupils because according to Brennan (1979) and Wilson and Evans (1980) they may receive a narrow and limiting curriculum which keeps them in special education and disadvantages them in the world of work after school. Croll and Moses (1985) also found that a few of the disruptive pupils were regarded as having no behavioural or emotional problems. It would have been most interesting if these cases had been probed in depth. They found that boys were twice as frequently included in all problem groups as girls, except for English as a Second Language (ESL) problems, in which there was roughly equal representation. Boys were nearly four times as likely to have discipline problems as girls. This is in comparsion with the ratio of 10:1 suggested by West (1967). West Indian boys were more than twice as likely to be regarded as having discipline and behaviour problems than white or Asian peers. Asian boys were slightly less likely to be recorded as having behaviour problems than white peers.

From these researches and those of Chazan (1964), Glavin and Annesley (1971) and Stott (1981) there would appear to be a strong correlation between behaviour problems and learning difficulties, although the relationship is not always precisely defined. For example, behaviour problems can result in lack of time on the learning task and so lead to failure. The emotional origins of some behaviour problems may result in 'mind time' spent on one's own troubles, excluding opportunities for learning. Learning difficulties and fear of failure can cause frustration and anxiety resulting in the rejection of school work and the erection of defence mechanisms against the likelihood of further failure and lack of self-esteem – an ego defence mechanism.

The Scottish Education Department, (SED, 1978), published a Survey of Scottish schools in which a startling 50 per cent of pupils were found to have learning difficulties of some kind. Only $1\frac{1}{2}$ per cent of the pupils with learning difficulties had problems with basic skills requiring specialist remedial help; the rest had difficulties in:

- understanding concepts and specialist terminology;
- using or being taught study skills;
- using higher order reading skills; and
- catching up on work missed because no one told them how to catch up.

The inspectors found that some, but by no means all, of the difficulties were accounted for by:

- frequent absence from school;
- too many different teachers in the same subject areas; and
- a lack of pacing and reinforcement in teaching methods.

The main causes of the learning difficulties were attributed to two factors:

- an inappropriate curriculum and
- an inadequate pedagogy.

The position would not appear to be significantly different in England and Wales in the 1980s. The recent HMI Survey of Secondary Schools (1988) reported that things were little improved since 1979 for lower attainers. There was still too much didactic teaching, too much copying and writing of notes and not enough emphasis upon oral learning and practical methods of teaching.

Schools across the country would seem to be poor at supporting the learning of their lower attainers and primary schools are no better in this, although they tend to be more understanding and give such pupils extra individual help. Primary pupils also obtain help from peers as they are more likely to be seated in groups and the pace is more leisurely allowing for different rates of progression. The content is less likely to be of the formal academic kind from which only the linguistically able can profit.

BEHAVIOUR PROBLEMS AND SPECIFIC LEARNING DIFFICULTIES

Although children with behaviour problems may, in addition, develop learning problems because of their lack of time on task over years of misbehaviour, some develop behaviour problems *secondary* to a specific learning difficulty which has not been diagnosed and taken into account. Rutter, Tizard and Whitmore (1970) found that:

- a third of boys referred for behaviour problems had specific reading difficulties;
- many showed serious educational backwardness;
- their IQ was usually in the normal range but, if it was lower than average, this was associated with an increased likelihood of aggression, antisocial or delinquent behaviour;
- the ethos of certain schools and styles of teaching and discipline may predispose to or protect certain children from conduct disorders. They said that 'the influences are, however, poorly understood'.

The findings from case studies and surveys carried out in the Kingston Polytechnic Learning Difficulties Project show that one of the major sources of learning failure predisposing to behaviour problems is in pupils who have difficulty in learning to write and, at a later stage, difficulty in writing neatly enough for their teachers. Their work is constantly marked as 'untidy' and 'careless' and they are continuously asked to rewrite work, take more care, and improve their writing without being told how to help themselves. Such pupils have a handwriting coordination problem which, without intervention, causes them to become frustrated and angry. They are then prone either to withdraw and silently cease to be noticed or to do nothing unless directly spoken to or watched.

Others use a number of strategies to avoid writing in any form, for example, losing books and pencils, continuously breaking and sharpening pencils, ignoring instructions and talking to others, and those who cause a distracting commotion or displace the teacher's attention on some other activity. Some able pupils use a cognitive strategy, they 'red herring' the teacher with interesting side issues and questions, or encourage or reinforce disgression into more conversational episodes and avenues, leaving little time for writing. These pupils' strategies may be summarised as: withdraw, avoid, distract, evade, digress, disrupt.

Moses (1982) confirmed this in relation to pupils with *general* learning difficulties finding a 'slow learner behaviour pattern' characterised by children spending higher amounts of time fidgeting, tapping the desk with their feet, fiddling with pencils and rulers, swinging about on chairs and similar off-task behaviours.

In most classrooms there will be four or five pupils who have untidy writing which, under pressure or over time on task, begins to disintegrate in form and style. In addition, where print script or italic writing has been taught, at least half of the pupils will be found to be handicapped by the writing task. We have found that when attention has to be diverted from the meaning of the writing to attend to its execution, the content becomes mundane and the spelling errors increase. In these cases, early identification of difficulties is essential and training in a flowing cursive hand will quickly help to overcome the problem. This can be undertaken within the class by the class teacher trained to identify the difficulties and willing to teach cursive. Coincidentally, the teacher will find an improvement in time on task, in behaviour, motivation and attitude to school. If other teachers notice the improvement too, and compliment the pupil, behaviour in their lessons will also improve. See Appendix 2 (p. 159) for some useful points on analysing errors in handwriting.

A similar situation will exist in relation to spelling problems, whether or not they are combined with writing difficulties. Peters and Smith (1986) concluded from their studies that whilst pupils coming to secondary school had had attention and remediation directed towards their reading, the same could not be said of spelling. In primary schools a teacher had always been on hand to help children with their spellings and to give them any which they found too difficult. In secondary schools, as HMI have reported, there is an over-emphasis upon writing and note-making which the lower attainers in particular, and some very able pupils with specific learning difficulties, cannot manage and so never demonstrate their real talents or grasp of issues. The major specific learning difficulties and resultant secondary behaviour problems in both primary and secondary schools frequently arise from unrecognised difficulties in spelling and writing. These may occur with or without reading difficulties. It is rare to find pupils with severe reading difficulties who do not also have even more severe spelling difficulties. See Appendix 3, (p.160) for approaches to remediating spelling problems. Some pupils, in addition, have handwriting coordinatinon difficulties or complex specific learning difficulties. The main patterns of specific learning difficulty are:

- reading and spelling difficulties;
- spelling difficulties;
- handwriting difficulties;
- reading, spelling and handwriting difficulties;
- spelling and handwriting difficulties;
- number difficulties;
- reading, spelling and number difficulties etc.

Specific difficulties in music, art and spatial areas are more likely to be condoned in schools because of our emphasis in them upon left hemisphere language-related activities (Ornstein, 1977; Hemming, 1988).

Some typical responses of distressed children with learning difficulties, or, as in Clare's case, 'fear of failure', are:

Reception class pupil 'Continuous wandering and never actually doing anything.'
Junior school teacher writing notes on a nine-year-old boy 'Restlessness, touching other children, picking nose, crawling under desks, etc., dropping things, thus providing excuses to grope around, rocking a chair, laughing quietly at nothing in particular, staring at neighbours until their attention is obtained, moving furniture about, losing worksheets or destroying them, humming, banging under desk with feet.'
Middle school pupil 'Always talking and out of his seat.'
Secondary school fourth-year pupil 'Clare suddenly started to become a problem in class. She talked almost continuously. At first it was muttering and asides. She just couldn't seem to stop herself and no threats, promises, understanding, help with work stopped her for long. When she was placed alone at the side of the room she talked to herself and took every opportunity to move about the room on any excuse. She became so noisy and irritating that other pupils and her

teachers became utterly frustrated. When she began to absent herself from school everyone was relieved to have peace and quiet again. She was quite an able pupil producing work of a good standard when suddenly it completely deteriorated and then she produced none at all.'

SUMMARY

There are a range of emotional and behavioural difficulties to be found in school children but there is not a simple formula for defining a behavioural or emotional difficulty. These difficulties tend to be relative and socially defined. There are no simple causal relationships to be found for difficult behaviours; there seems to be a set of interrelated factors which can predispose pupils in one setting or with one teacher to become attention-seeking, even disruptive, while in another they may remain quiet and attentive.

The main problems which teachers are concerned to overcome are attention-seeking and disruption, because these interfere with the progress of lessons. Boys are more likely to misbehave and be uncooperative in class than girls, but the girls are more likely to become subdued and withdrawn (Shepherd et al., 1971). Teachers tend to overlook this behaviour and do not always consider it to be such a problem because, of course, it does not interrupt classwork. However, it is nevertheless a problem for the pupil.

There seem to be strong links between learning difficulties and behaviour difficulties resulting in classroom problems. Many of these learning difficulties appear to derive from inappropriate curriculum tasks and poor teaching methods rather than from the pupils themselves. Some children are already vulnerable by reason of difficult, disadvantaging or distressing home circumstances, so that even the smallest stresses in school make them overreact or make them seek to work off their stress in characteristic ways. They may withdraw and become subdued and unnoticed or they may 'act out' as a response to distress and become labelled a 'problem' pupil. Those who 'act out' are more likely to be offered special provision or special schooling whereas it is often those with emotional difficulties who are more in need of this form of special provision.

15

2

The Teacher as Classroom Manager

INTRODUCTION

It is not always the pupil who owns the problem, as has already been indicated. Sometimes, the teacher may or may not act and so cause pupils' normal inhibition to fail so that they become 'at risk'. The teacher's skill in person perception needs to be continually exercised, for the classroom context is essentially a social context in which the teacher takes on the various roles of leader, adviser, guide, peer, supporter, controller, expert and so on. When operating in these different roles and relationships, it is a matter of *judgment* about which is appropriate and when. For example, in the controlling role it is important to identify a source of difficulty at its earliest stage – the frown or look of puzzlement which flashes across the face, the sudden blank expression, the hostile attitude, the quick exchange of looks or scowls – and then to judge whether to intervene or not. This aspect of the judgmental process in person perception is one which plays a very important part in keeping the social climate of the classroom at a tolerable, easy and facilitative level. There are dangers in overreacting, in not acting, in delaying and in generally getting the timing wrong. Appropriate action or inaction depend greatly upon the teacher's ability in person perception and judgmental processes. Research by Guilford (1959) showed that the good self judge should have the following characteristics:

> The good self judge is highly intelligent, emotionally adjusted and quite sociable. The good adjustment gives him the freedom to become aware of his own weaknesses and the sociability gives him the views that many others have of him. The good self judge is also said to have a good sense of humour and not to be conceited.

Knowing yourself before you can know about others is often a neglected aspect of teacher training. Here it is considered a key feature of the teacher's ability to function as an effective classroom manager. Before considering what constitutes good and poor management in the classroom, self-evaluation needs to be examined. In other words, if you know yourself then it is more likely you will make sensible judgments about other people and their needs. Inappropriate inter-personal responses can then be avoided giving greater opportunities for turning the classroom climate into a positive supportive one. If teachers need constant attention and support for their needs and for self-esteem, it is difficult for them to be positive and to support others, pupils as well as colleagues. The work of Argyle (1984) should be consulted to extend understanding in this field.

MANAGING A DIFFICULT INCIDENT USING CRITICAL INCIDENT ANALYSIS

Incident

A teacher on supply or a new teacher meets a class for the first time (choose an appropriate age group for the class in mind). She walks into the room the class is already there and noisy. She says, 'All right Class X, sit down and listen please', or for younger children 'Listen please, I want you all to come and sit quietly on the mat'. A large girl for her age turns and scowls and says 'F– off'.

Imagine the possible scenarios and how she could respond and the possible consequences. How would a number of colleagues have responded? Find a way of asking them. The key features which should figure in your final conclusions are:

1 Knowledge of the content of that particular response by the pupil, for example, with nursery and reception class children.

2 Determination of a strategy or strategies which deflect the potential confrontation without:
   (*a*) loss of face by either participant;
   (*b*) exacerbating the problem; or
   (*c*) the teacher's authority being jeopardised further in any way.

3 On deciding upon each strategy follow it through by examining all the hypothetical response chains which might ensue.

Critical incident analysis

Details of the steps of all the action:

'*All right Class X*'	– Attention gaining noise	
'*Sit down*'	– Instruction	
'*Listen*'	Instruction	
'*Please*'	– Voice lowered?	– Expects to be obeyed
	Voice tapers off?	– Enfeebled, does not expect to be obeyed
	Voice rises?	– Anxious, worried will not be obeyed
'*Large girl turns. . .*'	– How does she turn?	– Not expecting teacher
	– How is expletive directed?	– Mumbled
		– Not with hostility
		– With hostility–throws down the gauntlet

The crisis point

How does the teacher act at this crisis point? What are the possibilities and problems? For example, think of the possible implications of the following scenarios:

'Don't you speak to me like that!'
'Do you know what that means?'
'Go straight to the headteacher!'
'I told you to sit down!'
'What a remarkable paucity of vocabulary.' (*Turns to blackboard*),
    'Now I should like you all to take down the following.'
'I shall speak to you later. Now everybody . . .'

The important feature of the teacher's response is to *deflect the confrontation* at the critical point and, most importantly, quietly say to the girl 'I shall speak to you later'. This puts it on *hold* and prevents the other children from thinking she has ignored it or does not know what to do. She then gets straight on with the main part of the lesson. When the children have settled down to their own part of the work she, should *systematically go out to them starting well away from the girl* and look at each child's work and make some positive comment:

'Good, you've written the heading.'
'That is very well-formed handwriting.'
'Good! I like the way you have introduced your story, it gives it some mystery to start with.'
'Let me help you get started.'

When she arrives at the problem girl the teacher should treat her exactly as though nothing had happened – *bear no grudges*. The girl must be able to see the teacher *systematically working towards her* and be able to hear her positive comments to the others, see the cue smile as she approaches. If the girl has not started, the teacher should simply say, 'Let me help you get started', or 'Write the date and the title and then I shall come back and help you' thereby making *positive cognitive interventions (PCI)*.

At the end of the lesson, the teacher should make sure that the girl stays behind when *all the rest leave the room*. She must get rid of the potential audience. The critical phase now begins, as the tendency is for her to want to say things such as:

'Why did you say such a thing?'
'I will not have pupils speak to me like that' etc.

Each of these are provoking in their own way and may not only result in dumb insolence, but also set up the confrontation again with the teacher in the more powerful position. She must try, instead, to *open out the pupil* by gently saying, for example:

'Now, what was the problem?'
'What was all that about?'

It sometimes helps if, instead of standing bearing down on the pupil face-to-face (a confrontation pose) the teacher sits sideways on, on a chair or edge of a desk so that she is at the same eye level as the pupil. She should try to establish a counselling relationship within which she can talk about the whole scene and introduce the notion of a little kindness towards each other. At this stage, she should not threaten or give detentions or other punishments, even though she suspects the pupil will run off to boast about getting off. She will find that, *in later sessions,* it has had a modifying effect on her behaviour which eye contact, frown or quiet reminder can contain.

Cues for action

1 Deflect
2 Hold
3 Systematic PCI
4 Counsel

PERSONAL PRESENTATION IN THE CLASSROOM

Pose A – The 'meeting of friends' smile

This is said to be a fixed action pattern for humankind, an ethogram. It demonstrates the open-faced, direct gaze, mouth slightly open showing upper teeth only, tilt at corners of mouth and eyes and crowsfeet wrinkles. The chin is tilted slightly upwards and small bags are produced under each eye by the lifting action of the face muscles. In *the real event,* the eyebrows are quickly lifted and dropped in recognition. This smile is used as a greeting, even when no words are spoken. It is useful to give this in school corridors when passing pupils you know. It has a powerful effect of cueing them to the fact that you like them and helps make them feel significant in your eyes. This makes them more ready to give you time and listen when you next meet in lessons.

Pose B – The 'not sure if I can cope' smile

This is also thought to be an ethogram which other humans respond to without necessarily being able to identify the cues. The pattern is a fixed smile showing upper teeth, thin lower lip pulled in, upper teeth almost over lower lip as though biting (as children do when they have made a mistake), head down, eyes looking up slightly to the side, rather shyly. This smile signifies unsureness, submission and anxiety to the onlooker. If, in addition, the new teacher adopts a rather quiet, halting speech, with a high tense voice, this completes the picture of a scared individual. However 'good' the message, it will tend to be ignored or rejected by the recipients as from a source of no significance. The pattern of cues seen, do not represent or meet the expectations of teacher image which pupils hold. A class of pupils *of any age* will immediately recognise these signs of fear and give the teacher more trouble. Other signs of submission are showing the inside of the wrist and tilting the head to one side – appeasement gestures often used by people asking you to do some task they think you will not wish to do. Often the deputy head's posture when asking you to do an extra duty or cover! It seems to induce hostility and a desire to refuse in the recipient.

Meeting and greeting

Practise each pose by observing yourself in a large mirror. Try to switch easily from one to the other so that you know how each feels. On preparing to walk into the school or classroom, do so with a firm tread, head up, chin slightly tilted forward, shoulders back. It should feel a comfortable, easy, confident pose. Smile and lift eyebrows or nod and smile at all the pupils you know, making eye contact. Greet colleagues and the pupils of your own class or form tutor group by name. If you emanate such feelings and waves of calm and quiet cheerfulness, this will induce a more pleasant and supportive atmosphere in any group you work with and people learn to have confidence in you.

Telling

Practice asking or telling pupils and peers to do things. Do so firmly and kindly without giving off those 'limp' cues. Keep your head up, give a direct gaze, make eye contact, keep palms and wrists down, use a firm but quiet voice, and do not shout. The recipients of this message will quite happily do as they are asked unless unusually distressed.

> '*Open* the window, please, Darren,'
> 'Sit *down*, please, Sarah.'
> 'Be *quiet*, group two.'
> '*Listen*, please, Jonathon.'
> '*Not* now, Samantha.'
> '*Turn round,* Stephen.'

The italics indicate where the stress should come in the sentence, with a fall in pitch on the final word which is usually an individual's name. There is no need to stress a person's name for they will always hear this in the midst of any amount of noise. It is often referred to in psychology as the 'Cocktail Party Syndrome'.

Is there a suitable attire for school?

This is quite a contentious area. Some headteachers forbid the wearing of trousers and jeans by female members of staff in order to present the stereotyped role model for the girls in the school. Even more contentious is the issue of uniform for pupils. It is my view that school uniform should not be compulsory. This would quickly indicate whether or not pupils were proud to show that they belonged to their institutions and would enable those who wanted to experiment or demonstrate their individuality to do so in a relatively sheltered environment. Teachers could still make suggestions or give those few words of individual advice on suitability and style. A relaxation of such often rigidly enforced rules would prevent many thousands of daily confrontations and upsets. At the moment, schools are fussing about purple hair and shaved heads, although the relevance of these to the curriculum task and good interpersonal relationships is obscure.

Teachers should, however, consider what they wear themselves and the possible effect on pupils. A dirty, unkempt appearance shows little respect for the people who have to work with you and look at you. Pupils do model their behaviour and dress on the adults they meet. If a teacher feels insecure or worried about working with a particular group of pupils, especially for first encounters, it is often a good idea to dress up and at least look the part of a teacher, presenting as an authority figure by being more formally dressed. Pupils do appreciate the fact that many of their teachers dress well for work and follow fashion. Pupils are, in fact, exceptionally critical of their teachers' clothes, attitude and general presentation, and they have plenty of time for such study.

Once a teacher's position is established and the pupils' expectations that that person can fulfil the teacher's role are confirmed, it is possible to relax and become more informal. It takes a high degree of interpersonal and teaching skill to *begin* in this way, although it can be done.

WHO MAKES A GOOD MANAGER?

It may seem strange to emphasise the role of management skills in teaching but this is crucial because resources, groups of pupils and their behaviour problems require management. Management skills, as part of teaching skills, tend to receive insufficient attention in the normal course of training which can be a serious omission when teachers are faced with a difficult class. This is particularly characteristic of the short courses of postgraduate training. In addition, the role of the teacher is changing, particularly in secondary schools, with the introduction of GCSE. These studies require the teacher to manage the learning environment and to change from being a source of all information to being a resource, a coordinator, collaborator and so on. In infant classrooms such changes have been in effect for many years with integrated play, individualised learning programmes, vertical grouping and open-plan schools.

According to Eleanor Macdonald (1978), the principles of management are: *obtaining results through people*, setting objectives, devising targets, planning, organising, motivating people, monitoring results and developing staff (pupils in the teacher's case) to achieve the objectives. To achieve all this, the manager/teacher must have a high degree of technical, conceptual and social skills. From her experience in the training of managers, Eleanor Macdonald says that many poor managers assume that success in their organisations lies in pursuing their specialism relentlessly. They look upon the human relations aspect as a tiresome extra which can be ignored, whilst in reality it is the focal point of the whole activity. In secondary schools, in particular, there is a small proportion of teachers who hold this attitude, the 'content rammers'. They feel that the only worthwhile aspect of their work is teaching the fast tracking able groups or the sixth form. Eleanor Macdonald's solution is to make management training largely attitude training. As will be seen, much of what is written here is directed at producing an attitude change in the teacher, to view pupils as individuals deserving respect and being helped towards personal autonomy through practical advice and support in a positive learning environment. In fact, the following comment is quite a frequent one after a teacher has attended one of our Behaviour Problems courses.

What you are really about is changing us. Changing our attitude and updating us. Go on, admit it.

Good managers, like good teachers, according to Hall (1976) are deeply interested in both the people and the product. They need to find meaning in their work and strive to give meaning to others. Managers/teachers seek to make their pupils' work relevant. Good managers challenge and support their people so that innovation and challenge are opportunities for expansion and development and are not seen as a threat. Good managers, like good teachers, create opportunities for all their people (pupils) to succeed.

McGregor (1960), in his 'theory X' and 'theory Y' of management, suggested that some managers believe that workers/pupils are indolent, lack responsibility and so must be organised, controlled and their behaviour modified. This is achieved through extrinsic motivators such as rewards which control and structure the behaviours – *theory X*. On the other hand, others believe in the capabilities of the worker/pupil to have growth potential and assume responsibility. In this model, management must make it possible for people/pupils to achieve their own goals and direct their own efforts by arranging the conditions and methods of operation so that they can do this using intrinsic motivators – *theory Y*. The former is an *authoritarian* model of teacher/manager, the latter represents the *self-actualised* (Maslow, 1946) model which is preferred and promoted in this book.

Another way of representing what motivates individuals is through Argyris's (1971) *calculus*, thus: 'Individuals seek continually to increase their self-esteem or enhance their self-concept. They do this by searching for psychological success, setting their own challenging goals and meeting them. Therefore, if the goal is not relevant to an individual's self-concept and does not meet the need for psychological success, the whole sum of the calculus will be reduced and less effort will be expended'. From this we can draw the inference that the tasks the teacher sets must be meaningful to the learners and that they will only expend effort if they are and if by tackling them they will gain pyschological success and self-esteem. This underlines the essential nature of the interventions described as positive cognitive intervention (PCI) and catch them being good (CBG) (see pp.75, 97 and 99–101) where relevance can be explained if not already apparent. The brain can be engaged with the task, success can be constructed and then praised as it occurs. Once this pattern is established, pupils spend more and more time on task and less on disruptive behaviours. It is possible that the balance is such that all the time is on task and no time is spent in disruption.

If extrinsic rewards are used and the teacher acts as controller and source of power, then there is little opportunity for relaxation for anyone. The teacher polices the classroom and the pupils do not develop as autonomous learners capable of taking responsibility for their own learning or, giving attention to it, unless supervised. To observe this phenomenon, note the number of locked school libraries and supervised free periods.

TRANSACTIONAL ANALYSIS

Transactional analysis (TA) was developed by Eric Berne (1957) and is now widely used in businesses, schools and government training courses. It has become popular because it is a positive management tool which can be used to enhance life and work. An examination of

TA will highlight some areas of difficulty in the interactions between teachers and pupils, or 'bosses' and 'subordinates' and between colleagues and peers. The mode which is advocated here is:

I'm OK, you're OK, the CBG style.

According to Berne, the personality is composed of three parts, or ego states, which are systems of feelings and experiences derived from patterns of behaviour developed during the period of growing-up:

Child Ego State – when people, including bosses, feel and act as they did when they were children.
Adult Ego State – when people, including bosses, are thinking and acting rationally whilst gathering facts and evaluating results.
Parent Ego State – when people, including bosses, feel and act as their parents did.

Most people exhibit behaviour from *all three states* at one time or another. In any of the three states, you can adopt very different attitudes toward yourself and your subordinates:

The OK boss

Child state – is cooperative or creative.
Adult state – is responsive and analytical.
Parental state – brings out the best in people.

The not-OK boss

Child state – hostile or apologetic; scatterbrained behaviour.
Adult state – a mechanistic style.
Parental state – negative, opinionated, or over-nurturing, indifferent.

Through TA, these OK, and not-OK attitudes allow us to take any one of four positions:

1   *I'm OK, you're OK* – this is the get-along-with-people position.
2   *I'm OK, you're not OK* – this is the get-rid-of-people position which drives others away.
3   *I'm not OK, you're OK* – this is the get-away-from-people position.
4   *I'm not OK, you're not OK* – this is the I-get-nowhere-with-people position.

By understanding ego states as well as the OK and not-OK attitudes, we can make sense out of the different bossing styles that people use. Each stereotyped bossing style comes from one of the three ego states and has its not-OK side as well as its OK side. (**NB** 'P' = parental state, 'A' = adult state, 'C' = child state.) See page 24.

Whilst complementary transactions on the 'I'm OK, you're OK' level are good and denote sharing and communication between equals who respect each other, the others, particularly 'I'm OK, you're not OK', are not good. They are critical and overbearing and hold the potential for reaction and disruption. In the instance given, where the teacher says 'You are always making stupid, careless mistakes', the child is docile 'I'm sorry, I just can't get it right' and accepts

Complementary transactions

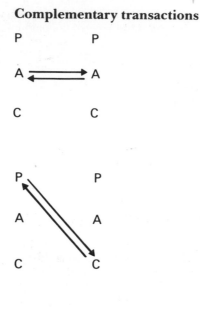

I'm OK, you're OK

T How long have you been working on this sum now?

P Nearly five minutes.

T This work is untidy!

P My pen won't work properly.

Complementary transactions

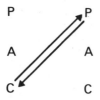

I'm not OK, you're OK

P I keep doing it wrong, Miss, will you come and help me?

T Yes, let me show you again how to do it (*supportive*).

Crossed transactions

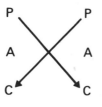

I'm OK, you're not OK

T How dare you speak to me like that!

P Aren't you going a bit over the top?

Tangential transactions

I'm OK, you're not OK

T Why didn't you do as you were told?

T Damian is eating the rabbit's food.

the blame. However, this interaction could have so easily turned into a provocative cross-transaction, with the following responses:

1   'Says you.'
2   No reply but builds up repressed anger and waits to score back.
3   'You are always picking on me!'
4   'That isn't true, you didn't teach us properly!'
5   'Rubbish!' (and other more robust ripostes).

A CASE STUDY SUMMARY OF A TEACHER'S MANAGERIAL PROBLEMS

Alix quit comprehensive schools after 15 years with the words: 'Full-time teaching in present conditions can drive you out of your mind'. She worked in South London, and she says: 'Some classes now are like battlefields. It's a battle from start to finish between teachers and children. There's a sense of struggle against overwhelming odds. You hear of teachers being cited in terms of war honours "She showed remarkable courage in an impossible situation." Children just reject your authority. They think that teachers don't understand the life they're living, and they're hostile to them. They take not the blindest bit of notice of what you say. They refuse to do what you ask. They swear. They fight. We're living in a depressed society. Everyone is distressed. Deep down in everyone there is a frustrated child who'd like to kick everybody, whom everyone wants to put down. The depression of the parents comes out in the kids and they tell us – some unknown teacher or social worker – to put it down.

A lot of schools are becoming more authoritarian now. That's fine where it can be done genially, but if you end up having to fight the kids, imposing authority on them in a harsh way, you're lost. Anyone who goes in with a sense of, "I've got to control this" is facing a pitched battle which you can't win. You can't teach or help children with this kind of strain. Teachers just tolerate it. They know they're not doing any good. They just think, "Can I survive? Can I manage? Can I cope?"'

Daily Mail (1979)

As can be seen, Alix's experience has shown her that policing is not effective, but has she worked out the way to succeed in this situation? Is her life in school made intolerable because everyone else is policing and she is not? Her conclusions lead her to suggest a 'benevolent dictatorship' but matching actions to this model is not as easy as it sounds and questions also need to be raised as to whether it would be in the long-term interests of the pupils.

LIAISON BETWEEN THE CLASSROOM MANAGER AND SCHOOL MANAGEMENT SYSTEMS

Teachers have to fit into a number of management structures as well as manage their own classrooms. In secondary schools, there are often pastoral care teams established to support pupils and to advise staff.

This type of role involves a considerable amount of liaison work and some teachers are better at this than others. Some are better at the great deal of paper work involved. Where there is poor liaison and insufficient attention to records and written communications, a wide range of communication problems and shortfalls can exist. A range of teachers may be included in the pastoral care team, for example, the deputy head or senior teacher responsible for pastoral care, heads of year, heads of lower, upper and middle school (where these exist), trained counsellors in some schools, heads of house, education social workers, and school psychological services, to which one can also add parents, community liaison workers and representatives from religious organisations.

According to Reid (1986) only a minority of pastoral care tutors are trained for the work although they attend short courses or have undertaken some study of the subject in their initial training or for higher degrees and diplomas. The quality of post holders is variable. Pastoral care involves work with pupils with major behavioural problems or learning difficulties, non-attenders, and those with personal or home problems and poor relationships. For case studies and good practice in pastoral care systems the following sources may be consulted: Murgatroyd, 1980; Galloway, 1981; Hamblin, 1986.

The Teachers' Action Collective (1976) voiced a number of criticisms of pastoral care which some teachers have held since pastoral systems were first introduced. They argued that the provision of pastoral care and special units is detrimental to schools. They put forward the view that staff appointed to such teams have to justify their scale posts and they and their activities direct resources and money away from basic education. Their very existence can remove responsibility from the classroom teacher for the management of pupils. On the other hand, in the control of hard working and sensitive staff they can enhance the work of the school and the well-being of pupils and staff. However, they very existence of a pastoral care system could suggest that there is system stress, that there is something wrong with the school curriculum and pedagogy and the school ethos, or there may be a core of problem teachers who are creating difficulties within the system. Alternatively, it could be that the very size of secondary schools necessitates some pastoral structure. Pastoral systems can also be regarded as promotion structures which recognise the worth of teachers good at developing therapeutic relationships. They can also be a means of removing dead wood from the academic system. The way in which the headteacher views the pastoral care route can, to a large extent, determine its effectiveness.

Pastoral care systems can prove very frustrating to class or subject teachers if they take away or override their responsibilities and authority. The introduction of heads of year and heads of upper and lower school could also be regarded as symptoms of system or school stress and can take over from the pastoral system or conflict with it in terms of power and responsibility if it becomes factionalised. The traditional subject departments and subject groupings can divide an organisation and, to reintegrate it and coordinate academic work across the curriculum, year teams have frequently been set up. This structure provides the warp and weft of the cloak of management in most secondary schools. It results in a matrix organisation. More recently the management structures of these schools have been undergoing further changes in response to many curriculum development initiatives and to falling rolls. Collegiate and faculty organisations have begun to increase. These have interdisciplinary teams which, when they work well, can have profoundly beneficial effects upon the curriculum and pedagogy for the pupils and thus reduce disaffection and problem behaviour. The work of these teams serves to cut the content of the curriculum whilst preserving the best features and isolating key concepts, methods and processes which pupils actually need to learn. The approach which seems to develop is one much more concerned with the learning process and with problem solving. The National Curriculum (1988) with its subject emphasis could reverse this trend and re-isolate subject learning.

In primary schools it is most often the deputy head or headteacher who is the referral point for difficult or disaffected pupils. Because staff numbers are smaller, it is possible for children's difficulties to be discussed with all of them on a more informal basis. Responsibility for management of all school matters lies directly with the headteacher rather than through other agents, as in secondary schools. There are, however, currciulum advisers and coordinators, most often in the areas of language, mathematics and science, and special needs. Other staff may take an interest in advising on curriculum areas but there are often insufficient incentive allowances for them. A well-led primary staff can act as an interdisciplinary team and keep under review and in balance both learning and subject demands.

In the matrix organisation, tension can often exist within a cell between pastoral, year and subject interests. The teacher within the cell, if he/she manages these relationships well, can improve the quality of information to each. By ensuring that all channels of communication are open, with information flowing freely between them, means that the quality of the pupils' experience of the system can be improved. One of the most frequent concerns of teachers, and particularly of middle managers, is of poor communication.

SUMMARY

Pupils with emotional and behavioural difficulties often have a low sense of self-esteem. Likewise, teachers who find it difficult to teach classes with these pupils in them, may suffer a blow to their own self-concept. They may come to *expect* to fail to control these pupils and present a submissive or 'failing-to-cope' profile in the presence of these classes. These cues can be picked up by pupils and will encourage them to become more assertive or provoking, leading to a downward spiral in work and in the relationship. Teachers who are successful, present a quietly confident profile and are firm, but not rigid, in their interactions. They have the air of expecting pupils to work for them and obey them, and pupils seem to respond in a positive way to this. Personal presentation can at least set the scene for positive action; after that, teachers like other managers need to identify the needs of their personnel. They should then try to adopt a supportive, constructive and intellectually challenging stance towards them if they are to get the best from them. Promoting good communications can be of great benefit to pupils and to the working of the school.

3

Social and Cognitive Factors in Behaviour Disturbances

INTRODUCTION

Research for many decades has shown that there are factors within the individual, the family background and the wider community, apart from within the school, which combine to cause problem behaviour to evolve. The major dimensions in theoretical terms on which such researches are based are:

- personality theory on temperamental differences;
- psychoanalytic theory where origins and explanations are sought in early psychosexual and oral frustrations;
- social psychological theory relating to rearing, reinforcement and interaction patterns;
- sociological factors which include some of the social psychology and in addition the effects of poverty, violence, criminality, housing, family size and socio-economics;
- cognitive theory, which suggests that pupils misbehave because they are bored or are seeking excitement to maintain a pleasurable level of dissonance, or that their cognitive strategies and knowledge are insufficient for coping with the task and so they succumb to learning failure.

The following outline presents a synthesis of some of the main findings of research over the last 65 years, without necessarily assigning it to a particular type, for most work lends itself to several theoretical explanations. The descriptions of results provide recognisable pictures of the problems teachers may meet in their classrooms. Understanding the possible different patterns underlying the same behaviour problem can help teachers cope with their own anger and enable them to select the most appropriate intervention. These research studies have examined the various social and psycho-social patterns underlying disruptive and delinquent behaviour, the extreme cases. The generalised heading of many of the early studies might be the socio-emotional origins of behaviour problems.

Many different reasons and mixtures of reasons have been put forward to try to account for pupils' misbehaviour while at school such as:

- social disadvantage in the schools' middle class milieu;
- inappropriate socialisation techniques in the home;
- inadequate social skills of pupils and sometimes teachers;
- inappropriate school ethos;
- over academic curriculum coupled with too rigid disciplining techniques;
- learning difficulties as a precursor to behaviour problems;
- emotional difficulties;
- inappropriate curriculum and inadequate pedagogy;
- boredom; and
- specific learning difficulties as a precursor.

It is of considerable interest that most of the studies in this area concern the plight of boys. The following is a composite list of the major cluster of problems revealed in various studies and concerns those who had been caught and punished – hence the term 'delinquent' was often used. The major clusters are derived from Hewitt and Jenkins (1946):

- Unsocialised behaviour problems (inconsistent desciplining or socialisation techniques)

  (a) plus rejection by parent(s)
  (b) plus neglect by parent(s)
  (c) by immature parent(s)
  (d) by indulgent parent(s)

- Socialised behaviour problems (consistent disciplining or socialisation techniques)

  (a) pseudo-social problems anti-authority – socialised to deviant norms and sub-culture
  (b) neurotic – over-socialised to rigid high standards

UNSOCIALISED BEHAVIOUR PROBLEMS

Rejection by parents

The rejected pupil shows *aggressive, violent and vengeful behaviour*. She/he gets on badly with peers and members of the family; is negativistic, disruptive and antisocial. The parents are usually hostile and quarrelsome, lacking in affection towards the child and are rejecting. The family is often of lower socio-economic status, with the parent-child interaction hostile and mutually suspicious and rejecting. It is most often *punitive and unjust*. The child's resulting aggression may then be projected outward on society. Jenkins (1966) blames the difficulty on the social rearing or socialisation processes in which the *inconsistency of discipline* builds up an inadequate 'shell of inhibition' around the basic impulsive core of the personality, the *id*. He explains that this gives rise to a personality who gives free rein to impulses, is defiant of authority, malicious, sullen, hostile, coercive, blames others, feels hard-done-by and persecuted. The child is unmoved by praise or punishment, showing little guilt or remorse.

The rejection and punitive nature of the relationship compound the problems which make it difficult to help such an individual in the ordinary classroom setting, without a large reduction in class size, so that more individual supportive and non-rejecting models of interaction can be offered. Details of the education of disturbed pupils may be found in a survey by Wilson and Evans (1980). These pupils are most often deeply emotionally disturbed and can be coped with by few teachers and schools. They are frequently suspended and transferred from school to school and eventually to a special school or secure institution.

In residential settings, many have been found to respond to a highly structured system of rewards and positive incentives for pro-social behaviours, often called *token economies*. Inappropriate behaviours such as swearing, lying, violence and absconding are dealt with by deducting points to a maximum level, say, 2000 and when this level is reached the young person is sent to a '*time out*' room for up to fifteen minutes. Points earned may be banked and spent later in a tangible form such as in the school shop, watching TV and buying snacks.

Less severe problems can be dealt with in a similar fashion at day school, especially if there is some supportive help through family therapy. Intermediate intervention treatment centres have been provided in some local areas but there are some teachers who are able to establish a good and stabilising influence on such pupils in ordinary schools, gradually building up their self-esteem, counteracting some of the effects of the parental rejection. For the sake of the teacher and the rest of the children in the class, the group size should be kept small. Two teachers to a group of four to six disturbed infants/juniors or adolescents have proved successful if the right teachers are selected.

Neglect by parents

The neglected pupil most often comes from a disorganised family where there are *gross inconsistencies* of discipline; the parents are unable to demonstrate firm self-control or firm standards of behaviour. The child's problems may start early and tend to be varied, but are not usually destructive or aggressive, consisting mainly of *evasions* of unpleasant things such as homework and tasks demanding effort. They often include mixed patterns of stealing (stealing for gain and as a result of emotional comfort needs, solitary stealing and joint stealing). Again (according to Jenkins, 1966) the family is often of lower socio-economic status and the 'inadequate shell of inhibition around the selfish and childish impulses has been built up through the inconsistency in discipline'. This pupil also seems unmoved by praise or punishment. It is possible to help this pupil more easily in the ordinary classroom if the teacher and the school have a consistent approach, using a behaviour modification scheme which emphasises positive aspects of the pupil's learning in a highly-structured and consistent manner. Some parents may respond to counselling and will help in the programme as far as they can.

Immature parents

An increasing reference is being made to parents who may or may not be young, but who are immature as adults and have difficulty in fully adopting the parent/adult role. They appear to seek to satisfy their own physical and emotional needs first, often expecting their children to act as mature persons supporting them. They too, demonstrate inconsistent rearing patterns, self-indulgent and often foolish behaviour. The children from this background will not have such severe emotional problems as the previous two groups and can more easily be helped in the classroom. They are more likely to follow others into undesirable activities, to seek attention and to behave in an inappropriate fashion.

Indulgent parents or 'compensating' parents

Pupils of indulgent parents are often brought up in an inconsistent fashion, characterised by sudden bursts of over-indulgence or general and inappropriate over-indulgence. In these circumstances, the 'boys will be boys' pattern is often apparent where any bad behaviour is likely to be encouraged as 'cute' or 'regular tough guy' or with 'she loves mummy really'. In some cases, there may be considerable sums of money spent on the child but a lack of attention to emotional needs. The children, although not necessarily having severe problems, are selfish, difficult to control in a classroom and often attention-seeking.

The 'compensators' try to make up for perceived deficits by being indulgent and over-lenient whenever possible. The deficits may be those which they themselves have experienced, compensations, or perhaps appeasements for absence of the other parent, death of a previous child, and so on.

The following case study is an example of a child with so-called unsocialised behaviour problems:

Case example by Christine Andrews (teacher)　　　　**Hospital Day School**
(Psychiatric Unit)

Name: Natasha
Date of birth: 29.2.74. C.A. 8.5 years
Date of admission to unit: September 1982
Family background: Father 53; London Transport Driver
　　　　　　　　　　　Mother 53; Factory worker
　　　　　　　　　　　One sister 26: College student
　　　　　　　　　　　Both parents born in West Indies, both children born UK

Emotional and social development
Natasha had a normal birth and babyhood. She showed disturbed behaviour in her nursery school. She was referred to Child Guidance Clinic 21.7.80, where she was seen by a psychiatrist. She presented with very disturbed behaviour and an EEG indicated some brain damage. The family failed to keep appointments and she was next referred to the psychiatric department of the hospital in July 1982, having been referred again by the school she was then attending for very difficult behaviour. She was soiling and wetting and had unspecified learning difficulties. The gap in her attendance at the clinic was due to her being sent to the West Indies.

School records
Nursery school at 2 yrs old, referred to clinic because of her behaviour.
The associated infant school would not admit her.

Commenced infant school January 1979.
Suspended March 1980.
Attended two schools in West Indies.
Admitted to junior school April 1982 (who initially thought she was a new immigrant).
Admitted to Day Unit September 1982.

Test results

1980 Verbal IQ 75	WISC 1982 Verbal 49
Performance 93	Performance 68

Query degenerative disease? Later tests and her EEG proved normal.

School report

This report shows that there were now admitted problems at home as well as school and it was apparent that there were disagreements between father and mother on how to treat Natasha. Mother refused to accept her low ability and felt that all discipline had to be done by father. The conclusion to the social reports shows that Natasha is an easily frustrated and angry child possibly because of unreasonable expectations. She expresses her anger in temper tantrums, wetting and soiling. The family need help to modify this behaviour and father and sister seem ready to cooperate.

Initial observation in the day unit

The behaviour reported by school was seen in any group situation. At the slightest criticism Natasha would react angrily, tearing up books, scribbling on them and then announcing she would 'wet' (which she did). First treatment programme was to wait until she had calmed down and then ask her to get a cloth and clear up. It was quickly apparent that she liked doing this and it also enabled her to get out of the task she had been set.

Programme A token system was established. Each day was divided into six sessions and she could get a token for each session when she had not wet and not lost her temper. She was not asked to clear up if she got angry. She was taken into the 'time out' room, a small room cleared of most of the furniture where she was held if necessary to prevent her throwing anything until she was ready to sit still and 'do a two minute silence'. All wetting was to be ignored and Natasha would return to the task to complete it in her play time. She had to be fetched and carried from the unit by her family because it was impossible to use hospital transport in case she wet and this involved particularly her father and made him very angry, but meant that he had to take some responsibility for his daughter.

This treatment was successful and after a full week of her being dry the hospital transport started to pick her up again. Since then there have been two other isolated cases of her wetting and each time her father has to bring her again for the following two days. The vital part of the programme has been to involve dad more, he finds out that since she is very attached to him he had to help with the discipline.

She is showing a gradual improvement with coping in groups, taking some criticism and we are beginning to increase the difficulty of her academic work. An ESN placement will be recommended for next September.

SOCIALISED BEHAVIOUR PROBLEMS

Pseudo-social behaviour problems

According to the Hewitt and Jenkins studies the socialised anti-authority individual has not been inconsistently reared but has been socialised into what is regarded as a *deviant family* or to a deviant sub-cultural norm. The models provided by parents and other siblings may be anti-authority, particularly with regard to school, and the child conforms to these norms and is suspicious, defiant and hostile to those in authority. The family, or some of its members, may belong to a criminal sub-culture and have a code of behaviour which is in direct contradiction to the school and classroom codes, resulting in such pupils quickly reverting to hostile, aggressive and disruptive behaviour at the least provocation or excuse. Relationships with authority figures are initially suspicious and negative, but they adjust well to others in the peer group.

Unsupportive and negative attitudes from the school will put such pupils *at risk* of developing severe behaviour problems, and those with any form of learning difficulty become particularly vulnerable. Behaviour modification and ego involvement strategies used in the classroom by a consistent, supportive adult model will help both this pupil adjust to school, and also the unsocialised neglected problem pupil who has not yet reached the extreme. Schools and teachers need to foster identification with the school and its models in a structured, stable, positive and supportive environment. A hostile, rejecting or neglectful environment will confirm the pupil in his/her reactive and disruptive behaviour. These pupils are those who may also seek to conform strongly to peer group norms and pressures, especially outgroups which differentiate them from the mainstream group, for example, in dress, behaviour, drug abuse, a form of counter-conformity in which *emotional support* is gained from association with the peer group.

Neurotic behaviour problems

These individuals, according to Hewitt and Jenkins, are found to be sensitive, over-inhibited, lonely and anxious with *strong feelings of inadequacy and inferiority*. They are most often children of small families of middle socio-economic status in which there are strong attachments. The mother is often over-anxious or there may be some emotional instability in either or both parents. These parents seem to set austere and uncompromising standards for the child; nothing he/she does is ever good enough, more and more pressure is always applied for the child to do better and work faster, however well the child may actually be performing. If the child falls behind at school, the parents may well determine to give extra teaching and 'drills' or insist upon extra homework for endless practice.

The pupil at school may appear to be submissive, apathetic and dreamy and is usually well behaved and reasonable, obedient and truthful. Jenkins (1968) suggests that this extreme form of social conditioning by the family results in inner conflicts which, in some cases, may lead to neurotic symptoms.

The behaviour problem pattern which *may occur* is found to be compulsory solitary stealing, furtive sadism sometimes culminating in sexual problems such as exhibitionism commonly called 'flashing', and voyeurism, the problem of the 'peeping Tom'. The problem, he suggests *does not always manifest itself* as a delinquency. The child may simply develop into an adult who is a highly conscientious and tense character who leads an impeccably respectable life. Instinctive desires are curtailed and this person cannot tolerate immorality in others. At times of personal crisis in later life, the stress may create a situation in which neurotic symptoms appear. These studies offer some interesting hypothetical groupings of types of socio-emotional difficulties which can predispose pupils to classroom behaviour problems.

DEVIANT PERSONALITY APPROACHES

An entirely different approach to the study of social deviance was begun by Jockelsson in 1961. Eight thousand hours were spent studying 255 men in prison for criminal offences (except hijacking and murder). The research was interested in how criminals think and found fifty-two so–called characteristic patterns of thought and behaviour of which the following were the most prominent.

The criminal was always a *victimiser*. At the pre-school stage he had been *restless, irritable,* had *wandered off* from home and, by four years, had *stolen*, for example, a neighbour's bicycle, money, etc. often with no attempt at concealment. By school age it was clear that he had already rejected mainstream thought and values embodied in family, school and work. He looked down on others, even in childhood, for being 'over-domesticated' – living within restraint was for 'suckers'. The researchers concluded that these individuals were seemingly born with such predispositions to think and act, not socialised into them, and that instead of rehabilitation schedules they need *habilitation* to develop in them the concept of trust, knowledge of injury to others and empathy.

This study was of extreme cases who were in prison and so the evidence is historical and still does not answer the nature-nurture question, that is, whether these individuals were born with criminal tendencies or whether they were 'made' by society. Is any individual born asocially conditioned? It would seem unlikely. By the age of four, their reinforcement experiences could have predisposed them to develop their antisocial tendencies. This 'deviant personality' approach has a number of precedents in the studies of the psychopathic personality. Particularly significant in this field is Professor David Lykken (1969) who found that GSR (galvanic skin response) of 'psychopaths' was not responsive in the same way as that of others. He found a small proportion of criminals who could, on other criteria, be said to be 'psychopaths' (or sociopathic in US terms) whose response to the lie detector (GSR based technique) was abnormal. Psychopaths were linked to the GSR machine which measures the electrical activity of the skin resulting from changes in sweating/skin conductance. They were asked questions to which there were factually correct and corroborated answers, such as name, address and so on. When normal subjects lie, the GSR reading fluctuates well beyond the normal fluctuations; however, when the psychopaths were lying the GSR showed no such fluctuation. The core attribute which the psychopaths seemed to share, although their patterns of deviance were quite different (sex, fraud, theft, murder), was the lack of empathy for the wants and feelings of others. What was not established, however, was whether socialisation could have caused this unresponsiveness or not. Other sources hint at the possibility of there being large numbers of successful 'psychopaths' in particular walks of life, such as the intelligence services, parliament, large and small companies, various notables in literature and many verging on the criminal (Ullman and Krasner, 1969). To a large extent the deviant personality approach has been superseded by the findings of the studies of deviant social rearing and social disadvantage, although studies of genetic factors (XYY sex chromosome) and deviant personality continue.

SCHOOL SOCIALISATION PROCESSES AND THEIR CONTRIBUTION TO BEHAVIOUR DIFFICULTIES

The research findings of Rutter and Madge (1976) showed that the differences between schools with high and low delinquency rates were due to factors connected with the school itself, as well as to the home environment. They found that some schools seemed to succeed in reducing pupils' delinquency rates while a few seemed to produce a higher rate. Pringle (1973) linked violent and disruptive behaviour with a curriculum which placed too little emphasis on individual, non-academic achievement and too much on competition. In such a setting, Hargreaves (1976, 1984) maintained that such pupils were unable to achieve academic success and so turned to disruption and bullying to gain attention and status. He argued that streaming merely aggravated this problem. In addition to this, Pringle also showed that a heavy and inflexible use of school rules was linked with bad behaviour and that vandalism increased in settings where there was lack of mutual respect between pupils and staff, or feelings of responsibility for one's own learning and to the school. It is this sense of responsibility, self-respect and self-worth which Hemming (1988) considers essential to the healthy growth of personality. The ethos of certain schools seems to have some profound effects upon its pupils (Rutter et al., 1979) in this respect.

Disruption and other associated behaviour problems seem to be on the increase, particularly in some schools. This increase seems to be associated with a curriculum which emphasises academic competition, places little value on non-academic pursuits or individual needs and aspirations, streams its pupils in this setting, imposes a heavy and inflexible code of school rules, and fails to involve pupils and staff in corporate development (Hargreaves, 1984). One could, perhaps, sum this up as inappropriate curriculum and bad management. The problem pupil's contribution to this equation is his/her condition, a lack of self-esteem, and a natural human tendency to want to supply this need or reduce this distressing condition by means which are often 'socially disapproved'.

School ethos, teaching and disciplining style seem to be inextricably related. A rigid authoritarian disciplining style would seem inappropriate, similarly too lax discipline may allow pupils to take over control of class groups and their aims may not always be educational. Authoritarian styles of teaching can give firm structure and direction to pupils' learning and behaviour and it is claimed that many difficult pupils can benefit from such a régime if it is a benevolent dictatorship. This style, however, does not provide the learning experiences leading towards autonomy which pupils need for life beyond school. It can, as has already been noted, cause problems with older lower attaining pupils whose learning difficulties have not been overcome. Research into teaching styles (Bennett and Jordan 1975, Bennett 1976) gave a number of insights of which perhaps the most significant was that 'good' teaching was to be seen in all style types from 'traditional' through to 'progressive' and most teachers used a mixture of strategies from the two extremes. What was not observed was the long-term and cumulative effects of style upon school ethos and pupil behaviour. HMI (1985) concluded that the single most significant variable contributing to a good school was the quality of leadership of the headteacher. The headteacher appears to set the tone and style of the organisation and only by concerted effort can a school staff counteract such an influence.

What can schools do to try to counteract the problems of ethos and style?

Many behaviour problems seem to derive from inappropriate sociali-sation strategies in the home and then the school. Socialisation consists of the régime of reward and punishment, given as reinforcement for the child's behaviour. Thus, manipulation of the reinforcement system could be the potential point of cure or intervention.

To counteract inconsistency and hostility the pupils need *firm, consistent* but friendly models and socialisation strategies. To counteract feelings of inadequacy and depression the pupils need *supportive, positive* and encouraging teachers. Evidence in support of this approach was presented at the British Educational Research Association (BERA) conference in Lancaster 1984. A Belgian research study was reported which had questioned more than 2000 fifteen-year-olds in the Province of Luxembourg. The study had concluded that punishments only aggravated bad behaviour at school and led to greater alienation from authority and to delinquency outside school.

The pupils expressed their alienation by mixing with other 'problem' students and became even harder to control. Their refusal to conform made them more likely to be 'caught in the act' by teachers or the police. The pupils *most at risk* in the Belgian study were found to have:

- changed secondary school several times;
- been excluded from school more than once;
- gained little prestige at school;
- made poor relationships with teachers; and
- developed a negative academic self-image.

The British authors of the BERA paper, Lawrence, Steed and Young, who reviewed research on disruptive behaviour, proposed an '*x*' factor to avoid the harmful effects of punishments as follows:

- strong controls at schools;
- characterised by *warmth, friendliness* and *participation*.

In their own research, Lawrence *et al.,* (1984) studied two secondary schools, one co-educational (1250) and one boys' school (800). Both were comprehensives. The report, although seeming to be couched in realistic terms, concentrated upon giving teachers strategies for dealing with trouble once it had arisen but not sufficient help guiding them to prevent it arising – their '*x*' factor. The teachers were asked to keep notes of every disruptive incident, how they dealt with it and what the outcome was, so building up a case file of successful interventions. During one week, for example, staff reported 77 incidents at the first school, including fighting in class, insolence, talking, whistling and eating sandwiches during lessons. As a result of their incident analyses, Lawrence *et al.* offered teachers the following advice:

- Nip the incident in the bud. If a problem is brewing up, try warning the pupil or order her/him to switch seats.

- Take account of group dynamics in class. Look for leaders, find ways of changing the group layout, stand in a different place.
- Do not accuse groups of theft when only one or two are involved.
- Talk to individual trouble-makers outside lesson time, especially when a pupil is becoming a persistent nuisance over several lesson periods.
- Give children the benefit of the doubt if they make excuses which cannot be checked, such as stomach ache.
- Defuse a potentially dangerous situation by cracking a joke.
- Think carefully before getting too angry about pupils eating in class.
- Avoid becoming personally involved and be alert to your own feelings and state of mind, be careful not to overreact if you are in a bad mood.
- If you do decide to have a confrontation, do it on your own ground and on your own terms and know what you are going to say.

The authors advised that schools themselves can cut down on disruptive behaviour by changing their timetables, curricula or internal organisation. They can space out periods with the same class and cut down the time a particular group of pupils spend together. They could find more efficient means of changeover between lessons and avoid over-rigid structures or sanctions for misbehaviour.

Now whilst this contains some useful advice, it conveys an attitude of teacher style and action that is misplaced, negative and unconstructive. Teachers are presented with a *policing* style of intervention. It has also to be remembered it was the 'successful' teachers who engaged in these 'successful' policing strategies. As will be explained, the 3Ms strategy, especially *monitoring*, will enable the first signs of inattention and unrest to be located, and the *maintenance* function and PCI will help prevent them arising, or overcome them when they do. These are harmonising rather than policing interventions. In teaching, one needs to work for harmony and involvement in the task, not aim to preside over suppressed resentment by the use of control devices and policing. It is an approach to disruption which is symptom-orientated, treating the pupils as trouble-makers and most often in the wrong. If, however, one is aware of the social and psychological context and content of their behaviour, it can be seen that it is the teacher who should most often change in attitude and approach to lesson planning and teaching in order to engage and involve all the pupils. Containment strategies are uneducative. Pupils come to reject school learning as a hateful, unedifying chore. They become alienated, rather than educated young people eager to seek further development. They become incapable of finding any fulfilment in educational pursuits and only derive identity through work or pleasure. In an era of unemployment, many of these young persons have a sad future. They can become depressed, lose self-esteem and feelings of worth. They may then become vulnerable to, for example, drug abuse.

Advisory teachers in health education at Hackney Teachers' Centre were quoted by *The Times Educational Supplement* (October, 1984) as follows:

> Young people may demonstrate antisocial or antiself behaviour even though they know that the behaviour is destructive. Drug taking, excessive smoking and drinking, exploitation of others, are only some of these behaviours. Low self-esteem and an inability to withstand peer group pressure may be at the core of this behaviour. Thus building self-esteem and decision-making abilities may have more impact than didactic information-giving sessions.

Blakeborough (1986) who has run the Kaleidescope project on drug abuse in Kingston for twenty years considers drug abuse as only one form of obsessional behaviour deriving from lack of self-esteem and from failure in life chances and at school. He and his team believe that teachers have an important role in preventing drug abuse or solvent abuse by building all pupils' sense of achievement and self-esteem in school. However difficult their social circumstances are, they maintain teachers are key agents in pupils' lives and this should be for good.

BOREDOM AND THE EXCITEMENT OF 'THE GAME'

What becomes apparent to most teachers is that there are pupils who have no learning difficulties and no traceable social problems (Croll and Moses, 1985) but who are disruptive – even severely so. How are these pupils to be judged? If we think of all the lessons which we found frustrating, all the teachers with whom we did not agree, however young and inexperienced we were, those ideas we wanted to try immediately and the silly things we said for effect, we can perhaps empathise with pupils now.

There are many pupils who feel excitement in challenging ideas, who enjoy disagreements for the interest of change and novelty and who find excitement in outfacing and outcountenancing adults, teachers and peers for the sheer delight, interest and stimulation it provides.

Excitement in some classrooms in relation to work and recognised achievement is in short supply. What did *we* do when we were young? We created our own excitement and challenge and this is what our pupils are doing today. They provoke us, they annoy us, they misbehave for the pure excitement of it all. It is cognitively engaging and pleasurable and avoids habituation. If we can *provide the challenge and intellectual excitement* in the course of school work, we can win together. Pupils need cognitive exhilaration which we can give them through work and then they will not need to seek it in other ways.

Excitement is probably the greatest spur to misbehaviour in classrooms (Reid, 1986) for all our pupils. The more boring the lessons and the less involving they are, the more likely the pupils will feel alienated and need to seek other forms of excitement through disruption. This area has not as yet produced much research evidence except as case examples, personal experiences of teachers, incidental evidence from appraisal research (Montgomery, 1984) and studies of teaching (Kerry, 1979; HMI 1986). The factors involved are less tangible than disadvantage and social conditioning but perhaps the time has come to begin such an investigation.

WHO IS MOST AT RISK?

What has to be recognised is that family socialisation patterns and strategies have different effects upon its members. Some children are more vulnerable to stress and disorder than others. In some families, only one individual may be selected to receive the hostility and rejection, or the extra pressure. Highly socially intelligent children may manipulate difficult situations to their own advantage; other reflective individuals may be able to win through their difficulties by intellectualising their problems. The slower mind may be unable to think in an extended fashion about problems and situations and easily becomes depressed or frustrated, and this can lead to aggression. Children with learning difficulties from disadvantaged environments are particularly 'at risk' for their intelligence may well be in excess of their school achievements, creating frustrations, aggression, disruption or withdrawal if not helped. Children from advantaged backgrounds with learning difficulties stand more chance of having their problem identified and receiving some formal help. The *most vulnerable* are generally children in disadvantaged families with an alcoholic father.

West (1982) distinguishes between temporary recidivists who have multiple convictions in youth which do not continue into adulthood, and *persistent* delinquents who tend to start their conviction careers at an early age and continue into adulthood. The former tend to come from relatively deprived backgrounds and the latter from the most deprived backgrounds – standing out as the most conspicuously deviant group from the earliest school years. According to Mitchell and Rosa (1981), the child behaviours most highly associated with later criminality are stealing, destructiveness, wandering from home, and lying. These showed the highest positive correlation with later criminality in their research. Excessive worrying and food fads were shown by these researchers to have a negative correlation.

Social background factors of 'at risk' children

Pupils who come from difficult or distressing home circumstances, with or without learning difficulties can become 'at risk' in a school system where little care and attention is given to the individual and his/her needs and concerns (Hargreaves, 1984). Secondary schools with their large numbers of pupils, continually changing timetable of rooms, teachers and subjects, can increase these pupils' vulnerability so that it is easy to feel alienated and lose identity and identification with the school and its purposes. This is the focus of concern in the Kaleidescope project on drug abuse (Blakebrough, 1986). These problems are not the necessary consequences of secondary schooling and large institutions. In some large schools shared common ideals and purposes between staff and pupils avoid such problems. Primary schools, because of their smaller size and continuity of staff contact with pupils, can more easily prevent the 'at risk' children from suffering further stress and alienation but, even this is not a necessary contingency as much depends upon the people in these schools and the *quality* of the relationship which they offer to the pupils in their care. Disruptive behaviours and attention-seeking often emerge under stress or at crisis points in a child's life. These factors which can put pupils 'at risk' and predispose them to become problems in school are often traceable to the following:

- during family upset and quarrelling;
- during family break-up and divorce;
- during severe parental illness and hospitalisation;
- when a new baby is born;
- in families where there is a lack of affection and support;
- at puberty with mood swings;
- under peer group rejection;
- when other children in the family are favoured;

- where there is selective oppression;
- in cases of abuse.

Some of these situations are temporary but the behaviour problem, whether 'acting out' or withdrawal, can be reinforced by the school so that the pupil becomes 'known' and has a label to live up to (Mongon, 1985) or overcome as well as peer reinforcement to contest. Stormer (1970) in observing the classroom behaviour of pupils, identified five different categories of behaviour problems for teachers:

- maladjusted children;
- revenge seekers;
- attention seekers;
- escapists; and
- power seekers.

These are vivid ways of drawing to our attention the different types of problems, but the categories identify them as belonging to the pupils themselves and not as a product of the interaction between the participants in the classroom context. The motives implicit in the categories *deflect* one to some extent from the origins of the problems which may be the same, but create a different pattern of reaction in different individuals, for example, a pupil who is suffering neglect in an inconsequential rearing pattern may seek revenge on adults or may seek attention.

In their survey of disruptive pupils Wilson and Evans (1980) recommended five effective approaches for all such disorders. The word 'disorder' carries an emotional and attitude loading which is not really helpful but their suggestions are most useful and consistent with behaviour management and the principles outlined in this book. They suggest:

- offering a warm, caring attitude in adult to child relationship;
- improving the pupil's self-image through success;
- giving firm, consistent discipline;
- offering a varied and stimulating educational programme;
- providing continuity in child-adult relationships.

SUMMARY

Family socialisation styles which may put some children at risk include:

- families using excessive physical punishment;
- families who are grossly lax in disciplining;
- families who are inconsistent in their disciplining techniques;
  (*a*) serious when associated with neglect;
  (*b*) very serious when associated with rejection;
- families who are excessively over-protective; and
- families who are excessively controlling in emotional terms, using withdrawal of love as a major strategy, made even more serious when coupled with the setting of too high standards for the child.

As a contrast, families and schools who are successful with children, according to Herbert (1975), generally display the following characteristics:

- they are strongly approving of the child and his/her activities and friends;
- there is a harmonious relationship within the family and home;

- there is a regular routine which is not too rigid;
- any demands made upon the child are consistent and supportive, where leniency prevails over severity;
- standards of behaviour and procedures are open to discussion; and
- the child appears to develop strong positive feelings towards the parents which later transfer to others.

Similarly, schools which adopt this supportive, positive and open style provide more effective learning environments for pupils to spend their fifteen thousand hours.

4

Emotional Origins of Behaviour Problems

INTRODUCTION

Fear is an adaptive emotional reaction in which we may feel physical sensations such as a pounding heart, butterflies in the stomach, dry mouth, perspiring hands and neck, shivering and dry coldness of the skin, immobility or shaking and sagging at the knees. These changes occur as adrenalin is released into the blood stream during emotion and are most likely to happen, in humans and animals, at times of 'flight or fight' where the bodily changes can be seen as a preparation for one of these actions. When these disturbing physical symptoms occur in the absence of objective fear-provoking situations, they are called 'anxiety attacks'. Although most people can shrug off the stress of modern living there are some who cannot and become oppressed by their fears. Fears may also, to some extent, be learned when a pupil links an unpleasant experience with a particular situation (Herbert, 1975). This can often be the case where learning experiences have been negative or teachers have been angry and fear-inducing over failure to learn, as has often seemed to happen in the case of fear of mathematics which many teachers themselves admit to.

In addition to learning to fear in lessons, pupils may become fearful of peers who bully or threaten and harass them. At home they can learn to become anxious too and Cameron (1963) listed a number of ways in which this might occur:

- when they are used as confidants by parents;
- when parents press for perfection and are never satisfied with their child's performance. This continuous 'must do better' pressure can create a child who is low in self-esteem and prone to feelings of anxiety;
- when parents are over-permissive and indulgent. The child, in order to feel secure, needs to have reasonable limits set, for without them he or she cannot predict or anticipate successfully what the world outside the home expects.

Anxiety can also have a useful aspect in that it can enhance a performance, unless it rises to too high a pitch when it begins to disrupt it. A little

Figure 3 *Main responses to stress*

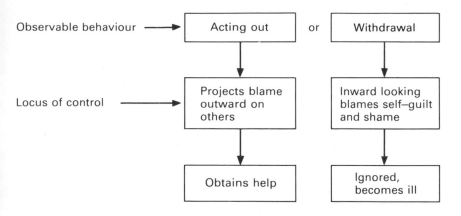

anxiety can do good and add a keen edge to performance, too much can do harm. Pupils who are excessively anxious tend to be self-disparaging, low in self-esteem and less popular with peers which can make them become isolated and a prey for other people's aggressive tendencies. Because of their anxiety, normal aggressive and protective responses to other children are repressed and they can become victims. If such fearful individuals do show or feel aggression they can become very apprehensive about their feelings and develop anxiety and inhibitions about all their responses. Although this state of inhibition and anxiety characterises the nervous child it nevertheless constitutes what may be called 'nervous health'. Neurosis is a state of nervous illness distinct from nervous health.

Where children suffer from nervous health the sources of their distress and anxiety can often be discovered, and the child helped to overcome them by rationalising, counselling and support for learning. Play and story talk can help younger children come to terms with their fears. A positive and supportive classroom climate will help many of these children and can provide a learning environment in which children can rebuild their self-esteem and their relationships. A distressed child who does not begin to prosper in these circumstances will be one for whom the teacher needs to obtain specialist advice and support. The following sections of this chapter give an outline of some of the main types of emotional difficulties which teachers may observe in their classrooms from pupils who are withdrawn, attention-seeking or disruptive.

EMOTIONAL DIFFICULTIES

Emotional health is distinguished from emotional illness, by children in the latter case being so distressed that they cause suffering and concern to themselves and those about them. They are often able to see that their behaviour is irrational or unreasonable but are incapable of stopping it. In emotional illness, the person is unable to maintain or undertake normal activities and becomes socially disabled, as with agoraphobia and school phobia.

Stress is the engendering of a higher than normal, or useful, level of emotion over a long period of time, maintained by some perceived unpleasant, or fear-inducing situation. Many pupils who suffer emotional stress may exhibit their stress in one of two major ways: they *act out* their internal conflicts, stress and anxiety by becoming disruptive or attention-seeking, or they may *withdraw*, becoming quiet and totally unnoticed in the classroom. The latter are often recognised to be those with the more serious problem in the long run. The more disruptive ones can become such a nuisance that eventually steps are taken to help them; the withdrawn ones may be ignored and left to sink deeper and deeper into distress so that it can become impossible to help without psychiatric intervention.

Social conditioning in this country is still such that girls are less likely to become disruptive than boys (Wheldall, 1988) in the ratio of about four to one. Boys, according to researchers, are likely to receive more attention and more information and support than disruptive girls.

Case example of a child with an emotionally-based behaviour problem – not an illness

It is often difficult to get parents to adopt simple strategies to help their children. For example, a mother was advised that her seven-year-old son was disruptive, attention-seeking, rude and sometimes aggressive in school and was near being excluded because other children were frightened and prevented from learning. The mother was distressed but also desperate herself because he was such a problem at home. She was, she felt, somewhat disorganised and really too busy looking after the new baby, a girl, of whom she was extremely fond. She preferred girls, she said, and wished he, Stephen, had been a girl. She was also worried about his nightmares which woke them all up and prevented him resting, which probably accounted for him falling asleep in the reading corner after his various tantrums.

The headteacher, on the consultant's advice, counselled that perhaps a first strategy would be for either the mother or the father to sit Stephen down on their lap each evening before bed, with the television off, and just cuddle him and talk to him about anything.

The parents did try the strategy but found ten minutes more than they could stand. The mother came back to the school each day and for long sessions would pour out an account of all that happened during the day but was encouraged to persist with the listening. Whilst the parents 'suffered' and persisted with what became five minutes' quiet time before bed, the boy suddenly became quiet, amenable and pleasant to work with at school.

ASPECTS OF EMOTION

There are three aspects to emotion:

- Physiological changes.
- Behavioural changes.
- Experiential changes or cognitive feelings of emotions.

The primary emotions, *anger* and *fear,* underlie most of the stresses resulting in emotional behaviour problems in classrooms. Frustration and hostility, leading to repressed or expressed anger; anxiety, learning failure and peer rejection leading to fearfulness, and anxiety, or frustration.

Physiological changes in emotion

There are ten physiological changes:

- Dilation of pupils of the eyes, widening eyes, increased or decreased blinking depending on the reaction.
- Increase in heart rate.
- Pilomotor reflex – goose pimples, hairs on skin stand up.
- Muscle tremor/tension – may shake, become immobile or weak at knees and sag.
- Blood composition changes – more glucose released, adrenalin or noradrenalin circulated.
- GSR changes – changes in sweat gland activity in skin – Galvanic Skin Response.
- Respiration rate changes – sighing or rapid breathing.
- Blood capillary flow changes – leading to blushing or blanching, muscles' supply of blood increased ready for 'fight or flight'.
- Intestinal changes – digestive activities stop, in severe emotion 'decks cleared for action' – involuntary urination and defaecation occurs.
- Salivation response – mouth may become dry (of the biblical story of the wisdom of Solomon and the thief).

Behavioural changes in emotion

These are as follows:

- Lunging forward, finger pointing, teeth bared, uttering high pitched noises in anger.
- Head back, open mouthed, teeth bared, baying, whites of eyes wide and clear, gesticulating in 'threat' prepared to flee.

In the classroom:

- Fixed smile showing both sets of teeth bared in anxiety and fear. Cross teacher often says 'Wipe that smile off your face', and the child is so frightened he/she cannot.
- Child sitting or standing reading but just noticeably jigging shows undue sign of tension on task, perhaps fear of failure.
- Fixed watchfulness – eyelids retracted showing whites of eyes, fixed gaze, child seems unable to approach or withdraw, white round mouth, possible perspiration on upper lip and mottled red around neck.
- Regression to thumbsucking when habit had previously been outgrown.
- Regression to temper tantrums and outbursts when this had previously been outgrown. Temper tantrums at an age after about three years when they are normally repressed.
- Regression to babytalk and babyishness often when new baby has arrived in the family.
- General attention-seeking behaviour.

Sometimes in cases of severe emotional stress there is wetting (enuresis) and/or soiling (encopresis) and at the extremes, self-mutilation and violence. Each of these problems requires specialist attention and the teacher should seek advice and refer the problem quickly.

Cognitive aspects of emotion

In many instances the child feels hurt and frustrated or justified in his/her behaviour, perceiving only a simple relationship between the 'trigger' and the action, rather than being aware of the deeper-seated emotional stress underlying the mechanism. Some sage children, even of a very young age, can be counselled to understand and cope with their problems, others may be provided with catharsis in the form of play, drama or music therapy to release the tensions, but the most effective strategy is to stop the problem arising at source by mobilising the support agencies in severe cases and bringing the parents into the discussion and, if possible, helping them to remove or deal with the problem situation which is causing the distress.

EMOTIONAL ILLNESSES

Emotional illnesses are referred to in psychiatric literature as neuroses. According to this literature there are four main types of neurotic illnesses: phobias, hysterias, obsessional-compulsions and depression.

Phobias

- Separation anxiety (school phobia is really a fear of leaving mother and not of school).
- Fear of personal harm (phobias associated with PE, bullying).

Hysterias
- Hysterical fainting fits in assembly.
- Conversion hysteria – neurotic blindness, paralysis in some, psychosomatic illnesses.

Obsessional-compulsions

Violent fear of, for example, filth, disorder, evil or naughty thoughts, thoughts that something may be made magically dirty by unclean thoughts with ritual behaviours and acts to cope. Only two mild cases were reported amongst all our case discussions. One boy with a preoccupation for order and neatness, and a girl overly preoccupied with cleanliness but not to the extent that it prevented either of them from engaging in school work as yet.

Depression

Often as a result of child abuse or, in adolescence, derived from seeming small origins or comments, the problem appears to be much more common than the literature would suggest. Only recently has it been thought that young children can suffer from depression.

Andrew – a case example

Andrew is 13 years old. His family live on the local council estate. Father has a criminal record and is at present unemployed. There is a family history of discord, fighting and quarrelling. His older sister (15) and mother are reported to be 'on the game' and his brother (18) is on probation for taking away and driving cars. In school, when he attends, Andrew is abusive to teachers, disruptive in lessons. He has a broken record of attendance and has little attainment in basic school subjects and so is in the lowest ability sets. Verbally, he seems quite intelligent and resents being in the bottom group. He does little to help himself out of this situation. Teachers are relieved when he is absent. Social Services have been involved with the family over a number of years and questions of abuse have been raised at intervals.

Could a supportive school environment and a positive approach to his specific learning difficulties help Andrew? Is he ill, or distressed?

CHILDHOOD AND ADOLESCENT DEPRESSION

This problem is also worthy of special note. Depression in children has only been recognised as an illness in the last forty years or so. Children may suffer depression in nursery, infant, junior or secondary school. Even babies in cots have been observed to be depressed and in unresponsive states. The child becomes subdued, fails to make eye contact, appears dejected, weepy and sad, and may even shed tears. This has often been noted in abused children. In addition, a state of 'fixed watchfulness' may also be seen in abused children; eyes wide, sclera showing above iris of eye, the child is impassive, watching others play, seemingly caught in the state between fearing to withdraw and fearing to approach in case attacked – the approach-avoidance conflict. These are extreme states of emotional anxiety and stress but teachers must note them early on and report them immediately to the headteacher and follow the LEA guidelines and procedures exactly.

Sadness and depression may also arise from bereavement in the family where anger and grief have not found expression. Depression is often regarded as repressed anger created by environmental circumstances and distress. Endogenous depressive conditions within the individual are sometimes a feature of hormonal changes, for example, at puberty, in post-natal depression and at middle-age.

Adolescent depression is thought to have many origins and can arise during puberty and when there are hormonal changes and accompanying fluctuations in mood. A harsh word about smells or spots, or a crude epithet, may cause anger and distress with which the adolescent cannot cope and which makes him/her feel outcast and ugly. It may, in some individuals, lead to a depressed state and, in extreme cases, attempted and even successful suicide. All attempts and threats of suicide should be treated as cries for help and as serious intents. A supportive school atmosphere and learning climate can help ease such times of stress. Being immersed in and earning praise for school work can take the mind away from anxieties and stress at least temporarily. One of the major sources of depression in childhood seems to arise from abuse, although bereavement is also a main source.

CHILD ABUSE

There are four main types of abuse about which the teacher needs to be aware:

Physical abuse

The child may have knuckle marks under eyebrow ridge; finger and thumb bruises on face, neck and arms; bites with adult-sized teeth marks; cigarette burns; weals from whips; unexplained bruises; scalds and burns; and fractures. Fixed watchfulness. The child will seldom, if ever, reveal the true source of these injuries. However, there are also difficult cases where children who bruise easily may be mis-diagnosed and their parents wrongly accused of physical abuse.

Neglect

The child stops growing; becomes pot-bellied, thin and bow-legged; hair becomes thin and coarse and begins to fall out; loses eyebrows; skin becomes coarse and scaly. With vitamin deficiency the child develops bleeding spots on legs. The child is always hungry and finds it difficult to concentrate until he/she finds food. Will eat other children's food, worms, or anything and is often found scouring the dustbins. In other cases, the child is fed but clothes, hair and body are not cared for or cleaned. Parents neglect to get child ready for school or fed before school. Child arrives late, sometimes not at all.

Sexual abuse

The child speaks of sexual matters with intimate and unexpected knowledge for age. May engage in overt sexual play and inappropriate behaviour. May appear fearful of adults, show fixed watchfulness, failure to learn, absorbed by own thoughts.

Emotional abuse

There are few overt signs of this but each of the former can give rise to severe emotional distress in the child. One reaction pattern will be withdrawal and depression, another may be for the child to imitate the adult aggressive models and act out anxiety and stress in the classroom. Examples are when one parent treats a young child or adolescent as an adult confidant and companion; overtly prefers another child in the family; uses emotional blackmail as discipline; is rigidly punitive and frightening for little reason and then immediately tries to placate and handle the child, cuddling, stroking and appeasing.

Case example of an abused child's behaviour

A twelve-year-old pupil transferred to the area and arrived at her new school (for children with moderate learning difficulties). She was in a foster home. The teacher found her to be a quiet, pale and small little girl. Underneath this quiet exterior she soon found a very angry and, at times, vicious and cruel person. When asked to make a 'Draw a Man' picture, the girl drew a stereotyped and simply clothed outline but coloured in a huge bright blue penis. The teacher was startled and took advice from the school psychologist and other staff. No one thought it of any significance. Later the girl's behaviour to a young man visiting the class and her language was sexually explicit, foul and quite inappropriate, expressing ideas and information not expected of a child of her age. She said she hated her father and some two terms later, when tested, had drawn another sexually explicit but uncoloured set of genitals. She needed help/treatment to gradually release this anger so that it would not continue into adulthood and make her become ill and incapable of making adequate relationships. The fostering alone would not necessarily do this as seemed to be assumed. This child's behaviour was characteristic of certain abused children and it was later discovered that this had in fact been the case.

Abused children may thus become depressed, withdrawn and weepy or they may react and model themselves on the aggressors and transgressors, becoming aggressive, stormy, brutal and unpredictable. In all cases of abuse, LEA consultation and report procedures must be closely followed. In addition, schools must be made safe and supportive places. When they are, these children are often found clinging to the teacher, arriving early and loitering until late, not wishing to go home. At least in this environment they have a safe place to be for up to ten hours per day, or longer in community schools.

Children with behaviour problems for which there is an underlying emotional origin are much more difficult to help by pedagogical and behavioural methods, for these attack the symptoms rather than the causes. In all instances a positive approach to learning and a supportive and positive attitude from teachers and the school will at least help the child survive in the ordinary classroom without contributing to his/her distress. The teacher must, however, seek advice and support through the headteacher or head of pastoral care from other agencies so that therapy can be obtained and the stressor removed where possible. Rutter (1975) concludes from his researches that children with emotional problems are much more likely to respond to therapy than children exhibiting behaviour problems without such an emotional origin. In school, music, drama, painting and play can be activities which provide some therapuetic outlet for pupil's emotions. It may be through observation of these activities that the teacher first notices the distresses and unhappiness of a withdrawn child. In some cases a morbid and excessive preoccupation with death, dying, and associated objects is noted often with an extraordinary predilection for the use of black paint in pictures and for interpretations of utter gloom and doom in stories. Although in middle childhood and early adolescence pupils often go through phases of interest and preoccupation with gloom and doom, taken with other indicators and cues these interests may, in some children, be important signs of inner distress which teachers should discuss with colleagues. Pupils often reveal their concerns when talking or writing about their interpretations of everyday scenes and events in pictures or videos, especially where these are slightly ambiguous and could be interpreted in several ways. Consider the following example:

> Five-year-old Tracy was asked to tell a story about the picture she was looking at with the teacher. The picture showed a man and woman sitting on a settee looking at the TV. The woman is holding a baby. Tracy said 'The man and the lady is watching it. He's drunk, she only loves our baby 'n he hits her.'

The question here for the teacher was whether this was the imaginative play of a young child's mind or whether something more serious lay behind it. As a result the teacher was alert for any other indicators which might have confirmed or denied either one of her hypotheses.

SCHOOL REFUSAL

School refusal is a general category within which there seem to be two different patterns of behaviour problems; one is truancy and the other has come to be called school phobia (Cooper, 1967; Barker, 1975). Truancy is wilful non-attendance at school often associated with social factors and alienation from school. School phobia as the name signifies has as its base an emotional problem or state of emotional illness in which the pupil cannot attend school for fear of distressing, and even catastrophic, emotional reactions which he/she cannot control.

An unpleasant or frightening event may trigger the phobia as in the case of a thirteen-year-old girl who went to do a regular babysitting session only to become involved in a ceremony with religious rites. The people for whom she was sitting prevented her returning home at her usual time and the whole event, it was later discovered in psychotherapy, had severely scared her. A few weeks later, the first onset of her school phobia set in. She became more and more anxious on leaving home and her parents finally had to drag her screaming and crying from the car into school. She showed many of the ten physiological and behavioural signs (see p.45). Generally, once pupils return home, the symptoms and the fear profile stop. Often, after one such traumatic uncontrollable experience, the pupil will develop a phobia about the phobia and will be so fearful of the symptoms that he/she will resist anything which might cause them to arise again. The phobic fear pattern can be very frightening, with pounding heart and temples, and massive uncontrollable sensations extending to wetting and soiling as has been often the case with fighter pilots going into battle.

This thirteeen-year-old was given tranquilisers and psychotherapy. After three weeks the tranquilisers were withdrawn and contacts were made with the school so that school work could be sent. At first, a friend from school brought the work, then a small group came along, later the teacher called and eventually it was arranged that she should go back to school and join a small remedial group. When none of this elicited the phobic symptoms she was persuaded to rejoin her original class and did so successfully. This return to school took place over a six-month period with the support of the child guidance services, a home tutor, the school, parents, class teacher and school friends. This pattern of treatment follows that known as 'desensitising therapy' and is based upon conditioning theory and research. In this case the underlying cause was not uncovered. 'School phobia' seldom occurs in this classic form and some children who refuse to attend school do so with the unwitting connivance of parents. These pupils may have learned to manipulate the adults around them, who condone their absence rather than confront their emotional response or psychosomatic symptoms. One twelve-year-old spent a week in hospital undergoing extensive tests and investigations, many of them quite uncomfortable, to try to find the origin of her morning headaches and stomach pains which were finally thought to be a combination of the desire for attention at home in competition with a younger sister and a need to stay at home to try to obtain it.

A mixture of responses and underlying conflicts and emotions is often observed with a fear of separation from the mother as a key issue in seemingly emotionally vulnerable individuals. The general advice from an analysis of case studies, in which different types of therapy have been tried, suggests that the most important factor is to return the pupil to school instantly if possible, but at least within two or three weeks. Treatment which involved lengthy periods from school with psychotherapy and home tuition proved less successful in the long-term in returning the pupil to school and keeping him/her there (Blagg 1988).

Janice was a five-year-old who had just started school. Each morning as her mother prepared to leave the classroom she began to cry loudly. The class teacher was able to reassure the mother that this was not an unusual occurance in five-year-olds and together they agreed to treat the whole thing in a matter of fact way. What was unusual, as the teacher soon found out, was that Janice continued to cry very loudly all day and could not be distracted by all the usual ploys and would not join in any activity. If the mildest of pressure was exerted to try to persuade her to join in or come and listen to a story she would simply cry even more loudly. All day she would stand in one place and cry. Both teacher and mother were very concerned. After several days the other children ceased to find Janice's behaviour interesting and the teacher grew accustomed to the noise. By the second week Janice was engaging in silent crying bouts and periods of watching what was going on around her. In the third week Janice silently observed, occasionally tears fell and she began to move her position to see things better, she was always given the opportunity to be included in, by look or gesture. Towards the end of the third week the real break-through came when she moved in close with the other children to listen to the story. No special fuss was made of her and after that she began to participate in the general run of classroom activities, quietly at first and then no differently from the rest. Janice proved to be an able pupil quickly learning to read and write well.

Children are most vulnerable to phobic symptoms at transfer times from home to school and from one school to another. Fear of leaving, or of separation from the mother is found to underly many school phobias. In others, it is a fear of personal harm at school, for example, in PE on the apparatus, from travelling, or bullying on the way to school. However, in some cases the origins cannot be traced.

Early patterns of anxiety may be observed when the 'Monday morning phenomenon' arises. The child, boy or girl, feels ill, complains of sickness, headache or stomach pains. These symptoms disappear as soon as the decision is made not to go to school and by 9.30 they are back to normal, doing a jigsaw or watching TV and eating breakfast.

The effectiveness of rapid return to school for particular cases of school phobia was first reported by Kennedy (1965). From the analysis of the effects of treatment in a controlled study of fifty children he was able to draw up the following guidelines to get phobic children back to school. His method worked in all fifty cases, without remission, and is still a recommended form of treatment according to Dawson (1985) in the teacher information pack (TIPs) Package, as long as this was only treated as the first stage of a longer-term strategy with a full follow-up and monitoring programme. The 'treatment' cannot work without the full cooperation of the parents.

Kennedy found that a forced, immediate return to school was an effective and rapid treatment if *seven or more* of the following ten symptoms were present:

- This is the first instance of unlawful absence.
- The unlawful absence began on the Monday following the period of illness during the later part of the previous week.

- The absence began suddenly and unexpectedly.
- The pupil is between four and eleven years of age.
- The pupil seems unduly concerned with notions of death.
- The pupil believes either correctly or incorrectly that the mother is physically ill.
- The parents seem to enjoy a harmonious relationship.
- The parents both seem to be relatively well adjusted and stable.
- The father helps with household chores.
- The parents are able to understand childhood and family problems.

After each day successfully completed at school, the parents were asked to praise their offspring extensively for staying there. They were told that within two or three days the children, unlike Janice, would settle down. Nevertheless, Janice remains happily at school now.

STEALING AND EMOTIONAL DISTRESS

When pupils are found stealing it is helpful to know that not all kinds of theft are the result of the same motive such as gain. This knowledge can, to some extent, offer understanding and guide the actions and attitudes that the teacher and school take. Rich's (1956) classification has been helpful in this respect in a number of cases. Attention should also be directed to the objects which they steal. For example, one Services girl stole only rulers and pens from class, and money from home and class, to buy sweets to give to other pupils. A secondary school second-year boy stole only small round purses and coins. There appear to be four main reasons for stealing:

- *Comforting offences* Most often solitary stealing engaged in by child seemingly as a substitute for loss or lack of affection felt from parents and peers. Most common in cases where there is a history of separation.
- *Marauding offences* Unplanned thefts engaged in by two or three young persons on impulse when seeing the opportunity. There is often peer group pressure and conformity attached to this and an element of 'proving'.
- *Proving offences* Usually solitary stealing by adolescents and young adults who are often said to be inadequate personalities. The theft usually consists of taking away and driving a car but may also be theft of cigarettes, alcohol, video-tapes and records.
- *Secondary offences* Stealing for gain, sometimes under the direction of an adult, a parent, older sibling or fence. Forward planning engaged in to avoid detection. Parents in Plymouth a few years ago were found to be organising and fencing the thefts of their seven-year-old children who could not, at that age, be taken to court and considered responsible for their actions.

Dealing with stealing

Most children take things belonging to others at some time and most people will admit to having stolen apples. Some admit to having taken school pencils and books and the firm's stationery if pressed, although they do not always altogether regard this as theft. A seemingly larger number of people feel able to help themselves to property 'left lying around' than in the past. Perhaps this is because there are more belongings to be taken and more people to take them, rather than just a straightforward moral decline. The word stealing is seldom used when pupils recount these experiences; they use euphemisms such as 'taking' and 'lifting' although the motive has been for gain. With regard to young children the word 'taking' is often the more appropriate one to use for it takes several years for the use of the possessive pronouns such as 'mine' and 'yours' to appear in the vocabulary and, even then, perhaps to the age of four or five for the concept to be fully understood. This understanding requires a range of appropriate learning experiences in context which the young child may not have had and so arrives at school without this knowledge or in some confusion. If the concept of ownership has not been developed, the finer moral concepts of right and wrong have little opportunity to establish themselves in relation to theft of possessions. Some children remain confused or insensitive to these issues until junior or even secondary school, particularly when the models they see at home favour and promote the art and skills of taking. Other young children may have been drilled in a moral code with little understanding of its rationale.

When children take things the teacher should show disapproval of the act and not the person. The disapproval should not be a public event. The teacher then needs to develop a teaching programme in which the concept of ownership can be developed together with notions of moral responsibility, rights and duties. According to Dawson *et al.* (1985) this must first mean that the child is enabled to enjoy the experience and rights of ownership of personal possessions, however small. The experience of sharing can be introduced and encouraged, together with the rights and responsibilities of the role of sharer. Acts of wrong doing and infringement of others' rights and freedoms need to be labelled so that their content and meaning can be identified and explored. Moral development comes slowly and only when the children themselves have a sense of their own worth and self-esteem can they begin to transfer this and learn to value others and their needs. Young children's stealing is often an indication of their need for affection and esteem, as Rich points out, to gain objects to give away to be attractive to peers and win their affection or esteem.

Persistent stealing in any classroom can be upsetting and the teacher needs to deal with it as unemotionally and quietly as possible. Contacting parents to gain their help and support is an essential part of dealing with the problem. It may be possible to counsel them on the possible origins of the problem, such as new babies in families engendering feelings of affectionlessness however much preparation has been made for the event. There are, then, ways in which the parents can guard against this once they are alerted to the problem. Similar problems can occur when children of the new step-parent arrive in the family or if there is family stress. At such times 'comforting' offences become common or bedwetting suddenly restarts when the child has been dry for years.

When a pupil has been caught stealing it is unwise for a huge fuss to be made in front of all the other pupils. The situation is best dealt with on an individual basis after the rest of the class have left, and in a counselling style. The nature of the act should be defined, the upset it caused to the owner should be stressed and an attempt should be made to establish the reason for the theft with the pupil. Strategies to avoid the situation occurring again should be planned and the teacher should keep a careful watch on the pupil making unobtrusive searches to ensure that, where possible, the behaviour is uncovered or preferably stopped before the theft can ensue. A simple and fair reparation for each theft should be agreed and undertaken, this will also need the cooperation or agreement of the parents. Taking care to provide little opportunity for theft is most important, for stealing and eating the chocolates or giving the presents can be so satisfying in itself that once the cycle is established it is difficult to stop. Increasing support and affection at home and school can be a difficult path for both parents and teachers to pursue. Whilst the teaching and learning programme is underway it is best that the pupil is not left exposed to situations which would be tempting. Petty theft, when it does occur, most often arises at about the age of eight or nine years, and can continue until around fourteen or fifteen when its nature tends to change towards breaking and entering or taking away and joy-riding cars. Seemingly comforting offences change to proving offences. In some cases this cycle can begin as early as four or five years of age. According to West (1982), in his studies of delinquent careers, most theft behaviours are abandoned between eighteen and twenty-one years of age and most youths do not go on to engage in criminal careers, except those from the most disturbed and deprived backgrounds who often do become recidivists.

Compulsive stealing for reasons of loss of self-esteem or loss of affection, as in proving and comforting offences, can be considered as examples of 'nervous illness' engendered by emotional distress. What must not be allowed to happen is that they are allowed to become a 'way of life' phenomenon as Mongon (1988) describes, where schools increasingly subject disruptive pupils to negative sanctions until they are excluded. In the case of theft the same processes can occur until the pupil finishes up with a criminal record.

Even in situations where stealing for gain is common and there appear to be no underlying emotional problems, there is most often a code of conduct known as 'honour among thieves' in which they would not think of stealing from each other, only from 'the rest'. In a school society in which individuals feel part of the purposeful activity, supported, helped and esteemed, they are far less likely to steal from it, deface or destroy it, for it becomes 'ours' not 'theirs'. However, not all schools are particularly good at developing such a sense of well-being and community amongst all their members, especially the lower attainers.

CHARACTERISTICS OF CHILDREN WITH LOW SELF-ESTEEM

Children with very low self-esteem will be recognised by their characteristic patterns of behaviours. There are, of course, a number of different patterns:

The lonely isolates are:
- isolate in playground;
- rejected by peers or ignored by them;
- derided by peers out of teacher's hearing;
- self-conscious;
- fearful;

- anxious for approval;
- unpredictable in behaviour;
- poor socially, with often inappropriate social behaviours;
- poor at joining in games and cooperative activities; and
- disruptive, but often unaware of this fact.

The able underachievers are:
- reluctant to join in anything;
- anxious for approval;
- over-sensitive to criticism;
- never satisfied with efforts;
- unrealistic in setting goals – they are either too high or too low;
- clowns; and
- unmotivated.

The generally disruptive:
- chatter continuously;
- move and wander around the room, if allowed;
- clown about;
- disturb other pupils' work;
- distract other pupils;
- are attention seeking;
- are negativistic; and
- are unmotivated to work.

The nature of self-esteem

Both disruptive and withdrawn pupils suffer from low self-esteem. Other terms which are related to self-esteem are the 'self-concept' and 'self-image'. Self-esteem reflects the evaluation that a person typically makes of him/herself. It contains an element of approval or disapproval and conveys the extent to which the person sees him/herself to be worthwhile, significant, successful and capable of dealing with life. It is, of course, a personal judgment and may undergo continual revision throughout life as new experience and information is incorporated into the concept of self.

In order for teachers to enhance self-esteem within the classroom, Purkey (1970) suggests six essential factors:

- *Challenge* – This involves bringing the pupil to the point where the chances of success are good and then to issue the challenge 'This is hard but I think you can do it'.
- *Freedom* – The pupils must have freedom to make real decisions.
- *Respect* – The teacher should never lower a pupil's sense of worth.
- *Warmth* – The teacher should provide a safe supportive learning environment.
- *Control* – The pupils must know that there are firm but reasonable and fair limits to what they may do, and should feel secure and safe in that knowledge.
- *Success* – The pupils must experience success rather than failure.

When we begin to recognise that some pupils, from their first day in school, experience daily feelings of failure rather than success, it is not surprising that after years and years they become antipathetic to school. As they become confirmed failures, and problems in the school's eyes, they cease to secure the respect and warmth which they need and sink further and further into a cycle of failure and rejection. Collaborative learning, conflict resolution and mediation strategies discussed in Chapter 10 offer a set of strategies to help deal with these problems.

SUMMARY

Teachers need to be aware that their pupils may be under emotional pressure and suffer from anxiety which can prevent them from learning. These stresses may be located in the home or school but the results are brought into the classroom. If children are in nervous health, the teachers and the school can do much to help and support them. If children become 'nervously ill' then their symptoms should be recorded and the appropriate advice and guidelines followed. Quiet, calm and prompt action in these cases is essential.

In addition to these children, there are also pupils with emotional problems resulting from learning difficulties who are allowed to fail in huge numbers in our schools, where teachers fail to adopt mixed-ability teaching strategies and techniques for differentiation of learning inputs and outcomes. As well as emotional difficulties arising from learning failure there are those which arise from pupils put 'at risk' by their socio-emotional conditioning, which makes them ill at ease and out of key in certain school environments. All these pupils suffer from systematic lowering of their self-esteem and concept of self-worth. This, in turn, makes some respond disruptively and others to become withdrawn. Faced with such problems teachers often seek to control, reprimand and use sanctions against the pupils who 'act out'. What is recommended here is that teachers address the issue of their own attitudes to learning and teaching and find ways of promoting pupil success, which will gradually counteract the feelings of low self-esteem. Pupils who find they are themselves respected in the school will learn to have respect for others; it is a reciprocal relationship.

5

Key Researches for Dealing with Disruption

INTRODUCTION

The early studies on changing unwanted classroom behaviours were mainly based upon the behaviour modification studies of Skinner (1953). He designed operant conditioning experiments in which rats' emitted behaviours were shaped to persuade them to press levers to obtain food and pigeons were taught to walk in figures of eight and play table tennis by the manipulation of reinforcement schedules. The principles which he derived from these and other experiments were applied, using token systems, to train mentally-impaired people and mentally-ill schizophrenic patients to become socially integrated, and autistic children to talk and become more social. He also wrote the book *Walden II*, showing how a society could be constructed upon the operation of these principles.

His behaviour modification techniques were also applied to classroom management problems and the following early studies selected for discussion illustrate this. Recent studies, for example, Wheldall and Merritt, 1984, 1985, 1986, with their BATPACK training programmes, follow in this tradition. Behaviour modification techniques are one subset of a variety of conditioning procedures, often called 'brain-washing techniques' and thus there are ethical issues related to this which will need to be considered.

School strategies for dealing with disruption had generally centred around punishment or fear of punishment, but the detentions and canings given seemed to have little effect on those who received them, they invariably seemed to misbehave again. Perhaps the supposition was that, without them, many more pupils would have misbehaved. Pupils themselves say that the deterrent effect only seems to persist up until the first detention or caning where these still exist. Once this barrier has been broken, pupils say they feel less anxious about getting another and some eventually become indifferent. This suggests that if punishments are used they should be used very sparingly indeed so that their effect can be maximised. 'Familiarity breeds contempt' would seem to be characteristic of most school punishment systems and there is little about most of them which is truly aversive. Fear of punishment seems to be the greater deterrent especially for the wide group of onlookers who learn to suppress their own undesirable behaviours because of what happens to others (Bandura and Walters 1963) in a process known as vicarious learning and vicarious reinforcement. Finding scapegoats on which to demonstrate the power of the system hardly seems to be a justification for the use of punishments. Perhaps their only advantage is that they are a short circuit treatment used under duress when there is insufficient time and energy to examine and deal with the reasons for the behaviour.

In schools today, there are few obvious sanctions left for teachers to use. They may give detentions but these are fraught with regulations. Notice must be given to parents, and periods of time adhered to. Exclusion from the classroom is often seen but is against many LEA rulings. Pupils sent out may miss important parts of work and so fail to acquire basic knowledge and fall further behind. They often go with bad grace and pull faces through the window. They may take themselves off and pull out the sleeves of coats in the cloakroom, write graffiti in the corridor, or run off. It can be dangerous and unwise to send young children out unaccompanied. They may run home upset and have an accident which has legal consequences for all concerned. In addition, once a child has been sent out or sent to the head of pastoral care, the deputy or the headteacher, discipline has been handed over to someone else and in a sense failure admitted.

The strategies which will be explained are those which involve gaining and maintaining classroom control and individual discipline without the use of punishment or bribes. Some are behavioural, others are motivational or cognitive strategies and should be tried before resorting to threats or punishment.

Understanding possible origins of behaviour problems may help one be less impatient and less likely to nag when a pupil does not do as asked, but teachers need to know more than this. Problems arising from both 'social' and 'asocial' origins, as already described, have their roots in the injudicious use of the reward and punishment system in the child's early years by the parents or guardians. It is not surprising, therefore, that treatments which are often most successful also manipulate this system. What is more surprising is that behaviour problems arising from other difficulties such as hyperactivity, learning difficulty, frustration and emotional problems also respond to the same system of use of rewards by the methods known as behaviour modification.

BEHAVIOUR MODIFICATION

Many parents and teachers exploit these methods without ever realising that they are doing so. Others, less fortunate, may begin by using the wrong strategy and get themselves into a position where whatever they do makes the problems worse.

Behaviour modification is based upon the principle of *reinforcement* of emitted responses. There is, however, one weakness. The behaviour modification may improve the pupil's behaviour but it will not improve the task performance (Wheldall and Merritt, 1984). This is why other methods also need to be introduced which will encourage this:

Positive reinforcement (+ve R) The presence of a positive reinforcer increases the likelihood of a response occurring.

Negative reinforcement (−ve R) When a negative reinforcement is removed this will *increase* the likelihood of response occurring. It does not stop the response. The presence of reinforcers whether positive or negative will increase a response rate or the incidence of unwanted or disruptive behaviour.

No reinforcement Ignore a response and it is less likely to be repeated.

REWARDS AND PUNISHMENT

In philosophical terms for something to be truly rewarding, the pupil must have *cognisance* of it and it has to be genuinely desirable to that individual. Rewards could be stars, marks, pleasant comments, smiles, approval, praise, support, prizes if this cognitive component is present.

Positive reinforcement carries no such cognitive requirement. Simply giving attention when the pupil is misbehaving can cause the behaviour to be repeated more and more often, even if the attention given is a sharp comment or disapproval. The *double bind* is that the teacher cannot always afford to ignore misbehaviour, otherwise the attention seeking may become worse and other pupils around will begin to imitate the unwanted behaviour when they see one of their number 'getting away with murder'. Punishments and tellings-off are sometitmes the only attention some pupils ever receive and to those deprived of attention, any form of it is better than none at all and so they 'act up' to be noticed and become a nuisance or class clown.

For something to be truly punishing it has to be aversive and, in philosophical terms, has to be accepted by the pupil as such. Thus, keeping a child in at lunchtime may be just what he/she wanted and is seen as a reward not a punishment. Knowing and understanding the relationship between the misdeed and the punishment and its *retributive* function is an added cognitive dimension which it is helpful to consider.

Estes identified a number of key concepts in relation to punishment.

- Mild punishment temporarily blocks behaviour. Pupils often ignore 'desist' instructions of low status person.
- Undesirable behaviour is not easily eliminated. We cannot unlearn unwanted behaviours, we merely inhibit or suppress them.
- Permanent weakening of undesirable behaviour occurs if it is simply unreinforced [ignored].
- Punishment, if severe, can lead to adverse emotional states which can suppress desirable responses.
- In the period of suppression of the unwanted behaviour, it is possible to reinforce some other more desirable behaviours.
- Punishment suppresses a response, it does not weaken it.
- Punishment only suppresses a response if it immediately follows it.

In Skinnerian behaviour modification, the 'organism need not know the goal towards which its behaviour is being shaped'. Thus, whenever discusson about intentions and purposes occurs or contracts are entered into, this removes the technique from the shaping-type ambit. In trying to change children's behaviours I find it helpful to distinguish between non-cognitive and cognitive interventions. Reserving 'positive reinforcement' for non-cognitive shaping procedures and 'rewards' for cognitive ones. This is not usually a distinction made in the studies of applied behavioural analysis (ABA). Thus we can read in Wheldall and Riding (1983) the following:

> In simple, everyday language consequences may be described as 'rewarding' or 'punishing'. Rewarding consequences, which we call *positive reinforcers*, are events which we seek out or 'go for' whilst we try to avoid punishing consequences; neutral consequences are events which affect us neither way. Behaviours followed by positive reinforcers are likely to increase in frequency. Behaviours followed by punishers tend to decrease in frequency whilst neutral consequences have no effect.

Reward and punishment will be used to describe cognitive intervention, and negative and positive reinforcement to describe behaviour modification processes. Often what occurs in practice is that both positive reinforcement and reward are used in the same intervention.

An important consideration in some researches and programmes is the giving of tangible rewards in the form of money, gifts, tokens to buy things such as time out of lessons, or time off task but playing sports. Token economies have been successfully used in the reintegration into society of mentally-ill adults and behaviourally-disturbed adolescents. The latter are often treated in this country to this régime in high security institutions. Their use, particularly in the classroom, brings with it such questions as whether it is right to bribe children to work in school. In fact it could be argued that if we have to bribe them, there is probably something wrong with the task and their ability to access it, or they have a history of failure which hinders them from being free to dare to make an effort. Stars and stickers which have individual information value and serve to give public acclaim are perhaps the furthest one might wish to go in this respect. Even so, they are to be avoided wherever possible. However, there is always the exceptional circumstances where, when everything else has failed, in desperation the 'bribe' is offered such as, 'If you sit quietly for five minutes and do your maths then you can go and play outside'. The danger is two-fold. When it works, as it so often does the first time, we are encouraged to repeat it. Eventually, the stakes and the expectations of reward rise higher and higher so that they can no longer be met. The second problem is that the pupil can come to learn that nothing needs to be done in the way of work unless someone is prepared to pay for it to be done and school work has no intrinsic value in itself now or even later.

A secondary school pupil who was very disruptive and spent little time on task was discussed at a recent in-service meeting. The teacher was offered two different sets of advice. The first advice was to find out what the pupil enjoyed doing and buy him something related to it which could then be used to negotiate a quiet session with a set time on task. He enjoyed painting, wanted some paints and it was suggested that these should be bought and used in the negotiations. The teacher was worried but willing to try. A second pupil enjoyed playing with cars. Time on cars, legally earned, would be used as a bribe to spend time on task in mathematics. This was easier to accept and implement by the teacher.

The second advice was to wait until both pupils settled at something and then 'catch them being good' and deliberately set out to build their self-esteem. Although the alternative of playing with a toy car was cheaper, it was no less questionable as a motivator. In addition, as all the other children who were good would not be getting the extra playtime it could reinforce their potential to misbehave so that they could be given special rewards. Giving gifts was worrying to all the teachers whereas time on activity of own choice used with the same intent was not, although in my view it was no less controversial. In the event, both teachers decided to try the 'catch them being good' strategy first. In both cases, it had a remarkable effect which persisted over the rest of the day and encouraged the teachers to go on using it. They therefore maintained their pupils' on task behaviours. They were surprised at this strategy's powerfulness and the fact that substitute tasks and tangible rewards did not have to be used. 'Catch them being good' has, however, to be used in an utterly sincere way and be credible and truthful if it is to work. Any insincerity on the part of the teacher or the fact that the teacher is not a credible and respected source will diminish the power of the technique. What is continually surprising to teachers is the regard and esteem in which they are held by the most unlikely pupils and how hard these pupils are prepared to work for the smallest crumbs of teacher approval.

Case example by Jan Holden

Name Nicky
Date of Birth 23.8.75. C.A. 7 yrs 7 mths
One sister born January 1982
Father: bank manager
Both parents are anxious that he does well academically.

Problem In September 1982 before the course:
Nicky would not read although he did not seem to have any problems with reading. The infant school records showed him 8.7 on Burt's word recognition test in July 1982. He scored 9.9 on Daniels and Diack's test on reading experience in September 1982.

Each reading time followed a similar pattern. Nicky would poke at his book, poke the children around him, or drop something and climb under the table to retrieve it.

He is a very strong-willed boy and said he did not like reading. Nothing shifted him. His mother came to see me (about some lost belongings) and as we chatted she said that neither she nor her husband were able to get Nicky to read much at home, although they both felt that this was important. As we talked, I realised that his mother and I both 'nagged' Nicky a great deal, so I tried to ignore his non-reading and tried not to make an issue of it, praising him when he did read.

Over the past few months this approach has worked better than nagging! He is reading more willingly; agrees when I tell him how good he's getting and the last fortnight has really enjoyed *Reading Workshop*, which is a new reading activity for this term.

TWO FOUNDATION RESEARCH STUDIES IN BEHAVIOUR MODIFICATION

STUDY 1

The research by Scott MacDonald (1971) is based upon behaviourist principles and demonstrates the shaping effect of positive reinforcement. 'Catch them being good', (CBG) by contrast, may range at one extreme from the nods, smiles and 'goods' of positive reinforcement to a mixed pattern of feedback and, at the other extreme, to positive cognitive interventions, (PCI) a positive, constructive explanation of what is good about a piece of work and how it can be made better.

The search for a good teaching style

Scott MacDonald and his co-workers were called into the Leeward School in Hawaii where the pupils were said to be out of control and causing great distress and concern. The researchers were not teachers or educational psychologists but, in this setting, naive observers although trained psychologists. They found some lenient and some permissive teachers unable to control classes or individuals, some authoritarians and one who terrified the pupils so much they were unable to recite from rote memory. Some classes were so overwhelmed by managerial detail there was no interaction. On the other hand, they found some representatives of each of these styles. The conclusions they drew from their observations were that the *search for style was futile*. Any teaching style could prove effective. In the course of their observation and recording, what they did note was that specific actions did evoke desired responses. Some teachers had what they called personal tricks and many used the *cold stare*. The cold stare stopped the activity of any pupil to whom it was directed. Several teachers gave responsibilities to pupils who maintained preferred behaviours. The researchers decided that it was unlikely that they could change a style and that it could prove more profitable to attend to the teachers' specific acts and perhaps change those.

They observed 11022 teacher and student behaviours and found that 90 per cent of all teacher behaviours fell into five categories, whether they were observing those teaching pre-school children, or fifteen-year-olds. This was true of all but two good teachers whose behaviours and interactions were so complex and so subtle it proved impossible for the researchers to analyse them or teach other teachers to use them.

Ten teachers were then observed in the main art of the study and another consistent factor which emerged was that the teachers spent *17–30 per cent of their time lecturing;* the rest was variable. The classes this time consisted of eight-, ten-, thirteen- and fifteen-year-olds. Inter-observer reliability in classifying and categorising responses was above the 80 per cent level. The researchers recorded teacher behaviour and pupil behaviour before and after the response, for example, pupil pokes peer with ruler. Teacher says 'Don't'. Observers wait five seconds and then record what the child is doing.

Pattern of teacher behaviours revealed

S (*Support*) Verbal or gestural (nod, smile, etc.) – when the teacher speaks to a student in a way which indicates by tone of voice, by content of the remark, or by gesture that the teacher unambiguously approves of the actions of the student.

A (*Approach*) When the teacher responds favourably, by her presence or postural attitude, indicating that she is attending to the behaviour of one or more students, clearly supportive movement toward student or contact of supportive nature such as patting on the back or shoulder.

I (*Information*) Long directions or lecture. (Turned the pupils off and bored them.)

V (*General Verbal Behaviour*) Short explanations and simple instructions not scored **I**. Usual verbalising which does not clearly fall into other categories. (Short verbals were excellent in directing pupils' behaviours and stimulating work.)

D (*Desist or Disapproval Behaviour*) When a teacher, either by gesture or word, asks a student to stop a given activity; when the teacher's behaviour is clearly designed to control a situation, as when she changes two students' seats to stop their talking, and the like.

(Talking to another adult, working at desk, pacing – not recorded.)
S and **A** were more enduring in their effects than **I** and **V**.

I – Short **I** improves student behaviour but the longer the lecture the more the students are 'turned off' and turn to misbehaviours.
Source: Scott MacDonald (1971) *Battle in the Classroom*, Brighton: Intext.

The researchers found that the effect of much teacher intervention was often temporarily to stop the behaviour for two or three seconds but then it was resumed, hence the five second delay in recording.

Support behaviours

Another major finding was that, when the teacher *positively supported* some behaviour, most often when no bad behaviour had occurred, this tended to not only improve the behaviour of the pupil to whom it was directed, but also seemed to have a positive effect on nearby pupils. The researchers called this the *ripple effect*.

Some teachers used support behaviours to terminate undesirable behaviours, a tactic which was previously unknown to the observers. For example, when one pupil was talking to another and was told by the teacher how good the work was which he or she had done the day before, the pupil showed no indication that the praise was valued at all, but five seconds later the student was busy working.

Desist behaviours

The desist behaviour seemed to work entirely against the teachers' own interest. In half the instances when desist was used, the pupils' behaviour showed no change and the desist did not stop the unwanted behaviour. In most of the rest of the instances it caused a deterioration in behaviour, for example, 34 per cent of the cases.

All teachers seemed to have little success with desist behaviours. The 17 per cent of cases where they were successful were with *sharp look* (stink look) and *sharp gesture*. Verbal criticism generated the most negative response – especially if lengthy, and also had a negative effect on the pupil's neighbours. Satire was one of the *worst* desist behaviours the teachers could use; only one or two teachers managed to use it in such a humorous way that they gained a positive attitude. In only one case was a teacher actually able to use desist effectively, but only because he was so *overpoweringly positive* most of the time that his pupils seemed willing to do anything to gain his favour. Another teacher used verbal behaviour (**V**) so effectively she needed no desists. She held the thirty-four pupils' attention all the time with an entertaining and vivacious style. The researchers deemed her an exception and concluded there was no way to teach the skill she displayed.

Scott MacDonald's conclusions were that teachers seriously under-estimated their influence and impact on their pupils. They often felt they did not have control when they clearly did, which made them nervous of experimenting with ideas and techniques. They observed the effect they had on the pupil they were talking to but they did not notice the marked effect that this behaviour had on the rest of the class. They discovered the powerful and simple means of influencing pupil behaviour, the deliberate *smiling teacher*.

One of the most interesting cases was that of the kindergarten teacher. The following is an extract from Scott MacDonald (1971) illustrating the problem:

> According to the teacher, a few of the 28 kindergarteners in her class were well behaved, but the majority – from the first bell in the morning to the end of school day – ignored her so completely that she was unable to complete a single lesson. The morning after the teacher had requested help, a consult-ant was seated in the back of her room before the tardy bell. He ignored all the children's attempts to gain his attention before and during the class.
>
> The teacher began by singing a song to gain the interest and attention of the children; they were to respond with the chorus. The students' responses varied: one boy continued to circle the room on a skateboard; one girl threw blocks at her tablemates; two boys continued to play on the lawn just outside the room, ignoring the teacher's demands to come in and sit down; four other boys were totally absorbed in a contest to determine who could scoot across the room without leaving their chairs.
>
> Under a portable chalkboard a boy was fending off thrusts of a long stick expertly wielded by a small girl, who punctuated her efforts with loud taunts. During these episodes, the remainder of the class momentarily sat attentive and ready to begin. When two of the previously attentive boys began to fight so vigorously that the teacher returned immediately to stop them; the other two boys continued to play on the lawn. While the teacher was absorbed with scolding the fighters, the skateboard boy crashed into a table, sending half a dozen children fleeing for safety; the teacher stopped her scolding and physically placed the skateboard boy in a circle of children and in the process delivered several more reprimands. This pattern continued for the entire 30 minutes the consultant stayed in the room.

The consultant found that during the thirty-minute periods observed, the kindergarten teacher did not exhibit a single example of support/approve behaviour. The teacher explained that the misbehaviour was due to the children's deficiencies, in particular their inadequate home training. She felt that the children were naughty, ill-mannered and disrespectful and that they required a firm hand. She did concede that she had not had much success so far with her methods of control.

The consultant suggested that the teacher ignored unacceptable behaviour and attended to the children who were ready to begin and giving her full attention. She should seek to support and approve of their behaviour. During the two days following this advice there was no change in the teacher's behaviour. She explained that she simply could not ignore misbehaviour; it was part of her personal ideology that 'naughty children must be punished'. On the fifth day, the consultant again recorded events, but every time the teacher smiled or approved, the consultant smiled and nodded approval. When she scolded and criticised, the consultant looked away. The effect was immediate. As she began to apply support/approve

Figure 4   *Maslow's hierarchy of human needs*

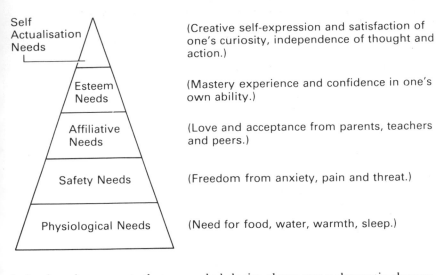

Self Actualisation Needs — (Creative self-expression and satisfaction of one's curiosity, independence of thought and action.)

Esteem Needs — (Mastery experience and confidence in one's own ability.)

Affiliative Needs — (Love and acceptance from parents, teachers and peers.)

Safety Needs — (Freedom from anxiety, pain and threat.)

Physiological Needs — (Need for food, water, warmth, sleep.)

behaviour in amounts that exceeded desist, there was a dramatic change in the classroom. For example, the boy who began each day on the skateboard, went and sat down, after a few passes which evoked no reprimand. When the teacher smiled at him he responded by sitting as close to her as possible. By day ten, this boy was attentive to the teacher for fifteen out of thirty minutes. After day ten, the teacher asked to try the new approach alone. The consultant withdrew. It was soon apparent that the teacher had returned to 'normal' and all the support/approve was gone. The teacher's ideological commitment to discipline through punishment apparently caused the reversal. The consultants were very depressed.

What Scott MacDonald and his co-workers were trying to apply were the Skinnerian principles of positive reinforcement to *shape* the kindergarten teacher's responses. If we are to use positive reinforcement and rewards, we need to know what is most reinforcing. Motivation theorists such as Maslow (1962) propose a tension reduction theory to explain human motivation and the role of reinforcement. The theory suggests that if we are hungry and thirsty, then it is likely that these needs will have to be satisfied before we can concentrate on school learning. If we are motivated to seek satisfaction for a need for self-esteem and affiliation with others, we will work to these ends. Thus, teachers need to construct the learning environment so that pupils can fulfil these needs by working on the task rather than fulfilling them despite the task by entertaining their peers. If we can find what motivates, we can also find what reinforces and rewards and leads to learning.

What are the most powerful reinforcers and rewards?

These have found to be:

- social approval of peers;
- social approval of teachers;
- getting something right;
- succeeding at some overall task;

- taking responsibility for work;
- taking responsibility for others.

What are the effects of punishment?

Both Thorndike (1930) and Estes (1964) found little evidence for the weakening effect of punishment and, in fact, found some signs that punishment strengthened the response. In analysing the situation, you find that when you tell people they are right, they only have to try to repeat the first attempt. When, however, you tell them they are wrong, they have to do something different, precisely what is not clear. They have to remember what not to do and form a hypothesis about what to do. This enables us to extrapolate a most important principle for guidance in using any desist behaviour.

Principle 1

If a pupil is told *not* to do a particular thing, that is 'desist from', within the shortest time possible, he/she must be told which behaviour will be acceptable. When this behaviour occurs, or its nearest approximation, it must be *immediately positively reinforced*.

Principle 2

An undesirable response which is intermittently punished and rewarded is stamped in (Wagner, 1963). This principle is in operation when children are reared inconsistently by their parents, or are in a classroom with an unruly teacher or a succession of ineffective teachers.

Parents also need help

Parents often demonstrate how they are manoeuvred into 'stamping in' bad behaviour. A common occurrence which can be observed in super-markets is the screaming two-year-old being dragged around the store by a red-faced parent, trying to prevent the miscreant from snatching things from shelves. The child wants sweets, the parent says no. The row goes and on until, arriving at the check-out queue, the embarrassed parent gives in. The child wins sweets and the argument. Researchers in the area of learning and reinforcement have shown that this type of interaction where the parent says 'No. . ., No. . ., No. . .,' then 'Yes' will stamp in all the unwanted behaviours of screaming, yelling and snatching when the child wants his/her own way. He/she learns to go on just long enough, especially in front of an audience, so that 'blackmail' will work. Adults are seen to lose their nerve and be manipulated against their will, having little power to deny. Inconsistent parents create a state of mind in which the child is indifferent to praise or blame, for a stable reaction pattern cannot be predicted. Such a parent might one night praise a child and buy him sweets for washing up and making a cup of tea, and the next night scream and rave if, in washing up, he had broken the cups or scalded himself with the hot water. Again, a type of double bind.

Indulgent parents teach their children to misbehave by encouraging them to be disobedient and praising them for it ('He's a real bad boy') and smiling. It may be attractive and clever when a two-year-old manipulates and controls an adult, but it is seldom the case later on when the two-year-old has grown into a selfish and attention-seeking seven-year-old and rules the household – the omnipotent child.

Infants grow towards the stage where they want to test out their interdependence and a teacher/mother described with horror the day she was taking her two-year-old son for a walk in the park and this moment of first testing occurred. They were walking back to the car. She unlocked and opened the door for him and went round to get in the driver's seat, to find he had watched her and, catching her eye when she said 'Come on, let's go home', had run off gleefully back into the park. She said she was shocked and angry and was just about to run after him when she thought of the consequences of her chasing him all over the place and bringing him back struggling and crying to the car. He wanted her to chase him, she thought. With great anguish, and in fear and trembling, she got into the car and drove slowly up the road a little way and stopped, door still ajar, and waited and watched. He came back when he saw her move off; when she stopped he ran up to the car and got in without a word. She had won the first round safely and he knew that she meant what she said.

STUDY 2

One of the earliest studies in which behaviour modification research was applied to classroom behaviour problems was carried out by Becker *et al.* (1967). The study was called *The Contingent Use of Teacher Attention and Praise in Reducing Classroom Problems*. The Becker study was undertaken in Urbana, Illinois, in an elementary school and showed that attention, praise, nearness and other social stimuli produced by teachers maintained the pro-social behaviours and the deviant ones. The researchers maintained that attention in almost any form maintained the deviant behaviours.

Their study was to demonstrate the differential *contingent use* of teacher attention and praise and was an exploration of ways of training teachers to be more effective in managing classroom behaviour problems. It was a study in which seven teachers volunteered to participate but only five completed the programme. The researchers undertook the following.

- They trained the teachers.
- They trained the observers.
- They selected *target* children, two (persistent problems) per class, in discussion with the teachers.
- They established *baseline* behaviour, that is the frequency of problem behaviour occurring. Problems arose when teachers tended to try out the techniques in advance and so altered the baseline behaviours before the study started.
- They established and tested coding categories for defining teacher behaviour.

The observer's (students) were trained and worked two to a class. The target children were observed for twenty minutes per day, for four days per week. The observers observed for twenty seconds and recorded for ten seconds throughout the twenty-minute period.

In the first five weeks, a baseline frequency for behaviour problems of the target children was established and the teachers were trained in behaviour modification strategies. There was a nine-week experimental period. Typewritten rules were given on 5″ × 8″ card and the teachers implemented a praise and attention strategy contingent upon any 'on target' behaviour of the target pupil. The following rules were given to the teachers:

1 Make rules for each period explicit to children (remind them of the rules when needed).
2 Ignore (do not attend to) behaviours which interfere with learning and teaching unless a child is being hurt by another (beware ignoring unwanted behaviours except under special conditions).
3 Use punishment which seems appropriate, preferably withdrawal of the reinforcement.
4 Give praise and attention to appropriate behaviours, for example, raising hand to answer question or to get attention.

One teacher was given general rules and instructed not to give target children any more special attention than the rest of the class. (This teacher used very negative control procedures and had a high level of disruptive behaviour from the pupils.)

After each day of the experimental period, the researchers gave feedback on the teachers' performance. For some teachers, the delivery of positive comments was difficult and initial attempts were stilted and stereotyped. After a week, however, the teachers were found to be changing:

– even the negative teacher was more smiling and spontaneous and actually enjoying her lessons; and
– another said she had fifteen minutes more, morning and afternoon to get things done.

Results

The average 'deviant' behaviour for the ten children in five classes was 62.13 per cent during baseline period and 29.19 per cent during experimental period when the positive intervention took place. This was a drop of over 50 per cent in behaviour problems. The system was not, however, very effective with all the children and did not produce much change in one child until his reading skills improved. In one case, instead of secondary reinforcers (praise and smiles), tangible reinforcement was used (bribes). The teachers were described as well as the pupils. For example:

Teacher A was sensitive, anxious, doubted her ability to use 'the approach' and whether it would work with her children's age group. Both children changed remarkably and so did the teacher and other members of the class. One of her target pupils was Albert, seven years, eight months. He was a noisy, disruptive child and could not stay in his seat. Teacher A said 'I could not have reinforced his negative behaviour more, for I caught him in every deviant act possible and often before it occurred. I lectured him and was only making a backward motion.'

Teacher B controlled the class by sharp command, physical punishment, and loss of privileges. She followed the programme effectively. Betty, nine years, seven months, was pestering, blurting out, thumbsucking, making loud noises and occasionally hitting other children. Her behaviour problems decreased as did her thumbsucking.

The findings of this research add support to the proposition that much can be done by the classroom teacher to eliminate behaviours which interfere with learning without having to rely on massive change in the home or intensive therapy.

(Becker *et al.* 1967)

CONCLUSIONS TO STUDIES

The conclusions which may be drawn from these studies is that positive attention, praise and support are *powerful reinforcers in the classroom* and teachers would be advised to learn to use them effectively. As can be seen, there are a few children whose behaviour demands further analysis and for whom the behaviour modification programme is not enough. There is also research evidence (Harrop, 1983 and Wheldall and Riding 1983) which confirms this but which suggests that, although behaviour modification will change social behaviours, it does not improve performance on task. Nevertheless, improving the social climate of the classroom does allow time for more teaching and learning to take place. There have also been criticisms that the effects of behaviour modification do not last. This is of some concern and may be caused by the teacher reverting to old habits or by the system not being sophisticated enough to maintain the improved performance. However, there are circumstances with children who have undiagnosed learning problems where this is true and the effects do not last. These criticisms do not seem to be unreasonable because, in order for motivation to work, there has to be interest in the task and a history of some success in similar activities. It would therefore seem necessary to use the positive approach derived from behaviour modification plus some cognitive component, for example, and investigate those principles which will make the task set intrinsically interesting and motivating (PCI). This cognition and resultant compliance can remove us from the dangers of 'brain washing'.

One can thus argue that for managing pupils' behaviour in classrooms, behaviour modification principles and practices are necessary but, they do not always provide sufficient conditions for eliciting good behaviour.

Within the Becker and Madsen study, one of the pupils, Carole, who talked out of turn and blurted out for 75 per cent of the time during the baseline period, only improved to 55 per cent deviant behaviour. The researchers were not satisfied and introduced a points system (week 9). At the end of the day, if she reached the required number of points, she could buy a 'treat' with them; initially this was sweets. Others in the class could earn sweets by helping her. The points were based on a shifting criterion geared to her progress. Carole progressed eventually to saving points over several days. On 3 May (week 10), she announced she was not going to work for points today and didn't. 'She was a hellion all day.' Over the next two weeks, she worked for a ring and the components of a make-up kit (she was aged seven and scored from 78 to 100 on various IQ tests) and was down to 20 per cent deviant behaviour that week. In the last week of May, she was back to talking and blurting out again. Most of us have met a Carole and, in this country, we should be less comfortable with this system of bribes and inducements than perhaps teachers in the USA. It is a token system involving knowledge of goals and purposes but for Carole the 'rewards' derived from blurting out and talking were obviously fulfilling a greater need than the tokens. This is characteristic of a child from a disturbed and disadvantaged background, whose affiliative and esteem needs are not being satisfied (Maslow, 1962).

THE DANGERS OF IGNORING UNWANTED BEHAVIOUR

The ignoring of unwanted behaviour can work when the behaviours to be ignored do not disturb other children or, when the child's behaviour is so disturbed and extreme that the other children can understand why and also be told not to encourage it. The child herself can be told she will be attended to when she is on target, and not when off target, shouting or roaming around the room. If, however, a teacher ignores the children's general murmuring or chatting during a story or explanations, this could build to serious inattention and disruption. Instead, non-verbal warnings or 3Ms (p.101) strategies can be used. During a story, for example, the teacher can pause and wait for a child to stop talking then resume the story without comment. Alternative strategies would be to:

- pause and give 'stink look' then resume;
- pause and quietly name the child then resume;
- pause and ask a question of the child then resume;
- pause with older children and start a nursery rhyme sequence to gain attention;
- put hand on child's head or shoulder to quieten; or
- gently signal child to be quiet and resume.

MANAGING TROUBLESOME BEHAVIOUR IN PRIMARY AND SECONDARY CLASSROOMS

Wheldall and Merritt (1984, 1988) carried out a research study over a period of ten years at the Centre for Child Study, University of Birmingham. During this period, they developed a 'behavioural approach to teaching' with teachers on in-service courses. The result of their researches is a skills training programme for teachers using behavioural methods called BATPACK. Their surveys have shown that, on average, four children per class were considered troublesome and boys were difficult more often than girls in a ratio of 3:1.

The most frequent troublesome behaviour reported by primary teachers in their West Midlands area was 'talking out of turn' (TOOT) 46 per cent, followed by 'hindering other children' (HOC) 25 per cent. No other categories reached over 10 per cent.

Similar results were found for secondary schools, TOOT (50 per cent) and HOC (17 per cent), with physical aggression reaching no higher than 10 per cent. These seem to represent the same behaviours with different category labels as found in the Kingston area; for TOOT read 'attention-seeking' behaviours and for HOC read 'disruptive behaviour'. The research presented evidence for the success of their behaviourally based methods with sets of case studies illustrating their effectiveness. Typical of their approach is to establish baseline behaviours, for example, time out of seat, and then show the miscreants this record, which often amazes them. The teacher then explains that he/she will continue to watch them and, if their 'out of seat' scores drop, they will earn a team point. The pupils are shown their progress charts and praised. As can be seen, extrinsic motivators are used, cognition is involved but the system is behaviourally based. It is directed to changing the pupils' behaviours by overt attention to them. These methods have clearly worked in the variety of settings they describe, to decrease unwanted behaviours and increase work output (except probably with quite a proportion of 'Caroles').

The researchers, in addition, found that their teachers did praise children more for work than they disapproved of it, but they did not praise good social behaviour. They set out to change this aspect of teachers' behaviour and encouraged them to approve of socially acceptable behaviours and to cease nagging unwanted ones. Where the BATPACK techniques differ from strategies developed at Kingston is mainly emphasis. The researchers' approach emphasises the use of *extrinsic* motivators whereas this book is more about the use of *intrinsic* motivators. Both use attention and praise as reinforcement and reward.

Wheldall's most recent survey report (1988) of behaviour problems in schools in the Birmingham area confirms his previous findings but, in addition, underlines the unequal treatment meted out to misbehaving and noisy girls. The girls receive the full disapproval of the system whereas misbehaviour of boys is largely condoned and, as a result, they receive more attention and are more likely to obtain help and support and do better than girls. Girls in these settings were found to be more likely to become withdrawn and disturbed. They thus suffer multiple discrimination and disadvantage by virtue of this different treatment stemming from attitudes to what is considered to be sex appropriate behaviours.

In a sense the studies mentioned in this chapter and the references to research in others have been about crisis management, the work of Kounin (1970) was different. In his book *Discipline and Group Management in Classrooms* he looked at how teachers effectively managed the ordinary behaviour of their pupils. When children do not quickly respond to the teacher's requests, the teacher may wait for attention, ignore the behaviour, switch to something more attractive, or decide to intervene or comment. How such interventions and comments are made can greatly affect the pupils. This was investigated by Kounin in studies of group management in a Detroit kindergarten and many of his findings are relevant today. He classified teacher desists, telling children to stop doing something, along three dimensions: firmness, clarity and roughness.

Firmness describes the degree to which children understand that a teacher means what he/she says, and that the instruction is to be carried out immediately. It involves following up the instruction and ensuring that it is done, watching the child, walking towards him/her and speaking emphatically rather than questioningly or quaveringly. Other children also respond to the instruction and stop misbehaving – the 'ripple' effect.

Clarity conveys who is to stop, what is to be stopped, and what should be done instead. This is in contrast with generalised admonitions to a class to 'keep the noise down' or 'be quiet'.

Roughness concerns the teacher's expression of anger or frustration, by look or tone and threats, or even physical punishment. Kounin found that 'rough desists' were less effective than clear ones and also caused more disruptive responses. These findings have been confirmed in subsequent research (for example, O'Leary, 1973), in particular, that quiet desists and quiet instructions were more effective than loud reprimands in controlling classroom behaviour.

SUMMARY

The research studies of successful interventions by researchers and teachers began in the late 1960s and, twenty years later, the same approaches are being confirmed.

Each of the foregoing studies emphasises the effectiveness of supportive teacher behaviours. They show that teachers who learned to attend to, smile and praise good work and good behaviour cause general and minor behaviour problems in their classrooms to diminish. These teachers were also effective in reducing the incidence of disruption. The studies showed that quiet instructions and calming approaches were more effective than sharp acrimonious ones.

Because the researchers were interested in the effectiveness or otherwise of behaviour modification or behaviour therapy their results can give a one-sided view of what may be needed in the repertoire of skills of the classroom teacher. The situation is one of 'not only but also'. The teacher needs not only a knowledge of and skills in behaviour modification principles and practices but also a range of knowledge and skills in cognitive intervention. This must include those of curriculum development and teaching methodology so as to match the learners' needs which may be expressed through behavioural difficulties.

6

Implementing a Behaviour Management Scheme

INTRODUCTION

When teachers attend in-service training courses to learn new information and new techniques, it soon becomes clear that although they may personally benefit it is not usually possible for them to implement profound changes in their schools unless they are the headteacher or deputy. Reading a text about behaviour problems can help teachers change their own practice, but in order for it to become a school-wide change they need to group together to influence opinion and practice. A small group of three can be just enough to create change. We recommend such groups attend in-service training courses because on their return to school they discuss the course, or in this case the book, and draw others into the conversation, spreading the ideas, and encouraging one another to change practice.

What has to be recognised is that innovation and innovators are beset by difficulties and resistance to change from others around them. Some examples of this resistance are:

'We have always done it this way' phenomenon.
'Its their problem and their initiative nothing to do with us, we do not need to think about it.'
'We are already doing it' syndrome. This prevents any consideration of the problem and the innovation (and they are not doing it).
'We tried it and it did not work.' This refers to something somebody did once which was only vaguely similar.
'Being nice to pupils will only make them worse and discipline will be destroyed.' The logical fallacy and conflation.
'It will mean a lowering of standards.' Any hint of standards being affected will cause ranks to form against the idea whether this is justified or not.
'I think it's a good idea, but the rest of the staff will not stand for it.' This is managerial opting out!

The lightning effect. If we put our heads above the fence or do something different we could attract unwelcome attention.

When faced by resistance to change and these ploys, it is essential for teachers who want to change things to work together.

A SUGGESTED PROCEDURE

1 Try to set up a working group

Although individual teachers can learn to implement the scheme in their own classrooms, greater benefits can accrue where several teachers or a whole school staff decide to work together.

2 Try to make your own and the school's aims explicit

(a) Each of us has one or several aims in the education we offer to our pupils, and it is important to make these explicit so that they can be examined and priorities established. It may happen that the aims we hold are too diffuse to be converted into practical objectives or that our priorities are actually working against our attempts to teach successfully. Aims might be framed thus:
  (i) to enable each individual to develop to his/her full potential;
  (ii) to ensure they learn 'the subject' properly, for example, mathematics, design technology, environmental studies;
  (iii) to develop each individual's basic skills in reading, writing and number.
(b) Write down what you *perceive* to be the school's aims and what are its *stated* aims.
(c) Make an opportunity to ask your pupils what they think school is trying to do for or to them; what its purposes are as they see and experience them.
(d) Ask them what they think your own most important aims are for them. What is your teaching geared to do?

You may not feel able at first to consult your pupils so openly. If not, try to do this at a later stage as you gain in confidence. Try to discuss your findings with other colleagues and you may find that this gains their interest so that a working group can be formed to discuss and compare notes as you proceed.

3 Compare the findings on your own, and the school's, aims with those of the DES (1981) listed below

(a) To help pupils develop lively, enquiring minds, the ability to question and argue rationally and to apply themselves to tasks and physical skills;
(b) to help pupils acquire knowledge and skills relevant to adult life and employment in a fast changing world;
(c) to help pupils use language and number effectively;
(d) to instil respect for religious and moral values and tolerance of other races, religions and ways of life;

(*e*)   to help pupils understand the world in which they live, and the interdependence of individuals, groups and nations;

(*f*)   to help pupils to appreciate human achievement and aspirations.

4   Learn over time to incorporate the following two aims into your own aims in education

(*a*)   To induce in pupils a *positive attitude to learning* (PAL) in all aspects of the curriculum.

(*b*)   To adopt for yourself a *supportive positive attitude* (SPA) to all aspects of pupil's learning and behaviour and other staff's work and interaction, and to parents' involvement with the school.

These two acronyms are deliberately introduced, first to be easily remembered because of their brevity in summing up a whole sentiment and second, because each describes the situation exactly. For example, PAL has the wider meaning that each pupil should find comfort and satisfaction in learning. Solace should be found by each pupil in learning since, for some, there will be little satisfaction or esteem to be found in any other area of their lives. A pupil who comes from a difficult or deprived home situation may become vulnerable to failure in school because of a number of predisposing factors which place him/her at risk. If such a pupil is subject to failure in learning on school tasks, then this will inevitably lead to a desire to seek attention and esteem in other ways, often through misbehaviour. Converting learning failure to success can provide pupils with the necessary emotional support to help them through difficult social and personal circumstances. Learning must become 'user friendly.' List:

(*a*)   the pupils who seem to be failing at school tasks;

(*b*)   the pupils who appear demotivated

and discuss these pupils' needs in study groups with colleagues.

The SPA acronym is to remind teachers that their attitudes provide the climate for learning and the atmosphere for classroom, staffroom and school. Where this is positive and supportive, pupils (and members of staff) will likewise feel able to be helpful and supportive. They will be less fearful of failure and will make greater efforts to win approval of their teachers whom they will learn to respect because respect has been shown to them. SPA can thus be conceived of as a therapeutic classroom and school environment.

5   Try to incorporate the following three objectives into your daily teaching

(*a*)   CBG – this stands for 'catch them being good'. In every lesson or every interaction with colleagues, you should try to find them 'on task', being good rather than trying to find them out and expose every little misdemeanour.

(*b*)   PCI – this stands for 'positive cognitive intervention'; in everything that is taught the pupils' brains should be engaged. Work which involves rote copying or reiterative behaviour in which the pupil does not actually have to think things through should be avoided where possible.

(c)   Process – concern yourself more, from now on, with enhancing the processes by which children learn rather than with end products only. If you make the process of learning enjoyable, this is highly motivating and pupils will learn more than they would have done before. They will achieve the end products you wished and do so more securely so that they no longer have to over-learn key points or learn them parrot-fashion with little understanding.

(d)   Methods – discuss ways in which these three suggestions can be implemented. Try to observe each other's lessons and count the incidence of each.

THE AIMS OF A BEHAVIOUR MANAGEMENT SCHEME

1   To promote a deeper understanding of teaching and learning processes.
2   To develop positive parental attitudes towards school and involvement in pupils' learning and behaviour.
3   To strengthen links between home and school.
4   To promote positive attitudes to pupils from teachers.
5   To increase knowledge and understanding of a range of classroom management techniques.
6   To help teachers provide a positive and therapeutic classroom atmosphere in which all pupils can flourish and learn to achieve success and independence.
7   To develop in pupils a positive self-image and sense of achievement and fulfilment in school.
8   To develop staff working groups or working parties to help promote the above purposes.

To this list teachers should, if they wish, add aims of their own.

Pyramiding

Pyramiding is a suggested method for exchanging information and defining ideas. After individuals have decided on their own lists of priority of aims and objectives in their subject areas, pairs or threes should meet together in departmental or year groups and produce a list in an agreed priority order. Next, pairs should meet in fours, threes in sixes, to review and discuss the lists and form an agreed rank order. Fours then meet in eights, and so on until the whole group formulates and finalises an agreed list. Ask the groups to sum up all the aims into one organised principle-centrating. This most often results in 'PAT' – a positive attitude to teaching (learning, pupils, parents, school, organisation, teachers, peers etc.) expressed in various ways.

A teacher working on his/her own should, nevertheless, try to arrange the list of scheme aims in order of priority, for the *process* of doing this will firmly establish them in mind. It then becomes unnecessary to learn them by heart and is a more interesting way of acquiring the information. This is an example of a process teaching strategy which can be widely used with pupils to help them learn more effectively. It is surprisingly effective with slow learners as well as able groups.

WHAT WILL THE SCHEME INVOLVE?

The techniques suggested take no extra time from lessons and will save time eventually. Initially the methods appear slower. Telling information is always quicker but is often not absorbed.

Teachers employing the strategies will need to be amongst the children, helping them as they work and being involved with both the process and the product. This method enables the teacher to get to know his/her pupils and place the results in an informed context. The scheme requires no extra resources; the teacher and the pupils are the essential resources to be found in a classroom. Changing to process methods of teaching does not require additional resources such as books, time or paper. Worksheets, for example, will simply be used in a different fashion.

The scheme can be employed within a school's formal approach to discipline. It is useful to obtain a list of the school rules and make further notes of those that are unwritten so that any areas of possible contradiction can be noted. Rather than ignoring petty school rules, it is better to negotiate a change in them. Loosening of arbitrary controls can be beneficial for both pupils and teachers. The scheme is *not designed to introduce a relaxation in discipline,* rather it engenders a more relaxed approach between pupils and teachers so that they speak as equals and bear each other mutual respect. However, there are clear classroom rules and the discipline is firm. Children are not allowed to upset others and get away with bad behaviour. As a result of using the scheme, the general classroom discipline will improve and work output will increase. Higher expectations about standards of behaviour can be shared and met. Although the scheme can be implemented in just one classroom, the more teachers involved, the better for all the pupils and the school as a whole.

Parents have an important role to play. Their help is not essential but they may well notice a difference in their child and want to discuss this with the teacher. The teachers should help them understand what is happening and encourage them to do likewise. In some difficult cases, it may be essential to obtain the cooperation of the parents and to teach them the strategies too because they may be creating the problem. Where they will not cooperate, keep working on them in the ways suggested; it is worth persevering for the child's sake.

The scheme will work with any group of pupils and the strategies outlined have been piloted with children/pupils aged from three to nineteen. Similarly, they have been used extensively with adults in training, and colleagues in schools. They have proved successful with urban and rural pupils and in classes where all the pupils are 'problems' and in situations where there are only one or two difficult pupils. Both young children and awkward adolescents respond well to them, as do those with mild to severe behaviour problems.

The more practice teachers have in the techniques, the more sophisticated and effective they become in their use. Practice can be enhanced by discussing progress with interested colleagues, who can often help by observing and recording data for collection and checking.

There are a number of ways in which various aspects of the scheme can be evaluated. Three types of measure are suggested. First, changes in attitude can be assessed using one of the pupil's motivation scales (Cohen and Cohen, 1981), attitude scales or the semantic differential (Osgood *et al.,* 1957). Second, an observer rating scale or observational recording system can help determine changes in classroom behaviour. The third type of measure involves a curriculum-based diagnosis of change. In this, teachers can record the change in response of the pupils to the work. This can be noted in their length of time on task, their constructive discussion about the task, the increased sophistication in questioning and their general motivation to start work and pursue their studies in their own time.

SUMMARY

Where teachers have identified a need to change the climate and ethos of their school to offer a more supportive environment for pupils, it is recommended that they try to group together with like-minded colleagues. Analysis by this group, or clusters of such groups, of the school's aims, curriculum, pedagogy and interpersonal relations can help each one to perceive the links between the achievement and motivation of the pupils and the support for learning and respect of the staff. Members of the group should try out appropriate techniques for pupils with behaviour difficulties and keep a record of successes and failures showing how these were brought about so that others can learn from them and improve upon them. When change must be brought about from the inside by a small group which seeks to influence others the following tactics may be found to be helpful:

- Let the project remain an eternal experiment if you have to explain it to anyone.
- Never ask permission, make a start and report progress.
- Help the project by helping senior staff 'recall' that day they threw out the suggestion which started it all off.
- Spread the good word like an infection.
- Ask for the smallest amount of money possible to promote or move the programme along when it begins to be noticed.
- Adopt some acronyms or make some to implant the ideas in peoples' minds.
- Keep everybody informed with 'inside' information.
- When the whole school finally adopts the policy, plan to go public, conference and disseminate with the aid of colleagues. None preach like the converted.

7

How to Identify and Record Behaviour Problems

INTRODUCTION

Observing pupils is an important part of a teacher's job. How else are they able to respond to thirty different pupil's needs and demands? Of course, this observation takes place during teaching and moving around the class facilitating learning. It also occurs in all those small moments when teachers stand back and monitor what is going on. Skill in this form of observation can mark out the successful from the unsuccessful teacher. So often teachers who are in difficulties have failed to notice the beginning of unrest amongst their pupils. As classroom observer offering teacher support I have witnessed fights, card schools, and one pupil who simulated three sexual exploits in succession without ever attracting the attention of the teacher although half the class dissolved in merriment. If the observer intervenes the teacher's vestiges of discipline and confidence are undermined and so other strategies need to be discussed in the debriefing session afterwards, such as the management, monitoring and maintenance strategies outlined in Chapter 8.

Where there are pupils with behavioural difficulties, it is imperative that teachers increase the amount of time they spend on discreet observation to help identify the precise nature of the pupil's difficulties, how, when and where they arise. The observations need to be made unobtrusively and should be spread across the time the pupil is with the teacher. All possible situations should be sampled both positive and negative. Data also needs to be collected on how the pupil behaves with other teachers, in different types of lesson, behaviour in school and outside when supervised and unsupervised.

Spreading the observations, sampling different behaviours and activities and focusing the attention, where necessary, upon key indicants can provide valuable information not usually available for analysis. Ways in which teachers may undertake these observations without predjudice to the pupils and how they may record their findings during a busy teaching schedule are suggested in the next sections.

STEPS TO BE TAKEN

1 Determine the *behaviour problems* by careful and detailed observation and recording. Identify the one which you wish to change – the target behaviour.
2 Determine what or who *rewards and maintains* the behaviour problems in your classroom – an important step in the process of change. Change the setting, move the children but stop them reinforcing the unwanted behaviours.
3 Determine the *environments* which are opposite and incompatible with the behaviour problems which may then be reinforced to *redirect* learning in a *positive* or *prosocial* direction.
4 Determine the *environment* which most frequently evokes the unwanted behaviour and that which does not, for example, as soon as writing begins. This could indicate a handwriting or spelling problem needing help.
5 Determine *the tasks* in which the problem behaviours are *most and least* evident.
6 Determine *with whom* the behaviour is most frequent and least frequent (which teacher or parent). It may be their behaviours that need changing rather than the pupil's.

PROBLEMS IN TARGETING

Determining any of the above requires careful observation of the pupil in a number of settings. It is this observation which is difficult to accomplish successfully and which requires a little practice and some caution.

Observation is the act or practice of noting and recording *facts* and events as they happen. The targets of observational techniques are signs, indicants, or behaviours and the data may be used to make *inferences* about *constructs*. *Inferences* are extrapolations or assumptions drawn from the factual data. *Constructs* are systems of ideas, concepts, attitudes or beliefs which are not overt or public.

Observation of human behaviour is a phenomenon of everyday life and therein lies the danger. It must not be assumed that so-called 'observations' made at the scene are necessarily valid. It is only with great care and practice that such observations can be a true and factual record, or even a sample of what was seen. Immediately a sample is taken judgmental processes are involved about what should be sampled and therefore about what is significant. In order to overcome this problem, osbervers use various strategies, for example:

Diary description – an attempt is made through continuous rapid writing or audio and video-recording to record everything that is taking place.
Sampling – a cycle of ten seconds looking, followed by ten seconds writing throughout a session is maintained.

Both methods should result in a factual record of what took place including 'scratches head with pen in right hand, turns round to boy on left, puts out tongue . . .' etc., but very often a teacher will give his/her 'observations' meaning opinions and thoughts about a child. These should not be included. In classroom observation, as in observational research in general, there are three main problems:

1   Observation versus inference

'Robert punched Chris on the nose' is factual data. The user of the data may then suggest that Robert is an aggressive boy. This is an *inference* and should *not* appear in the observation notes or raw data. In fact, if this is an *isolated* event, one should not on any account make such an inference.

2   Paradigms

These are *guiding frames of reference*, what Goethe called 'Zeitgeist' or 'Spirit of the Age'. The frame of reference is there in our minds without us necessarily being aware of it, such that we use it to guide our interpretations of what we observe. In some degree, our civilisation is subject to the scientific paradigm, the belief that scientific evidence will reveal the truth. The Freudian analyst interprets the adult's problems as resulting from repressions of infantile sexuality, the behaviourist from early social conditioning or socialisation. Unless a teacher's training is *eclectic*, then certain paradigms will be unavoidably embedded in the construct system and will limit both actions and thoughts. Thus it is that several theories are drawn upon in this scheme, for example, *behaviour modification theory*, *cognitive theory* and *motivation theory*.

As will be noted from reading this material, other theoretical frameworks have been drawn upon, including Freudian personality constructs and social psychology. Paradigms might also be called 'fashions in thought' and thus the researcher most often tries to interpret the data in relation to at least *two* frames of reference. The practitioner and applied psychologist, by relating theory and research to practice, constructs a web of knowledge about what works and why, developing, what some might term, a humanistic psychology of learning and teaching.

3   Bias

The observer most often thinks that he/she is making an accurate record of what is seen, but a problem to guard against is *seeing what you want* to see. The following observations (Figure 5) demonstrate this. The actual record of what took place is given in the first column. This is compared with the consultant's record who has been told 'We think the child is autistic.'

He is, however, a normal little boy playing whilst waiting for his mother to fix up a play group place.

The observer constructs the profile thus: 'seems to treat all people as objects; social gaze avoidance; seems emotionally cold; ritualised perseverative moments; very limited or no language comprehension and expression – must be autistic.'

Figure 5 *References between observer recordings*

Actual observation	Consultant observer
2.45 Child pulls chair towards him across the floor. Snatches at B's pram. Desists when his mother says quietly 'No, Robin'. Spins wheeled chair. Goes back to ordinary chair, pulls it round and spins it.	2.45 Child pulling a chair around the floor. Interested only in furniture and not in the people. Takes B's pram just as object with wheels, spinning everything. No notice of people.

When the biased observer's notes are examined, it can be seen that:

Pulling chair around the floor.	Is untrue, he makes a highly structured movement: pulls chair towards him.
Interested only in furniture.	Inference.
Not interested in people.	Inference.
Takes B's pram just as an object.	Inference
Spinning everything.	Untrue.
No notice of people.	Untrue.

(Source: Wright (1960) in *Handbook of Research Methods in Child Development*, Harper and Row)

Control

Since the major problems leading to the error are *observer errors* and *interpretation errors,* the first control to institute is:

(a)   that the factual record is *kept separate* from the inferences which are drawn; and

(b)   that where possible a second observer is available to record the same problem event(s) at least on one occasion, for example, that another teacher is asked to record the pupil's behaviour for a short period where possible.

Days 1 and 2
It is rarely possible for classroom teachers to sit and observe their own classes for ten or twenty minutes uninterrupted, as an outside agent might do in the research studies quoted. This is not essential, instead:

1   (a) Choose the target pupil.
    (b) Keep a notepad to hand.
    (c) Set the pupils working and go round to help them.
    (d) Mark the frequency of unwanted behaviours of the target

pupil throughout a timed period thus '1111 11'.

(e) Repeat morning and afternoon. (See *Record Sheet A*, p.84.)

2   If possible withdraw for thirty seconds to one minute and record everything you see the target pupil do, whenever possible, starting new activity, activity change, halfway through task. (See *Record Sheet B*, p.85.)

3   At the end of each day write down the *main types* of nuisance behaviours that you recall and any 'historical record' of the more vivid incidents. Decide what to record for the third day, the *target* behaviour which you want to change. (See *Record Sheets C and D*, pp.86 and 87.)

Record in a range of settings *if possible*, for example, at activity change, activity start, halfway through and at the end of: English, mathematics or basic skills, PE, art, music, eating behaviour, with peers in playground, with another adult.

Day 3 (Record Sheet D)

1   Record as a specimen diary description as fully as possible *any* occurrence of the *target* behaviour. Write down *post hoc* if recording 'as it happens' is not feasible.
2   Record the point in lesson/day at which each occurs.
3   Record the environment or the location of the target behaviour and who else is present.

Very often, in the real world rather than in a laboratory classroom, it is both necessary and desirable to intervene on several pupil behaviours at the same time.

SUMMARY

The main obstacle in identifying the nature and origins of pupils' behavioural difficulties in the classroom is lack of systematic and careful observation. Too often we see only what we want or expect to see rather than what has actually taken place. On top of this we may add our judgmental inferences and prejudices. In these circumstances the pupil is at a grave disadvantage. When a range of observation strategies has been applied and some systematised recording has taken place inferences and prejudices can be separated from facts and instances. This will allow a more accurate appraisal of the situation to be made. The intervention can then be appropriately structured and focused. Quite frequently it will be found that although the pupils are the ones who exhibit the difficulties, a major set of provocations may lie within the curriculum and pedagogy. It may also be noticed that the difficulties arise from particular ways in which the pupils are treated or after particular lessons, with other teachers or in relation to particular tasks. These patterns of reaction will become clear when systematic observations are made. The results will mean that key issues can be brought into focus so that appropriate changes in the learning environment can be made which will harmonise the pupils' and the school community's needs.

Record Sheet A

RECORD SHEET 1

TARGET PUPIL: _____

DATE: _____

Chronological age: _____

Position in family: _____

BASELINE RECORD

TIME	DAY ONE	DAY TWO (multiple baseline)
am		
TOTALS		
pm		
TOTALS		

1   Days one and two – record *frequency of undesirable behaviour.*

2   It may be possible before day two to develop a code to represent the different problem behaviours, for example, 'H' (hit), 'S' (shout), 'W' (wanders).

BASELINE FREQUENCY: _____   _____

AVERAGE PER DAY: _____   _____

Record Sheet B

RECORD SHEET 1   TARGET PUPIL: _____

DATE: _____

OBSERVATIONAL RECORD (copy extra sheets as necessary)

TIME OF	OBSERVATIONAL RECORD	ACTIVITY/LESSON
(30 secs)		
(30 secs)		
(30 secs)		
(30 secs)		

Record Sheet C

RECORD SHEET 1

TARGET PUPIL: _____

DATE: _____

HISTORICAL AND ANECDOTAL RECORD

Note down from the other records the *main types* of problem behaviour observed. Note down *any additional observations*. Now identify the *target behaviour* which you wish to change ready to record in detail in *Record D*.

TIME	List of problems noted DAY ONE	List of problems noted DAY TWO
	Additional notes or activities	Additional notes or activities

ANECDOTES – QUOTES ON BEHAVIOUR

IDENTIFY
TARGET
BEHAVIOUR

Record Sheet D

| **RECORD SHEET 1** | TARGET PUPIL: _____ |
| | DATE: _____ |

TARGET BEHAVIOUR

When the target behaviour occurs write down an exact behavioural record of what you see.

TIME	OBSERVATION	ACTIVITY & SETTING

Action to be taken

When the various records have been completed and appropriate checks made, review the behaviours and identify key aspects and the patterns of the problem. Discuss these findings with colleagues or others engaged in similar work to help determine whether there are other patterns or interpretations which can be revealed. Complete as many sections of the *Record Sheet E* (p.88) as is possible at this stage, and on the basis of these entries, and with reference to the next chapter, draw up your proposed plan for intervention.

Record Sheet E

STATEMENT OF PROBLEM AND INTENT

1 Problem behaviour to be changed: Baseline
frequency

2 Strategy to be used:

3 Changes to environment:

4 Who maintains behaviour and how to be stopped:

5 Setting in which behaviour occurs:

6 Setting in which, or with whom, behaviour does not occur:

7 Intervention period:

8 Evaluation of progress of intervention: Frequency of
problem now

8

Intervention Principles and Practices

INTRODUCTION

Behavioural psychology and its use in education has become an area of increasing interest to those concerned with special educational needs and, of late, there has been a profusion of training courses for teachers. These courses concern themselves with teaching basic behavioural principles to enable the teachers to manage pupils' behaviour problems using behaviour modification techniques, and are marketed in the form of in-service training materials, for example: BATPACK (Wheldall *et al.*, 1984), SNAP (Ainscow *et al.*, 1981), PAD (Chisholm *et al.*, 1986), TIPS (Dawson, 1985). Behaviour control techniques have been a second and related group of strategies according to Nuttall and Snook, (1973) which have been recommended for teaching pupils with both learning difficulties and those with certain types of behaviour problems. This second group of strategies are interrelated and referred to as 'task analysis', 'direct instruction' and 'precision teaching'.

TASK ANALYSIS

Task analysis is most often applied to the basic skills curriculum, reading, language, writing, number and movement. These are the so-called core skills areas which the pupil needs to be taught in order to gain access to other areas of the curriculum. The techniques are also applied in the teaching of pro-social behaviour to children with severe learning difficulties, also called the education of the developmentally young (EDY Project of the Hester Adrian Research Centre).

There are seven steps in the task analytic model:

- Subject area for intervention is selected, for example, sharing.
- Units for each subject are identified, for example, sharing toys.
- A goal for each unit is written, for example, handing over toys on request.
- A behavioural objective or task for each goal is written, for example, hands toy to teacher on request on four out of five occasions, without protest.
- The task is analysed into a sequence of skills which are also written as behavioural objectives.
- Slice tasks and skills as behavioural objectives. If the task and skills are too difficult then they are made easier without changing the nature of the activity.
- The order of the teaching units is selected.

Behavioural objectives must contain three components:

1   a verb which contains an observable behaviour from the pupil;
2   a description of conditions of the performance; and
3   a description of the criterion to be achieved.

As can be seen, the technique is concerned with behavioural outcomes which the teacher then reinforces, often according to a predetermined schedule. Precision teaching is not a method of teaching but a system of recording pupil responses. Recording is highly systematised and may include the use of mechanical or electronic counters, tallies and so on. Rates of response, times to completion, time sampling or time-ruled checklists, checklists for criterion-referenced performance, ratings and graphing of cumulative results and tests are all possible targets for recording. Often pupils assist in the collecting and recording of their own responses as, for example, when they use stop clocks to record their time on task. In a typical precision teaching activity the teacher might decide that the pupil must 'be able to read the first five sight words on the reading scheme by the end of one week with 95 per cent accuracy' and set up a series of test and training sessions to accomplish this, using flash cards in a word tin and rote practice. Robert had serious problems with this task and so it was 'sliced' so that first he would learn two words to criterion. He accomplished this but found it too difficult to proceed to the next level. He was seven years old, a mildly slow learner with specific difficulties in the reading, spelling and writing areas and could not benefit from this technique. However, many other children have and it has enabled them to overcome barriers in learning and given them confidence to proceed. What needs to be analysed in these cases is what *metacognitive* events make one child able to learn and not another, but this is not part of the process of recording, the interest is in correct performance to criterion.

Although it may be stated that task analysis has been undertaken, questions should be asked:

- Has the task been suitably described and defined?
- Has the task been suitably analysed or broken down into relevant units?

The answer to these questions is often 'no' especially with regard to the complex area of reading, writing and spelling skills. Hierarchies of relevant skills have most often not been defined and taught, so that programmes can occupy a pupil's time interestingly but

with little profit. Pupils can work through some of the programmes without having established the concepts but learn the
correct response through repetition.

The first significant endorsement of the curriculum defined
in terms of the objectives-based model appeared in the Warnock
Report (DES 1978). It required for pupils with special needs
the presence of 'well-defined' guidelines for each area of the
curriculum, and 'programmes . . . planned for individual children
with clearly defined short-term goals within the general plan'.
The 1981 Education Act endorsed these practices by defining
assessment procedures for statementing in terms of the categorical
distinctions made in the objectives based/skills analysis approach to
the curriculum (Wood and Shears 1986). The national curriculum
with its criterion-referenced assessment and subjects defined in
terms of ten levels and targets seems one more step towards
a closed curriculum and a dependent learner. Is it that the
alternative model, the process model proposed by Stenhouse (1975),
is insufficiently understood by those who observe education and by
many practitioners because of its often indefinable outcomes and the
dangerous autonomy which it offers to the learner?

THE PROCESS OF ASSESSMENT THROUGH TEACHING

This process described by Solity and Bull (1987) moves through the
following stages:

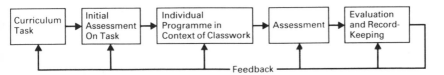

Matching pupils' needs and tasks can significantly reduce attention-
seeking and time off task which can be used in disruption. In assessment
through teaching, the curriculum task is used to determine what the
pupil can and cannot do. Hospital teachers, for example, have to become
particularly adept at this when they meet patients for the first time and
need to continue these pupils' educational studies. By presenting text to
read or a subject to write about, the teacher can make a rapid assessment
of the level of reading and writing skills and find a better match of
reading and writing materials and subjects. Diagnostic questioning
about a subject can reveal the previous knowledge base from which
the teacher can work. Decisions about teaching method and resources
can be made and then records of progress can be compiled.

DIRECT INSTRUCTION

Direct instructional approaches begin with trying to find the most
effective way to *teach* children and concentrate upon teaching them
to generalise what they have learned to new and different situations.

As children with learning difficulties fall behind they have to be taught more in less time in order to close the gap. Becker *et al.*, (1966), who first devised these techniques, focused attention upon language skills, and more recently it has been applied to the teaching of reading, writing and number. A clear illustration of this style of 'teaching' may be found in the following quotation from Solity and Bull (1987):

> Direct instruction encourages us to plan every aspect of our teaching thoroughly and well in advance.

This, I think, we can all agree with but they go on to say:

> By doing this a teacher can place himself in the shoes of the child and look for any lack of clarity or ambiguity in the presentation of new skills. Is the presentation consistent with only one interpretation? Are the instructions straightforward, clear and easy to follow?

Whilst I can see the benefit of such clarity in very narrowly defined skills areas, such as teaching a particular phonic blend, the enthusiasm which such success may generate should not lead us to think that all children with learning difficulties or lack of this piece of knowledge may best be taught in this way. It is best applied for a well-defined purpose for an individual child. The kind of structured environment that such 'teaching' requires can often only be successfully accomplished by the use of instructional technology as in the case of the DISTAR programme or with individual instruction. These techniques were, of course, first devised by psychologists working with individual cases, their interests and background were in behavioural psychology not in teaching. The use of the word 'instruction', for example, is inconsistent in my view with education and teaching, it is concerned with rote training and drills with learner autonomy very much a minor consideration.

The main model of instruction in direct instruction is:

MODEL – TEACH – TEST

The methods recommended are small group teaching, which can easily be arranged in primary classes and in 'remedial' settings in secondary schools and special schools and, 'unison oral responding'. This latter method, according to Solity *et al.* (1987), '. . .ensures a high degree of active student involvement and gives the children an opportunity to practise the skill being taught.' This type of interaction is termed 'academic engaged time'! When the child performs correctly, then the teacher praises him/her and may ask the child to model the skill for the others. The instructional hierarchy has five stages – acquisition, fluency, maintenance, generalisation and adaptation. Rewards and reinforcements predominate in the early stages, whilst later on it is hoped that the task becomes intrinsically interesting.

Other behavioural techniques to help the pupils succeed are cueing and prompting correct behaviour and then 'fading' so that they cannot become reliant on them.

BEHAVIOURAL APPROACHES

The techniques which follow are based on behavioural psychology, but have been adapted to be of use to the class teacher who may have thirty or forty pupils to organise and teach while at the same time trying to give individual attention to those children with special needs.

FOUR BEHAVIOURAL STRATEGIES

Inhibition and positive reinforcement (IPR) and modelling and positive reinforcement (MPR)

It appears that it is not possible to unlearn a response or an unwanted behaviour and so suggestions that we can extinguish behaviour problems are unwarranted. What seems to happen is that the learning is stored and then must be suppressed to be overwhelmed by new reaction patterns so that stimuli in the classroom do not provoke the misbehaviour. One of the ways in which this can be achieved is through a behavioural strategy which we can call inhibition and positive reinforcement. The teacher must ignore the unwanted behaviour and immediately *positively reinforce*, by giving attention and praise, to an opposite and desirable behaviour or the nearest equivalent. The pupil is not told or made aware of the ultimate purpose of this intervention, the pro-social goal towards which the teacher is shaping the behaviour. This technique often goes wrong because the teacher ignores the unwanted behaviour and forgets to reinforce the opposite competing behaviour. Totally ignoring unwanted behaviour can cause it to increase in the classroom because the pupil is deliberately testing the teacher because he/she has an emotional need for attention, or because peers support the unwanted behaviours. Therefore IPR has to be used with considerable skill and caution. It is particularly effective, however, in PE and group activities where there is general bustle and some noise associated with the task. Teachers usually report that the pupils' behaviour becomes worse before it gets better. The reason is often that the positive reinforcement is not contingent on (following immediately as a consequence) the desirable response. Teachers usually say that the pupil has done nothing desirable to support, but then this situation can be constructed or another child's behaviour can be reinforced. One of our teachers, Pauline Beaumont, records:

> When I could not find something positive in her own behaviour to reinforce I found something in one of the pupils sitting next to her. This had a remarkable effect and she eagerly sought to emulate them and spent more time on task!

This is the strategy which Blackham and Silkerman (1972) called MPR – modelling and positive reinforcement. If the teacher feels that the pupils' behaviour must be stopped *non-verbal cueing* can often suffice as a warning. If the teacher resorts to shouting this becomes progressively less effective as a quietening strategy and the work and behaviour deteriorates. This is a common sequence of events for inexperienced teachers whose classes gradually become beyond their control. An example of one teacher's intervention follows:

> Darren, nine years old, is continually getting out of his seat to borrow pencils, chat and annoy other pupils. He himself is not noisy but leaves a trail of disruption behind him.

Target Sitting in seat behaviour, on task behaviours of any kind.

Questions Does he have a learning problem since he is avoiding task? Is the task inappropriate for him or unmotivating? Is he just highly sociable or does he need peer attention?

Strategies Try IPR to extend in seat behaviours. This should cut down disruption and may help to involve him more in the task and so improve success rate. Observe task and work behaviours closely to diagnose difficulties.

Later Provide more opportunities for social interaction on task, for example, using *oracy* skills and observe.

As can be seen, careful observation is an important part of making the technique work. This enables more information to be collected for later use. All of this can contribute to *curriculum diagnosis of learning difficulties* and appropriate intervention on task.

Intervention Every time Darren was noted sitting in his seat, the teacher smiled at him or said 'Good, Darren!' When he was on task in his seat the teacher went to stand by him, put her hand on his shoulder and they looked at work together. She said 'Good' or 'Let me help you'. Every now and again, the teacher passing Darren at work said 'Keep up the good progress, Darren'. At the end of the day she sometimes said 'You've had a good day today, Darren'.

The results were two-fold and this is not surprising since IPR was applied to two aspects of Darren's behaviour. He sat in place or stood near his place for most of the time in the lessons. His behaviour only became worse when packing up or changing activities and this needed to be dealt with by further IPR and MPR interventions. Because the teacher kept remembering to look at his work Darren became more involved and interested in it, which brought with it greater success because of time on task. Some of the on task comments, however, were informational and so added the dimension of cognitive intervention to the strategies. This mixture of methods so often proves the most effective in the end.

IPR is extremely effective when used by teachers during PE, games, drama and music lessons where behaviour can quickly deteriorate. For example, the pupils are set to 'Move quickly and quietly, as though you were a very tiny person'. The music starts, the pupils move and the teacher moves through the group complimenting individuals on their performance: 'Very good, Emma', 'Very nice, Stephen', 'Good, Sarah', 'Well done, Jason', 'Good try, Ram'. All of this amounts to a shaping procedure through which small silly behaviours can be ignored but the approximations to desirable behaviours can be reinforced.

Role shift and positive reinforcement (RSPR) (Blackham and Silberman, 1972)

When a pupil or an adult is acting out a role which is inappropriate in the situation, RSPR should be used. For example, a pupil may be behaving in a babyish fashion, or a teacher may be behaving in too authoritarian a manner. Each should be watched for any behaviour which is incompatible with the unwanted one and this should be immediately positively reinforced. Again, there is no overt comment on the purpose or nature of the behaviours. As can be seen, behaviour shaping does not address itself to underlying causes and origins, it simply serves to redirect unwanted behaviours. Most experienced teachers use these techniques to a greater or lesser extent. Knowing the details can bring the strategies into the open for inspection and enable them to be used more effectively and selectively.

Time out from positive reinforcement (TO)

'Time out' was originally conceived to stop all reinforcement which might be maintaining a particular unwanted behaviour. This involved silence, stillness and removal of any peer responses which might be supporting or encouraging the behaviour. The individual was ignored and left in isolation which extended to placing the child on a stool, in a quiet place or in a time out room. Use of time out in these ways is also found to have many beneficial side effects for all concerned and these additional benefits are outlined below:

A time out chair
When a child becomes upset or angry and starts to shout or becomes excitable, refusing to settle down, send him/her to sit on the time out chair for thirty seconds. This must not be treated as a punishment place or as an old-fashioned dunce's stool – that would be cruel. The time out chair should be a *neutral* zone for calming down and regaining composure. Time out should be of short duration, ten to thirty seconds only, especially for younger children. At the end of the designated period, the child should be asked very quietly if he/she is ready to resume activities. Leaving the chair during the thirty seconds is not allowed unless there is an invitation by the teacher to do so, or unless the child tells the teacher he/she is ready to do so.

A time out cushion
For very young children, it is useful to have a very large, soft, fluffy greeny-coloured cushion for them to lie on for thirty seconds or so. Seriously upset or disturbed children can be left for longer to sleep off their distress.

A time out room
It is common in schools for pupils with severe behaviour problems and autistic children to have a time out room to which a child can be taken and left for a few minutes or longer to cool down. This room is bare, devoid of furniture and fittings, with a secure window. It is often enough to say 'time out' and the pupil marches him/herself off into the room once the routine is established. The important factor for the teacher is not to forget that out of sight can mean out of mind.

In psychiatric settings a set of old telephone directories are often left in the room for the pupil to tear. This can help to distract and prevent head-banging which is not uncommon. When pupils are in time out, other children must *not* speak to them or attract attention. This is absolutely forbidden. During time out, the pupils must be *ignored*. At the end of the period, any questions or instructions should be kept to a low tone so as not to raise the tempo again. The pupils may decide to stay in time out. The teacher should not try to cajole or persuade them back into the class activities otherwise pupils will withhold their participation as a weapon. Return time can be indicated by a questioning look from the teacher, the pupil nods, and the teacher beckons him or her back. It is important to keep time out short.

Sending out

Teachers often view sending a pupil outside the room as a form of time out. This is not really the case as it is usually preceded by a row and raised teacher's voice. The tolerence level snaps and the frustrated teacher drives a pupil out of the room with threats and admonishments delivered in a high, sharp tone. A punishment is intended. Time out is a low-key quiet exchange, involving movement to a neutral quiet zone.

Sending out is *not* advised. As already noted, the pupil often runs home, wanders off, hides in the cloakrooms and vandalises or steals from pockets, or stands pulling faces through the window. If the pupil has an accident, the teacher is responsible.

Always check the school rules and accepted procedures. Most school rules do not advise or allow you to send a child out of the room unattended. Do not send pupils out of the room. Send them to a quiet neutral area of the room or into time out instead. If you must send a pupil out, first send a responsible child to fetch a helper, such as the headteacher or duty member of staff, to escort the pupil. Alternatively, leave the class with another teacher and escort the pupil yourself. *Never leave your class unattended.*

Tokens

Tokens such as dots, stars, smiling faces drawn by the teacher, dragon and ladybird stickers are all used to signify good behaviour and good work. These are akin to smiles and ticks and can be used to encourage effort and motivation without any real cognitive component.

Tokens can be useful for young children to have because they are a public and highly visible sign of recognition which they are proud to earn. The system must, however, be fair and all children must have an equal chance of earning them, even if they are slow learners, otherwise they can defeat their purpose. It is much better for pupils to work for teacher's praise and supportive comments than extrinsic motivators such as stars and tokens.

COGNITIVE INTERVENTION STRATEGIES

Often pupils do not know what is acceptable behaviour or that they are off task, irritating and misbehaving. They may also not perceive the reinforcements and the rewards of a particular teacher as positive and constructive. It can therefore be helpful for a pupil to know what the teacher considers to be desirable behaviour and to agree that it is desirable. The limitations of behaviour modification approaches are that they enhance the behaviour but do not improve the task work. Behaviour control approaches or task analysis and direct instructional techniques are needed in addition to help progress on task. Nevertheless these techniques with their highly structured reinforcement schedules, goals and task gradients do not transfer easily to classrooms where teachers are seeking to develop learner autonomy, self-direction and creative problem solving.

It is for these reasons that more open, less rigid behavioural strategies have been recommended and in addition the following cognitive and mixed strategies.

Catch them being good – a mixed strategy

CGB is a straightforward and simple technique to learn. The teacher should literally catch the pupils when they are *on task* being good rather than when they are not. Catching them off task is much more typical and applies to both social and task work. It is usual for teachers to make little comment when children are behaving and doing good work, seemingly it confirms their expectations that this is how things should be. They have little idea of the effort their pupils are making in maintaining an interest in, and concentrating on what often appear to them as seemingly purposeless and time-consuming activities. If pupils are asked why they are doing such-and-such a task they will frequently respond 'because our teacher told us to' and will not be able to think further than this. As they grow older they begin to question the relevance of such experiences.

The teacher should move around the class and deliberately find instances of all pupils on task being good. It is an extraordinarily powerful technique giving the pupils the attention and recognition many of them crave. It will extend time on task and will also give the teacher information on how well the task is progressing and how effective it is. CBG can be used to shape pro-social behaviours and to direct and inform on task behaviours. It acts as a form of direct feedback on performance for pupils keeping them on target. Although the information content is not high it is nevertheless useful to the learner. CBG is often accompanied by smiles and supportive proximity as well as attention, but it has to be genuine. If the teacher gushes and says everything is 'good', 'wonderful' or 'brilliant', in the end it will be discounted by pupils and derided and so will the teacher. CBG requires practice. It is helpful to ask a colleague to come and record the number and types of CBG a teacher gives in a session. This helps to ensure that it really is taking place in a way in which the pupil can feel affirmed and in a way which can be recognised. CBG demands a genuine interest in pupils' learning and a real desire to help them with great pleasure taken in their smallest successes.

Behaviour contract (BC)

This is used in many situations and contracts can range from simple verbal agreements to semi-legal documents of the type drawn up by Social Services with young people said to be beyond their parents' control. The essence of a contract is that the behaviour should be discussed with the pupil so that there is an understanding of the issues and their ramifications, and an agreement is entered into by all parties to remedy or bring order and some compliance into the situation. The Social Services' contract involves discussion with parents and the pupil and in drawing it up all parties have to discuss the problems that divide them, and negotiate some best fit solutions. The resolutions and actions agreed are written into the contract, they are signed and are held to be binding by all the participants. If the contract is broken it may be renegotiated or the sanctions of the law may be brought into play.

Secondary school contracts often take the form of pupils being 'put on report'. They agree to carry a card or book which teachers must sign to confirm no disruptive behaviour has occurred. As can be seen it is a tenuous hold or hedge against temptation. It can serve as a constant reminder to pupil and teachers to note the behaviour and may provide sufficient attention and observation to be successful. Daily and weekly results should be examined with the pupil and the parents. Exclusion may follow if the contract is broken. If something goes wrong in the chain of negotiations and the LEA for example overrides the headteacher and governors' decision, a truculent and even more disruptive pupil may return to harass the teachers. If all goes well, the keeping of the contract can give an opportunity for teacher attitudes to the pupil to become more positive and supportive. It gives each party respite from their adversarial roles and time for relationships to be healed.

A good contract is an outcome of a considerable amount of negotiation and counselling. With such detailed attention to a pupil's problems, the opportunity to relate in a more adult way in a one-to-one situation can be just the therapy the pupil needs. The daily and weekly reporting brings the two together for legitimate discussion and, in the hands of a skilled teacher, can prove very effective. The teacher becomes a respected and significant adult to whom the pupil can refer at other times, preferably before getting into difficulties. Establishing a contract should therefore be given sufficient time and should be carefully carried out in an unperfunctory manner. The interview discussions should be probing and tension releasing.

When primary teachers establish contracts it may often be with parents, to persuade them to give their children more of their undivided attention and time, for example, for perhaps twenty minutes per day whilst the teacher gives the pupil's reading more individual attention in class to help him/her catch up. It may be an informal contract with a pupil involving a verbal agreement such as 'If you will concentrate on your work without getting out of your seat once during writing news, I shall come and help you with your writing.' Implicit in the contract is some contribution by both parties. The pupil tries to control unwanted behaviours and the teacher usually gives time or special support. Offering time off task, running about in the playground or feeding the rabbits, would be more in keeping with dispensing rewards rather than sharing and easing some of the problem.

Case example

Lisa was described as a highly disruptive five-year-old with an alcoholic mother. She was very noisy, banging and shouting and roving round the room, she prevented all the other pupils from working and was creating nervous strain in Sara, her teacher. We discussed the case. The advice was difficult to believe but Sara was determined to go through with it. She had tried CBG and ignoring to no avail. Sara warned the headteacher and her colleagues that the next day her room could be a bit noisy but she would be trying an experiment with Lisa. She took Lisa on one side and explained that her behaviour was very noisy and was stopping other children from working. Sara said she would completely ignore Lisa when she was noisy and being a nuisance and so would all the children. When she was quiet she would be helped to join in. Sara called the class to come to the story corner and listen to the story. Battle commenced. All the children came except Lisa who bounced and clattered about the room. Sara told the children they were to ignore Lisa completely, as she was going to, until she was quiet and sensible like them, and began the story quietly. Lisa observed and began to sing. Sara continued the story. Lisa suddenly found a tambourine and jumped up onto a table and banged it. Sara continued the story, not looking at her. Lisa continued to bang the tambourine for fourteen minutes, then she suddenly stopped, put it down, ran over to the story corner and sat down touching Sara. Sara put her arm around her, smiled and continued the story.

Since that time, six months have elapsed and Lisa's behaviour has never reverted to disruption again. Sara discoverd that Lisa wanted to earn stars for her work and so has been helping her to do so.

COGNITIVE-PROCESS INTERVENTION PRINCIPLES AND PRACTICES

Four critical factors have been identified in the Learning Difficulties Research Project in relation to managing pupils' behaviour problems. These are:

1   Developing *positive self-images* in the pupils and the teachers.
2   Stimulating *thinking and communication* through the medium of any subject, or in skill training.
3   Engaging in *classroom management strategies*.
4   Developing *tactical lesson planning*.

From these factors three principles have been derived which experience and research have shown have the desired potency for effecting change. It is noticeable that 'classroom control' which might be expected to be among these principles is not. The reason for this is that a measure of control is achieved through each of the rest. The three principles, as already touched on, are: CBG, PCI and the 3Ms.

The principles are represented by acronyms for ease and speed. Each summarises a whole practice and theory of intervention which is easy to remember in this form and which can be recalled instantly in difficult circumstances, when decisions have to be very rapid and books cannot be consulted or research pondered upon before action is taken. Teaching involves sets of dynamic interactions where implicit, primitive theories and 'ad hocery' can and will prevail over rational judgment when time is short.

DETAILS OF THE MAIN PRINCIPLES

Catch them being good (CBG)

The CBG strategy is one which teachers *think* they use but, if you record the number of desist and negative unsupportive comments against the number of positive supportive ones using tally strokes or mechanical counters, you will find that the less successful the teacher, the more negative the interactive responses and the fewer the positives, both in relation to the task and the social behaviours.
CBG requires:

- The teacher to reinforce positively any pupil's correct response with nods, smiles, paraphrasing and statements such as 'Yes, good', 'Well done'. Incorrect responses should not be ridiculed but the pupil should be encouraged to rethink, have another try, or responses given such as the following: 'Nearly', 'Yes, and what else?'; 'Good so far. Who can help him/her out?'

- The teacher, having set the task, should move around the class discussing the work with individual pupils *not* just those having difficulty. During a lesson the teacher should make personal, positive contact with every pupil in the class, saying *something supportive* about their work, its content, quality, the way it is written, and receive some of the pupil's thoughts and attitudes about it.

- The teacher cannot afford to stand apart at the front of the class whilst the pupils read, write or practise the set task, for this creates division between the teacher and the pupil. It can imply 'She/he is making us do this but is not interested as long as we finish it before the bell and keep quiet'. In this circumstance, if the task does not appear to be of immediate significance or relevance, the pupil will turn to peers to supply interest and light relief, or to relieve frustration and boredom.

The longer one person, in this instance the teacher, talks the more frustration seems to build up in the listener which needs release in some form of personal response. Some pupils use jokes to relieve the tension, others become disruptive and are more difficult to handle. Thus long informational sessions are to be avoided with difficult pupils and the material presented in a different way, or several ways, to enable the pupils to participate more and become active rather than passive learners.

CBG includes the use of behaviour modification techniques such as inhibition and positive reinforcement (IPR) and behaviour contract (BC) where appropriate, with individual difficult pupils. CGB involves more than shaping behaviour. It includes the direct personal involvement with the learner in the task and can provide qualitative comment on it, so overlapping PCI.

Teachers are nearly always convinced that they do operate on the basis of CBG, but when they observe themselves in action, or the events are recorded by an observer, they find that they do so much less than they think. Record your own CBG to task responses and social responses separately.

Positive cognitive intervention (PCI)

Much of the learning taking place in classrooms seems to be of the kind which requires children to learn large amounts of factual information in what is called the pursuit of knowledge. The pupils, when questioned, often fail to see the point or relevance of much of what they learn and the less committed refuse or avoid much of what they are set to do.

- When tasks are set in such a way that the learner can contribute his/her own ideas to the project, and the teaching strategies encourage the process of 'accommodation' – adapting internal schemata or knowledge to the new information in a meaningful way – pupils begin to want to learn and perceive the work as relevant.

- When the methods of learning are set so that the learner is required to think about the material and use it in a meaningful way in problem solving and concept formation, then motivation is reinforced and the learner gets on with the task. This technique can be applied to all subjects of the curriculum. The distinction is made between *telling* information and pupils writing it down, and *teaching* as a result of which pupils learn.
- When the teacher uses more open questions, rather than questions requiring closed or factual one-word answers, pupils become more intellectually responsive. If the learning strategy is set so that in structured settings, in dyads and triads, the pupils can question and respond in an extended way about the content, all pupils have a chance to engage in legitimate dialogue. This is important as many pupils do not know what they think until they try to explain it to someone else.
- When the pupils have written or made something as a response, it should receive more than a cursory look or tick. During the lesson, it should be given some qualitative appraisal by the teacher with some structured guidance on methods and techniques for further development. Some sharing of ideas and opinions should take place.

Teachers need to question if the information telling, question-answer and writing down strategy is the best method of learning information, when not all information has the same structural and hierarchical priority within a subject area. The ORACLE project (Galton *et al.*, 1980) found that only 0.6 per cent of the teachers' time was spent on interactions designed to promote thinking. PCI is thus a much neglected aspect of teaching. It is also one of the most difficult of the strategies for teachers to develop (Montgomery, 1988). Even the very best of teachers can always learn more in this area.

Management, monitoring and maintenance (3Ms)

In any lesson there are basic strategies which teachers use in order to gain and maintain pupils' attention, whatever teaching method they subsequently use. The 3Ms strategy represents a net of related tactics which the effective teacher uses time and again to gain and keep classroom control. It fits most circumstances.

Management phase
The teacher makes an *attention-gaining noise* or *signal* which his/her class learns to recognise and respond to. The signal may be the sharp closing of a door; a sharp noise of ruler on table; a hand-clap; a speech noise such as 'Uhmm!', 'Now then!', 'Right', 'Class 4', 'Good morning, everybody', etc. Some teachers stand quietly and wait.

The teacher gives a *short verbal instruction,* such as 'Everybody sit down', 'Sit down and get out your books', 'I want you to listen carefully', 'Everyone come over and sit on the mat'. A lively class of pupils will respond well to this instruction but we all know that a number of pupils will continue talking and doing their own thing. A common mistake is for the teacher to repeat the instruction louder, and again louder still, so that pupils are startled and stop. This is because, next time round, they simply talk louder themselves. The teacher may also anxiously begin the lesson over the noise of the talkers who will now continue with others, perhaps, joining in. Some very difficult classes who have experienced a number of teachers with control problems will continue talking whilst the teacher shouts 'Be quiet' or some other instruction, louder and louder. The pupils thus demonstrate that *they* are really in control and finally drive the teacher to threaten, bully and perhaps get him/herself into an irretrievable position. To avoid this situation, it is important not to rush into this inescapable route to disaster and, after the short verbal instruction, follow it with an *individual instruction*. This simply means following up the 'Everybody sit down!' instruction with a pause, looking carefully around and then quietly addressing by name any individual still standing talking, for example, 'John sit down', 'Sarah, open your book', 'Richard, turn round please!' We can always hear our own name amidst noise. Quietly done the effect of this is to cause the group around the individual also to fall silent or get out their books. It creates a *ripple effect*. This indicates the importance of learning names or having a classroom plan as soon as possible. Without them the teacher is powerless.

When there is a lull, *immediately* introduce the *main theme* of the lesson. The longer the teacher spends on activities other than this, for example, dealing with late-comers, minor administrative matters involving individuals, keeping the rest waiting, the more likelihood there is of other pupils starting to behave in undesirable ways.

The introductory sequence should have a good pace. Soon a habit of getting on with the work will be established so that all the teacher has to do is enter the room or call for attention and the children will respond appropriately.

Monitoring phase

Once the individual or group work has been set, the crucial phase of monitoring begins. Not all children will settle immediately and not all will want to. The usual response is for the teacher to deal with individual requests and then go out amongst the class to help some pupils get started or to iron out difficulties. A few teachers remain at their desks, withdrawn from the class, issuing occasional instructions or giving information, sometimes engaged in other work. This can create an attitude in the pupils of 'them and us' or represent to them an authoritarian style of teaching which is not interested in them or what they produce, only that they should do it as they are told. Pupils who feel even mildly anti-authority in this depersonalised setting may be prompted to undermine the teacher representative of authority. Thus, whilst the teacher is *in* legal authority and must be *an* authority in terms of subject content, this role is to be distinguished from displays of overt authoritarianism, because the cues are very easily picked up by pupils who particularly resent this style in a young, inexperienced teacher.

Monitoring involves casting one's eyes over the whole class and observing individuals who are the focus of disturbance or those who have not yet settled. The teacher then needs either to mention the individual by name, for example, 'John, hurry up and get started please', 'Susan, if you have a problem I will come and deal with it in a moment, just settle down now', or quickly to move round the work groups, quietening the loudest member. It is important to settle the whole class down to work before giving detailed help, otherwise some may never start at all. Once the pupils know that you are engaging in this monitoring activity, you will only need to make eye contact with ringleaders or a hand gesture to settle or move them. The whole session can often be controlled by *conducting* the class by eye contact and gesture *non-verbal cueing*. It is much more restful to achieve control by non-verbal methods than verbal ones, for any noise the teacher makes can contribute to the pupils modelling and using their voices even louder. The noisier the teacher, the noisier the children.

The monitoring phase should be short, but can be repeated as required throughout the next phase when noise level seems about to rise or one or two pupils can suddenly be heard above the general work murmur. Pupils continually test even the experienced teacher's level of observance, only resuming work if eye contact is made.

Remember the '*3 second rule*'. On naming pupils be sure to look back at them to check that they are back on task. If you do not do this, they soon learn they can resume their disruptive behaviour.

Maintenance phase

Once the pupils' part of the work has been set and they have been settled to work, it is advisable for the teacher to move around the class to find out how well the task is going, to help those with difficulties, to involve those whose motivation is hard to encourage. The pupils should know that *each one* of them can expect to receive some positive comment from the teacher about their work or some help during the lesson (PCI), not just those who are having difficulty or are being a nuisance.

It is this individualised attention to the task that encourages interest and effort. The pupils come to want to work for the teacher because he/she treats the work as important by taking a personal interest in it. Each pupil comes to feel significant and believes that his/her effort is an important and useful contribution. It enhances self-esteem and generates an active interest in school work. The teacher meanwhile, through close observation of performance on task, can obtain feedback on the effectiveness of the teaching content and method, modifying future work, diagnosing difficulty and preventing learning failure. Most difficulties will arise at the 'now write it down' point, so each teacher needs to know how to help with special needs in handwriting or spelling. This needs to be an in-service training priority to which there is a whole-school approach.

The most important thing to remember is that the comments the teacher gives on the pupils' work, whilst moving around the class, should be *positive* and *structured*. Negative comments engender negative attitudes and demotivate the pupil. Therefore the technique suggested is to *find* something positive and helpful to say about the work which will show how it is good in this or that respect and how it could be improved by doing (*a*) or (*b*). It is essential to adopt this approach with those whom you know will have made little effort or little progress. If they have written or done nothing at all, then the positive approach has to be in sharing and developing ideas, however poorly articulated, written or constructed they might eventually be. This second aspect may be the subject of other forms of specific help, for example, do not prevent a pupil from writing ideas and gaining on understanding in his/her own phonetic code by presenting a severe attitude to poor spelling. The first stage in the treatment of the spelling problem should be to check that the pupil can at least represent speech phonetically and *does* have sound-to-symbol correspondence. Mark the ideas expressed separately from the mechanics of its expression. Similarly, pupils with poor pencil control do not deliberately write untidily; they *cannot* learn to write legibly and tidily without specific help.

During the maintenancing period, when the pupils are getting on with their part of the task and the teacher is working in detail with an individual pupil, it is always necessary to keep alert for the sound of diversion and to look up, making eye contact with the 'offender', thus reverting to the monitoring function as circumstances require teacher's interest and guidance.

The teacher needs to take a detailed and careful interest in any work produced. This can make the effort seem significant and important to the pupil. The ORACLE project showed that the maximum time any pupil received teacher attention for any purpose in a day was forty-four seconds. Researches by Hegarty *et al.* (1981) and Croll and Moses (1985) showed that most teacher attention was actually directed to the children with learning difficulties. Thus, the chances of every child receiving their 'ten penn'orth' are fairly slim.

Case example

A seven-year-old boy who had been very disruptive since he had been at school was described as well able to read and write but spent much of the lesson calling out, shouting and talking. In between these outbursts he would throw himself on the cushions in the quiet corner shouting 'shag', slap himself and rock vigorously but not actually masturbate but seem to be close to it. The home circumstances were not happy. Father favoured an older child and mother was now very much concerned with a new baby. His reception class teacher found one way to quieten him was to let him sit on her lap during story and frequently whilst she was talking to other children, but was unable to control his behaviour at other times. His present teacher who has only had him in the class for two weeks is much concerned that as he grows and moves up into the Junior School, he will no longer be able to be accommodated in the ordinary classroom and wants to know what will help him now. She has managed to be so encouraging about his progress in curriculum activities that he often works well instead of refusing to do anything or cooperate at all. He reads well, for example, but cannot seem to make progress on the calling out, shouting and rocking. She is concerned that the other children may start to take an interest in his behaviours and perhaps imitate or encourage him. At the moment they do not seem to take any notice of his odd behaviours. She is worried that the parents working in the class may complain. The boy's parents are not the sort who will come willingly to school or attend school functions.

What advice would you give to the teacher and how could she be helped to help the child?

You will need to:

1   Identify target behaviour(s).
2   Determine strategy(ies) to be used.
3   Decide how to explain these to the teacher.
4   Decide how you would support the teacher in her intervention.
5   Consider approaches to parents and other agencies.
6   Determine by which criteria you would identify and monitor success or failure.
7   Decide if there are any factors to be considered which could underlie the overt behaviour but for which there is no background information?

GENERAL GUIDELINES ON CLASS CONTROL

Rule 1   Never make a threat you cannot or do not intend to carry out.

Rule 2   Select the *lowest likely level* of intervention to obtain the desired response. Do not wade in, all guns blazing, or with a huge hammer to crack a very small nut. Save yourself, keep something in reserve or you will tire easily and pupils will quickly have been exposed to all your techniques. For example, use 'observe', 'frown', and 'stink look' before 'naming' and IPR. Try IPR and 'time out' before behaviour contract.

An example has already been given to show what to do when a confrontation looms, namely: deflect, hold, systematic PCI and counsel. Any problem, if mishandled, can set back relations greatly. Another gross error which a teacher can make is to make a joke at a pupil's expense. It may seem that all the pupils laugh and the difficulty has been overcome, but sarcasm breeds resentment and emotion which can colour all future interactions so that the pupil becomes more uncooperative and seeks to undermine classroom discipline whenever possible.

Rule 3   Distinguish very carefully between misbehaviour in situations which are *rule governed* and those which are *non-rule governed*. Different techniques must apply. For example, 'rule governed' means that the *pupils are well aware* of classroom rules such as not calling out, not shouting each other down or not talking whilst the teacher is trying to achieve quiet and begin the session. What they are doing is keeping the teacher waiting, testing his/her patience and skill in classroom control. As soon as the 3Ms strategy is operated, order is restored and the lesson can begin. This happened recently when I went to give a lecture, in place of an ill colleague, to a group of PGCE students in training. The group entered the room just before me. As I entered, they were sitting down, talking and getting out books and pens. I waited. They observed me sidelong but continued talking. One or two looked interestedly at me, expecting me to quell them. I decided not to bother but to sit quietly on the side of the teacher's desk and wait. It was, after all, a session on classroom control. I waited and they deliberately exercised their withholding of attention and talked, not making eye contact. I smiled at one or two. One or two officious persons, guessing that this could go on for some time and wanting to start, 'ssshed' them several times and the group fell quiet, watching intently, wondering what I should have to say. It was an opportunity not to be missed. Never lose power by ranting or nagging. I, of course, said 'thank you' to the quieteners and, with a warm smile to the rest, 'I do hope your pupils will treat you as you have just treated me. I wonder what you will do?' Irony is sometimes irresistible.

The students knew I was waiting to begin, courtesy demanded that they should stop talking and listen but they did not. I wondered what experiences they were having on the course which made them want to put up this hostile front. Why did so many wish to demonstrate their personal power behind the group protection and anonymity? Had I known any names at all, I could have quietly called on one or two to attend and the rest would have followed suit. This is akin to the woeful lot of the supply teacher who is moved from school to school, who never has a chance to learn the pupils' names and so cannot easily gain control and attention. It is always strangers of dubious or unknown status, and often women, who are treated to this form of contempt.

The non-rule governed situation is one which pertains in the early days of schooling, in nursery and reception classes, where many pupils have been used to being the centre of attention at home. The teacher, calling for attention or saying 'Everybody come here', is not noticed rather than ignored. This reaction is not deliberate but the teacher's commands do not necessarily create a change in or structure the child's behaviour. Parents are indulgent about instructions; if children disobey they often let them and smile encouragingly and the child fails to learn to follow directions unless individually directed or physically handled. Pupils have to learn that when a teacher says 'Stop', they must do so. Later, they may be able to read work-card instructions but, again, they fail to follow them until they or the teacher reads them aloud and the words are internalised.

In these non-rule situations, the teacher has to call those children who he/she knows will come to him/her, and then do something interesting which will attract attention and draw the others in. Meanwhile, the nursery assistants and helpers can go around encouraging others to come. Using the same word formats and giving advanced warning that 'story is due' or something nice is about to happen can cue attention and bring children together easily.

With older groups, a series of bad experiences and poor teachers can allow them to lapse into ungovernable egocentric behaviours, more typical of five-year-olds. If, in addition, there is a group of hostile adolescents who deliberately set out to prevent teaching taking place and who refuse to do any work, this makes the job more difficult. These pupils know they will only be given detentions from which they will absent themselves. They may know that the school management will not back the teacher, or that the governors would not approve suspension and investigation of the case, and this puts all the power, if they wish, in their hands. In this situation, the teacher has to begin the lesson as fast as possible, cutting the class introductions and discussion. Instead, worksheets can be put in front of the pupils and some will start. The teacher must then go around the class and try to engage the rest of the groups in the task, keeping the noise down as far as possible, rather than trying to gain total silence. If the work can be made relevant and interesting, actually requiring and legitimising talking, the class will gradually settle down. If the teacher works hard at CBG and PCI during this period, the pupils' attitudes to this lesson will begin to change and they will be more ready to listen, especially to someone who has enough respect for them to support and encourage them in their work. This cannot be achieved instantly but can, with time.

In such a group, a large number of learning difficulties will reside and these need remediation or teaching method change. An easy beginning will be to tackle handwriting and spelling. The handwriting errors need analysing (see error analysis sheet, p.159). Correct letter shapes to be taught for a cursive hand, and joining should be introduced immediately at *all* ages (Montgomery, 1989). Teach this as far as possible on an individual basis, and other pupils will overhear and take an interest, and often ask for help for themselves. For poor spelling, a set of cognitive strategies are recommended (p.160). These strategies make the pupils more confident in their own abilities to help themselves, and time spent in these two ways can help many of them begin to enjoy writing their thoughts down for the first time. These methods are extensions of PCI. A structured handwriting programme for the cursive hand may be found in Morse (1986).

Another problem pupils have, is that many are inarticulate. Work which involves paired discussion, in order to resolve problems and develop hypotheses before or instead of recording, will encourage oracy. A succession of HMI reports have pointed to insufficient development of oral communication in both primary and secondary schools. Recommended materials and packages for this are *Ways and Means* (Bowers *et al.*, 1985), *Developing Oral Skills* (Brooks *et al.*, 1987), *Study Skills* (Montgomery, 1983), and *Able Pupils' Needs* (Montgomery, 1985).

GAINING AND MAINTAINING ATTENTION

When starting a lesson, use the 3Ms strategy (p.101). Once the lesson is in progress, many other strategies can be used to maintain quiet or a working atmosphere:

- *Monitoring* – Often during work the noise level rises. When this happens look around the room to locate the area of disturbance and quietly name one of the children in the group. This should quieten him/her. It also gives a ripple effect – a spreading wave of quiet.

- *Ripple effect* – The other children near the noise-maker also settle down and become quiet. Whatever you are doing, you must have your ears and eyes tuned to the class as a whole, rather than just the group you are dealing with. Pupils expect teachers to have eyes in the backs of their heads and to be 'on the ball' in this way. If they are not, the noise spreads and disruption will ensue if unchecked.

- *Reprimands* – Occasionally it is necessary to reprimand a pupil. Keep it very short and very quiet. Reprimands should be delivered so that only individuals can hear because loud reprimands increase the disruptive behaviours of other pupils whereas soft ones decrease the frequency (O'Leary *et al.*, 1973).

- *Observing* – Often observing and recording the frequency of misbehaviours of an individual can cause the behaviours to disappear (Dawson, 1985). The teacher who stands back from the group work at regular intervals and just looks around to see what is going on (monitoring) may note a misbehaviour and simply look at the miscreant or appear to look at him/her. This will often cause the pupil to attend to the work again.

- *Cueing* – There is a wide range of cues which the teacher can use to indicate disapproval, or that attention to work is required. Each of the following is preferable to a verbal instruction. Try cueing first, before a reprimand and, if necessary, couple naming with a particular cue to gain the attention of individuals.

  Visual cueing
  eye contact;
  eye contact and raised eyebrow;
  frown;
  'stink look';
  shake of the head;
  pointing with finger;
  calming gesture with the hand;
  finger on the lip;
  smile;
  nod.

Auditory cueing
a light cough;
a snap of the fingers;
quiet naming of the child;
a tap on the desk with a pencil.

Proximity and contact cueing
a calming hand on shoulder or top of head;
removing object of distraction;
walking towards pupil;
moving towards and standing near pupil;
sitting next to pupil;
gently turning and propelling pupil towards place;
holding hand and leading (young pupils);
arm lightly round shoulder (younger pupils).

Wheldall and Merritt (1986) report that teachers in their research project have found that making physical contact has facilitated their pupils' learning. Clearly, at secondary level, physical contact should generally be avoided in case it is misconstrued. Sometimes teachers put a hand on a pupil's shoulder as they look at the work, this often generates face pulling and asides.

- *Calming* – Move quietly to a shouting or agitated pupil and put a calming hand on the shoulder, forearm or top of the head and very quietly say 'Sssh, sssh, don't shout, calm down' in a soothing manner. Make eye contact if possible and say 'Settle down, now – good, that's better'. Keep an eye on the pupil for a few minutes after this and cue for quiet, or soothe with a calming hand gesture again. If the disturbance continues, go over and quietly sort out the trouble. Do not become involved and excitable yourself. When one child begins to shout, stop it immediately otherwise others will join in or shout louder to be heard. It is very important that the teacher does not become involved in this spiral of noise. Step in quickly but do not do so negatively or harshly.

DEALING WITH CRUSHES

Men and women teachers are the subject of crushes from both male and female pupils. This happens in particular when pupils reach adolescence but can occur earlier. Sometimes these attentions can be attractive to the teacher. They may be characterised by pupils hanging about or shadowing the teacher in school to engage in conversation, particularly trying to collect personal information and to talk in a familiar way. Anonymous 'love' notes may be put on the windscreens of cars or in briefcases and so on. Teachers who are given friendly supportive attention tend to respond by being more open and expansive. In class, they may smile or speak more to a pupil who reinforces them.

This should be as far as things go with the teacher remaining aloof in all other respects until the crush gradually subsides. Some pupils are, however, more demanding and more manipulative and exploitative. Very often they involve one or two friends who act as confidantes with whom details of each little interaction are discussed and further contacts planned. They may brag to each other or pupils in the wider group about what they have said and done. These accounts, can in a few cases, develop into flights of fancy and could, if broadcast, compromise the teacher. Cases of this kind have been known where the teacher is quite innocent of any accusations made by the headteacher or parents who have these things brought to their attention. Occasionally, a teacher may succumb to a pupil's advances and exploitation.

If a teacher becomes aware that a pupil is developing, or has developed, a 'crush', then it is important that:

- The teacher should be seen by other pupils not to be encouraging favourites or accepting more chat from them. In this instance it is important to be *scrupulously fair* even to the extent of ignoring the individual a little more than might be expected in the classroom.
- The teacher should tell another, or several colleagues that the crush is building. Often they can walk together to and from rooms or cars so that the pupils cannot lay in wait between lessons or after school with any likelihood of a successful encounter.
- The teacher should not allow him/herself to be alone in the classroom with the pupil after other pupils have gone. Always move with the class whilst perhaps talking with the individual *out into the corridor*. This is a more public place and colleagues can intervene.
- The teacher does not enter stock cupboards, etc. with pupils and close the door.
- The teacher does not send pupils, particularly girls, up ladders to reach stock whilst holding the ladder steady.
- The teacher avoids physical contact in secondary schools (particularly male teachers with female pupils). If contact is made it should be confined to the socially legitimised touch areas (Jouvet, 1966) – lower forearm, top of shoulder, top of head. In addition, the front of body and pupils' backs, especially those of girls, should not be touched. In PE some of these rules are adjusted as appropriate to enable support over apparatus to be given.
- If the pupil with the crush is showing signs of obsession, the teacher takes advice from senior colleagues and the headteacher so that timetabling changes may be planned. Advice can also be obtained from the School Psychological Services and, in some cases, the parents may need to be consulted.

Parent crushes on teachers

With the increasing access of parents to school, for various parent involvement projects, it is not uncommon for a parent to develop an attraction to a teacher. The teacher is often oblivious of the effect he/she is having and somewhat enjoys the attention or extra flattery that might be involved. When personal notes arrive and conversations turn from the pupil or task to personal issues, the teacher can easily be caught in a trap, being made to feel guilty about having been the cause of the attachment and the heightened feelings of the other person. The tendency is often not to speak but to hide and avoid the situation. This is the time when advice from peers and senior colleagues needs to be sought.

Headteachers often find there is one member of staff who takes more than a dislike to them and, after some triggering misunderstanding, are reported at every turn for an illicit act or 'corruption'. Corruption and sexual misdemeanours are favourite accusations for which there may be no foundation but people will, of course, foolishly say, 'There is no smoke without fire'. The accuser may even step beyond the bounds of irrational interpretation of ordinary events actually to fantasise about being the subject of sexual or other harassment and report the headteacher or classroom teacher for it. It is obviously very important to take advice early on and have this kind of behaviour identified for the schizoid illness it is.

The difficulty which any person in authority faces is that his/her actions are imbued with a greater significance and deliberation than was originally intended. Entirely random and insignificant details are observed and can be made into a pattern of relevance by someone if they really wish to.

POSITIVE CUEING

The examples already given show how control can be exerted across the whole classroom non-verbally and how unwanted behaviours can be temporarily stopped. What is equally important is to *support* and *extend* desirable behaviours such as: on task behaviour, sensible answers, attention, quietness, sitting in place, helpful behaviours and so on. When these occur, it is extremely important to *give recognition* to *reinforce* them so that they will continue or re-occur. Reinforce *both* work and social behaviour if you want to encourage more of it. Therefore:

- *Smile* when children give you correct answers, sit in their seats, wait quietly, work hard and so on.
- *Nod* and smile at them when you approve of behaviour, answers or work.
- *Look at them interestedly and attentively* when they speak.
- *Stand or sit companionably* beside them to help with work.
- *Paraphrase* or repeat their answers and smile.

SUMMARY

In this chapter a number of principles and practices have been derived from behavioural psychology for application to the ordinary classroom. These approaches have mainly been applied to basic skills areas in the form of task-analysis strategies and to behaviour management in the form of behaviour therapy techniques. In addition to these a number of other techniques have been developed in relation to cognitive psychology, forming what might be regarded as a humanistic psychology of learning and teaching. Teachers will need to evaluate the pupil's behavioural difficulties very carefully and then select appropriate techniques from those outlined. The results of these interventions need to be carefully evaluated and changed if appropriate. Where the problems extend to other members of the class, then classroom organisation and task management will need to be examined along the lines suggested in the next two chapters.

9
Class Control and Organisation

INTRODUCTION

Classroom management advice is more often based upon rich experience than grounded research or experimental studies and is none the less valuable for that. It would, however, be helpful to teachers if more research could be done in this area. As yet we are really only in the position of developing a theory and practice towards a form which can be empirically tested. Aspects such as room management and group work have been increasingly well-researched but more attention needs to be focused upon the strengths and weaknesses of vertical grouping, open plan, the 'wheel' organisation in infant classrooms and individual learning programmes. The methods and the results of their use need to be researched on a long-term comparative basis where each is in the hands of good and satisfactory practitioners. Herein lies the difficulty in determining with accuracy what is good practice when the researcher often has only minimal knowledge and experience of teaching, and usually none of teacher training. This is a key issue, for my researches show that even very good teachers seldom, if ever, know what constitutes good teaching and how they have constructed their success. This is particularly true of those teachers who have only received a one-year post-graduate course of training. The suggestions which follow are based upon substantial experience and grounded research.

SETTING THE CLASSROOM RULES

When you first meet a class, it is helpful to make clear the classroom rules. It is not usual to say 'Class 3, here are my rules' but to introduce oneself and begin the lesson or session and, at the first minor infringement, give the rule or social agenda.

Social agenda

'Don't talk whilst I am.'
'Don't run in the classroom.'
'Don't touch other people's property.'
'Treat other people with respect.'

The rule should be given quietly and firmly as each infringement occurs, and the pupils reminded of it at intervals. In the first few weeks with a new class, much time may be devoted to these social agendas and also to explaining why the rules are needed, Wragg (1979) investigating 313 different lessons found that classroom rules centred mainly upon the following:

No talking when teacher was talking in a public situation.
No disruptive noise.
Rules concerning entering, leaving and moving about the classroom.

Explanation of rules helps understanding and gains compliance

'Listen to instructions, then you will not miss anything.'
'Put your hand up if you wish to interrupt or say something.'
'We only move out of our places if we really need to.'
'Running about the room can be dangerous when there are a lot of people around. Things are knocked over or can be spoilt.'
'Treat other people as you would like to be treated yourself. Kindness and pleasantness improves relationships. The reverse spoils them for much longer.'

So often the pupils do not perceive the long-term consequences of their actions or the general social usefulness of some of the classroom rules, and so explanations can help. It is particularly important to avoid petty and unnecessary rules and procedures which almost encourage the mischievous to flout them. The reasons why pupils flout rules in the majority of cases can be put down, not to socio-emotional difficulties in the home etc. but excitement of 'the game' as has already been indicated, so the less excitement and attention created by the teacher through quiet control statements the better. After the control statement the teacher should *look carefully* around the class to stop further infringements, stare and switch to the activity in hand or to a new activity, distracting the attention elsewhere. The sequence is:

CONTROL STATEMENT → STARE →
SWITCH or DISTRACT

If another member of the class, or the same one, is still attention-seeking or talking at the same time as the teacher, then give:

STINK LOOK → SWITCH or DISTRACT

If this is insufficient, then:

NAME quietly or ASK QUESTION about the work

SWITCH or DISTRACT

These are all variations of the 3Ms strategy.

DISCIPLINE TACTICS DURING INFORMATION SESSIONS AND STORY

When children start to talk during story or explanations, or poke and pull others, instead of always stopping and telling them not to do what they are doing, try *pausing* in the story and looking at the child. On making eye contact, if the child becomes still and quiet, simply resume the story telling. This avoids nagging and spoiling the story for the rest of the children. Another tactic is to try *quietly naming* the inattentive pupil and, as soon as he/she settles and makes eye contact, resume the story.

With older pupils, break off in the middle of an explanation, smile and say 'And Goldilocks said to the three bears . . .' Direct this to the inattentive child. All the others will laugh or smile and look at him or her. Not quite understanding what is going on, he/she will quickly realise they are the focus of something and pay attention to find out what it is. Smile and resume the explanation.

Another tactic to gain control instead of reprimanding children who are inattentive, is to ask them a question about the story or the talk to gain their attention and to keep that of the other children. If they cannot answer it, ask another child to help them out and praise them for doing so.

How to avoid shouting and still gain young children's attention

Useful phrases for gaining the children's attention are:

'All show me your hands.'
'Show me your eyes – I want to see everyone's eyes looking at mine.'
'Show me ten fingers, six fingers . . .'
'All children with lace up shoes . . .'
'All children with fair hair . . .'
'Tiptoe quietly to your table . . .'
'Touch your elbows, touch your nose . . .'
'Go sit on your chairs and rest your heads.'
'Close your eyes.'

Try to avoid saying 'girls' then 'boys' line up, so that you do not encourage stereotypes.

LINING UP AND GOING OUT

Always make a definite end to a session or lesson, do not let the lesson just peter out. Call the class to attention and issue brief packing up instructions. Ask them to sit at their desks to show when they are ready, then, table by table, tell them to go and line up quietly at the door. Noisy tables of pupils can be told to return to their seats and others lined up to go. Children like to be first in queues and prefer not to sit and wait. Noisy individuals can also be extracted from the queue and sent back to their places to fold arms, sit up straight and stop talking.

Show me who's ready!

With children aged between five and nine years, do not allow the door to be opened until you arrive at the head of the queue and say to them 'Show me who's ready!' This will produce a stiffening in posture, quietening and a more orderly queue. Make eye contact with all of them and congratulate those who are obviously quiet and ready to go.

> 'Very good, Sarah, I can see you are ready.'
> 'Good, Damian is ready now.'
> 'Face this way please, Stephen. Good.'
> 'You can lead on now.'

Open the door and let them lead out to the hall to lunch, or through school and out. Always try to send them out in a calm and orderly fashion. If you have a door which leads straight outside, still make sure you have the control of it. Again, release them by lining up or directly table by table. Alternatively, stand still and wait for silence, especially with older pupils. Use one or two names if necessary.

Children coming in and out of the classroom

Meet and greet all the younger pupils as they arrive with their parents first thing in the morning. Make sure each child has a few moments to tell you important things which have happened and that games and apparatus are already out or accessible for them to settle happily before the parent leaves. Reserve a few minutes at the end of the day, after story or other work, to tidy up and collect coats and say 'goodbyes' calmly and pleasantly. Try not to let them rush off in all directions, late or in a hurry. Children in a rush out of school can become careless and forget to check for oncoming traffic. For older pupils be in the classroom ready and waiting and adapt the above. Allow them to choose an activity *or* direct them to the appropriate area. Encourage all pupils to come in and out of the classroom in an orderly and calm, quiet manner. Bring them in yourself if necessary.

If the class is boisterous and noisy, make the children *line up outside* the classroom and *walk in quietly* to stand at their places and wait for you to invite them to sit down. As they become calmer, they can be encouraged to come in, sit down and get out their work, or in an integrated setting to settle down straight away to their own work. At the end of the morning, day or lesson when they move out of the room, wait until they have put away their work tidily and returned to sit at their tables quietly before dismissing them.

GAINING QUIET BEFORE AND DURING GROUP WORK

Before the group work begins, ask pupils to suggest signals which might be used to ask for quiet, for example, one or two hands raised, finger on lips, arm(s) raised fully extended, standing up, etc. Vote on each one to find out which is preferred. Once a signal has been voted on, explain that when any member of the small group or larger class wants quiet to think or speak, all they have to do is to make the agreed signal. Other pupils, on seeing the signal, must be quiet and make the signal as well until all is quiet for the speaker. Young children enjoy sharing control of the group in this way and become very responsive to each other's needs.

When dealing with older pupils, ask them before group work begins to suggest signs which they might choose to use to gain silence from the rest of the class. List the signs on the board and vote to find the most popular. Each pupil then designs their own sign card (using paper, thin card, coloured pencils or felt-tip pens) with the agreed sign on it. When they want quiet, they must raise their card. Others follow suit and when all are quiet, the first signer may speak.

Arrivals

When a child is brought to school and is in tears and starts to scream and cry when left, quickly show him/her something bright and colourful or noisy to distract the attention. If you suspect the child is going to cry when left, try to engage him/her in some form of play before the parent or guardian leaves. As soon as the child is engrossed it will be easy for the adult to leave. Only a few children (and parents) need a period of weaning when the parent stays in the room for a while.

Dismissing pupils

Very often young children will be sitting on the mat listening to a story before they go home or go to lunch. Before dismissing them, say 'Watch me carefully and do what I do'.

'Hands on knees.'
'Hands on heads.'
'Fingers on lips.'
'Very quietly stand. (*Teacher quietly stands with them.*) Creep quietly out of room and find your coats.'
or
'Show me who is ready!'

Young children most often respond to this by sitting up straight and keeping quiet. To those who are quietest say 'Good, Sarah, good Leon. You can fetch your coats', and so on. Then, as they return with their coats, say softly, 'Come back quietly', and 'Well done'. Use this and other forms of praise to each child who remembers to come back quietly.

Alternatively, ask the pupils to sit quietly, 'With eyes closed'. When they feel a touch on their arm or hand they can get up and fetch their coat. Anyone who peeps loses their turn. Pupils at their desks or on the mat respond well to this strategy.

When dismissing older pupils, wait until after the bell has gone and for quiet to descend. When pupils fall silent and are sitting ready packed, waiting to go, allow them to leave one by one, table by table or row by row. If they want to stay and talk, avoiding the next lesson, use naming.

Leading into the hall

Line children up quietly at the classroom door. Noisy children will most often make up the rear of the queue. Ask those in front to lead the whole class responsibly into the hall. Walk with the children, two-thirds of the way back so that you can see the front of the queue and control the back of it – the noisier ones. *Do not* remain behind in the classroom dealing with trivia, leaving the children to their own devices.

An alternative strategy is to line children up at the classroom door quietly. Lead the front of the queue out of the classroom towards the hall and at the corner or at a critical point where you can see most of the children *stop*. Allow the queue to file past you so that you can make sure they are quiet and under control. Move forward again with the last third – the potentially noisy section.

EQUIPMENT AND ADMINISTRATIVE ROUTINES

Most disturbances occur when books, pencils and apparatus are being distributed, collected or replaced. It is a great time for movement, conversation and release of all kinds of tension under the cover of general noise. Early on, the teacher should establish equipment routines and rules.

- Rules should be discussed so that pupils know why the procedures are thus.
- Rules should be reviewed and changed if the pupils offer better ones or would like a new method for a period of time.
- Rules can be posted on the wall as a reminder.
- Equipment areas can be colour-coded to make collection and return easier.
- Allow time for these routines to be properly completed. Do not be left with all the clearing up.

Examples of routines

- Pupils enter the room over a period of time and settle themselves to an activity of their choice where a wide range is already out and available. This is typical of many nursery and infant settings and the teacher monitors and records the progress of individuals, ensuring that they are exposing themselves to a range of learning experiences but, in the order of their own choice.

- In other settings, pupils enter the room and wait until everyone is assembled and registered before the teaching begins. The waiting period can be when disruption begins and when the funny voices and odd noises are introduced, causing great amusement (and excitement). Experienced teachers handle this easily with humour and good grace. Less experienced teachers would be advised to have something on the board – a five-minute filler (Montgomery *et al.*, 1987) or a worksheet, paper, pens or pencils to occupy these idle and potentially difficult moments.

- Some pupils responsibly take charge and distribute books and papers to their class or group; some do not. The teacher needs to make a number of decisions about the tactics on these occasions, for example:

Trusties

1   Three 'trustees' deliver all the books, leaving the teacher free to control the rest of the class (or mark the register). The problem is that other children need to have a turn at helping the teacher in this respect and to share a little responsibility.

2   Train other children so that there is a rotation, and praise them for their skill, speed and quietness. All should have a turn during each half-term.

3   Keep a careful watch for the tendency to throw books over desks at other children. Stop the proceedings, making the aide give the book to the nearest pupil to *pass* to the others.

Tables

1   Sometimes it is just as quick for the teacher to move quickly around the tables, planting materials down for *one of the pupils* to distribute to the rest. Name this person and ask them to do this.

2   If you put things in the middle of the table, all the group grab and become noisy and difficult to settle.

3   Pupils can be asked to collect or replace materials *one table* at a time to avoid fuss and crush.

4   A disruptive class can be quietened by only allowing pupils to leave when their table is quiet and ready to go. If they start to rush out in a clamour, stand by the door and send them back to their table to move out quietly. Practise this a few times and the routine will quickly become established. At least you will ensure that, at the end of the lesson, you have gained control and they are sent off quietly to other lessons. Do not let them all rush for the door at once.

Independence

1   It should be the aim of the classroom teacher to have such a well-ordered class that each individual is capable of collecting and returning books and materials or moving about the room quietly and in a sensible, self-disciplined way. This does not come about without training for independence. This can be achieved by beginning with 'tables', setting the rules with them and slowly training towards independence.

2   It is mainly in primary, rather than secondary, classrooms that pupils are trained towards, and achieve, this greater autonomy and independence. After these self-respecting and motivating experiences, it is not surprising that when they move to situations where they lose this autonomy and are herded from one place to another, their behaviour correspondingly deteriorates.

3   Colour coding or cupboard, shelf and alcove labelling all facilitate the finding and replacing of materials and some considerable thought should be given by teachers to this aspect of classroom organisation.

SETTING THE CLASSROOM CLIMATE

It is essential for a student teacher in training to learn the names and places of most of the pupils in the class or classes he/she is going to teach. This information should be collected on observation visits. The names of the disruptive pupils will easily be learned but this is not enough for effective classroom control and can even single these pupils out for attention and encourage their misbehaviour.

Effective classroom control and the right climate cannot be achieved without knowing the pupils' names. If names are not known, instructions to individuals become difficult to make and impersonal, for example, 'The boy at the back with the red jumper'. He can pretend it is not him but someone else in the row in front. The attention-calling has to be louder to gain attention, whereas we always hear our own name in any din and the sentence is long and elaborate when a name would interrupt less. Pupils like to be known to the teacher and expect to be, it makes them feel significant. They know the teacher's name and feel somewhat injured not to be known likewise.

The extra preparation of learning the names is very useful but particularly difficult for teachers of large class groups whom they see once a week. It can help if you draft a seating plan which you fill in and ask them to keep for a few weeks. When you ask questions, you can practise using the names until they become familiar. In seminar or discussion groups, a list for signing can be sent round and then used by the tutor to put names to faces in the ensuing talk. Pupils have expectations about the way they should be treated by teachers and a number of important studies have referred to this (Hammersley, 1976; Woods, 1979; Docking, 1980; Robinson, 1981). The general conclusions are that pupils expect teachers to be:

Firm – and able to control the pupils and the class. The methods by which this is done however, are not punitive or domineering.
Fair – if reprimands or punishments are given, then only the 'guilty' receive them. A whole class is not kept in because one child talks out of turn.
Consistent – the teacher is well-ordered and work is structured. Praise is given for worthwhile things and can be seen to be so.
Teaches – the teacher explains things well and gets work done. The pupils feel they are making progress. Boredom is avoided.
Respect – the teacher respects the pupils and allows them to retain a sense of dignity, receiving respect in return.
Friendly – the teacher is friendly but not over-familiar, can 'take a joke' and laugh with pupils.
Supportive – helps pupils to achieve good results for their efforts and praises them for doing so (CBG and PCI). Most teachers are not supportive enough.

These are the attributes of the good teacher as perceived by the pupils and they are also the attributes which lead to the setting of the right kind of classroom climate (a supportive positive attitude), as has been suggested in previous chapters. It is this firmness, respect and kindly interest which many pupils have not met and desperately need. Such a teacher can thus provide a model for the pupils' subsequent behaviours in dealing with conflict and stress.

This profile of a good teacher has not always been so, and it helps sometimes to know what the opposite is so that it may be avoided. Back in 1932 Weller wrote 'Teacher and pupil confront each other with attitudes from which the underlying hostility can never be altogether removed'. Each, he argues, is trying to achieve his/her own ends at the expense of the other. In that period, and even in some classrooms today, this uneasy truce is still observed where the teacher perceives his/her role as one of *domination*, using the 'drill sergeant' and policing strategies. In these strategies, the teacher unilaterally imposes order on events, demands automatic obedience to his/her commands and insists on a high level of regimentation. Denscombe (1985) argues that this order of rules, regimentation and rituals serves to structure pupils' consciousness and becomes embedded in it so that they accept it. It also serves to enhance the teacher's ability to cover syllabus material without challenge. This 'covering' of the syllabus is done by dictate, rote and copying, without any necessary recourse to understanding. The pupils may, therefore, function well in objective tests and provide stereotyped answers, but have to parrot learn much at revision times and cannot apply what they have learned to new and different situations or questions other than those for which they have been primed.

With domination therefore, goes a tendency to give didactic lessons which, lacking feedback from the consumers, are repeated year after year without enhancement. Punishment by threats of, or actual detentions tend to be used to bolster up this strategy where pupils become defiant. Some schools still retain corporal punishment. Teachers should, if they are to be successful, avoid *domination, didacticism* and *detentions*.

Some teachers use partial approaches. In one of our classroom appraisal sessions, an unruly third-year secondary class entered the maths session with its usual noise and hullaballoo. The teacher quietened the pupils fiercely and they settled down to the work which was out ready for them. Warren, as usual, began shouting across the room, and Darren, as usual, was doing no work unless given individual attention and was encouraging Warren. Suddenly the teacher, from a few yards away, darted towards us, eyes blazing, shouting and instructing Warren to sit still, not move, get on with his work and many other more unpleasant things. He showed the full human aggression profile of arched back, finger pointing, half screaming and half shouting. He thoroughly shocked and frightened us all. He was bigger and more powerful than us but I could imagine one of the fifth-year class taking him on, and what then? The work was interesting, a practical problem-solving maths session set at the right level. There was no need for him to have behaved like that. Presumably, he was tensed up because I was there. He is known, too, to have 'a short fuse'. The pupils were subdued and resentful even though, after this, he worked round to each group to help them. He did not praise their achievements but the work did proceed.

When there are teachers on the staff who predominantly use domination strategies, they make it more difficult for their colleagues to gain discipline in more equable ways. They set up resentments which pupils expiate in other teachers' lessons. In a school committed to domination, anyone who tries to use other methods, unless they are skilled, will run a serious risk of having major discipline problems. In these settings, it is best to get to 'know the ropes'. Use the school routines and rituals at first, but then gradually wean your lessons and classroom routines towards independence and cooperative or collaborative learning. In dominance settings, the first time a teacher tries group work with all the class a *novelty* effect is created and enormous noise, even bedlam, can break out. Train in on group work a stage or a group at a time. Do not expect regimented pupils to take responsibility for their independent learning. To determine your school's domination, answer the following questions.

Dominance checklist

1 Does the school library have to be supervised or locked up (other than supervision involved in using books)?
2 Do pupils' free periods for study have to be supervised?
3 Is there bullying or scapegoating going on?
4 When you leave your classroom does the noise level rise?
4 Do pupils not make eye contact with strangers in school? Do they ignore and hustle them?
6 Does graffiti and vandalism occur frequently?
7 Does the place look bare and the corridors empty?
8 Are corridors a bad place to be when pupils are on the move because of too much noise and lack of order?
9 Are teachers often heard shouting at their classes next door, above or below you, or when you walk down the corridor?
10 Are many discipline problems handed on to a senior member of staff, for example, deputy head or head of pastoral care?
11 Are pupils sent out of the classroom to stand in the corridor?
12 Are detentions used as a means of asserting discipline?

If your answer to most of these questions is 'yes', then your setting would appear to fall into the domination domain and only with determined effort over a number of years will you, and a group of like-minded colleagues, be able to change some of it. A new headteacher, however, could turn the situation round in about three years. Research has, in fact, shown that the headteacher is the major contributing factor in determining between good and poor schools.

In your own lessons

1 Count your CBG versus desist for social activities.
2 Count your PCI versus negatives on task-related activities.
3 Ask a colleague to record the number of smiles you give in a session.
4 List the different punishments you give in a week.
5 List the different rewards you give in a week.
6 How many problem pupils do you have?

Draw your own conclusions!

In a study by Holt (1962), he found that although many pupils were disruptive, most of the others spent their time in a fearful state. They were scared of physical punishment, verbal abuse, sarcasm, being shown up and generally being demeaned. This was no environment in which learning was likely to be fostered. Withholding work or support, avoiding and evading are the only means such pupils have of exerting any control over their own actions.

Figure 6   *Table plan*

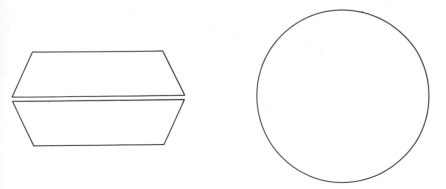

THE ORGANISATION OF THE SETTING

Tables

Most primary classrooms and some secondary ones are laid out with table groupings so that a class of thirty is seated around five or six tables, rather than in rows. Research by Wheldall *et al.*, (1981) showed that pupils did more work when organised in rows and spent less time in social interaction off task. Table organisation was introduced to foster cooperative work in groups and also to encourage linguistic interchange. The difficulty often arises when the interchange is *social* when it should, or could be *task related*.

In Figure 6 above, the tables are of two types to lend flexibility and to provide for individual working conditions when the need requires. The odd single table is very useful for isolating pupils from distraction or when they are feeling in need of seclusion.

Cone zone
When teaching a class, the teacher tends to focus maximum attention in an arc in front, slightly deflected from the mid-line, to the side of the hand preference, and makes most interaction during introductions to lessons within that area. Anxiety can reduce this field to 'tunnel vision'. The interested, worthy and compliant sit in the *cone zone*. They answer the questions and pay most attention. Try to teach from different vantage points and move around the room at least twice during the major teaching inputs. At times teach from the back and from different sides to extend your influence.

Discipline and problems with queues

Try to move around the class looking at children's work and helping them, instead of allowing a queue to form at the teacher's desk. Once children form a queue, they stop work altogether and chat. Even if you deal with them quickly, some children spend all lesson joining and rejoining the queue to avoid working. The queue often blocks the teacher's view of the rest of the class, allowing misdemeanours to occur and the noise level to rise. Try never to allow a queue to develop.

Task-directed arrangement

Rearrange the positions of the desks and other furniture to suit the demands of the task.

- Move the furniture to the sides of the room to make an arena for acting out role play and simulations.
- Arrange tables together for group work in fours and fives. Larger group numbers than five lead to less efficient organisation and lower task completion. Fours divide into pairs; even fives break down to twos and threes and work separately.
- Provide separate double tables for pair work; do not leave them as for groups.
- Individual work can be at either group or separate tables.

It has been recorded many times that what is often said to be group work is more likely to be individual work at grouped places. The significance of this is that there is very little real group work taking place, even in those schools who believe they have adopted the principle and its practices (Bennet, 1986). If the pupils could actually do the work sitting at opposite sides of the room, then it is not group work. Nor does sharing apparatus and recording automatically mean the work is group work in nature.

- Carpeted areas for story are common in primary classrooms. Carpeted classrooms create an entirely different and calming atmosphere and are extremely helpful in easing background noise.
- Small story areas for large groups can often be improved by having carpeted 'steps' on two sides for pupils to sit on. This means the children are not so on top of each other, craning necks over heads, but can make direct eye contact with the teacher.
- Story chairs need to be large to accommodate two children or a child and an adult for reading together.

The size of rooms and density problems

This is a significant factor in increasing noise and creating density problems such as quarrelling and disruption. Where rooms are large, pupils can have more space to organise themselves and their belongings. There are fewer opportunities to knock things over and snatch property. Space gives more room for access by the teacher to areas of disruption and to exert a calming effect by his/her proximity.

Size of furniture and fittings needs to be carefully planned when space is small. Smaller furniture with personal trays underneath can give additional room and shelf space. Difficult classes are noisier and more difficult to control in small rooms crowded with furniture. If you have to have a difficult class, argue for the largest, best-fitted room. All pupils need a home-base if they are not to feel rootless.

Ambience

Make the classroom as pleasant-looking and as safe as possible, with a noticeboard for pupils' own use, and room to display their work around the walls. In specialist rooms, make sure there are regular periods of time when a year group's work can be seen by its contributors. Hold special displays and exhibitions. Encourage older pupils to select and display work or collections and to help you in your preparation for display.

Ensure that dingy rooms are put on the list for decoration and check to see if stronger lights would brighten the place up. Big posters and display backing paper can be used to cover unsightly cracks, peeling paint and dirt.

Furniture

Check the furniture regularly to see that broken chairs and tables are quickly removed and replaced. Try to requisition an old piece of carpet to lay and note the effect it has on the pupils. Make sure that the furniture is the right size for the pupils. Work can become very tiring and progressively untidy under the strain of too high a table or too low a chair. This is especially difficult and tiring for a left-hander pulling the writing hand in to the body across the page. Seat left-handers on the left-hand side of pairs so that their arms are not hampered by their neighbour's, and allow them to tilt their paper more for comfort.

Teacher's kit

One of the attention-seeking ploys of pupils is to arrive without, or mislay, materials such as books, papers, pens and pencils. Alternatively, pencils continuously break and need sharpening and pens run out of ink. The mobile teacher must always carry:

    two or three sharpened pencils;
    biros or pens with ink;
    paper; and
    chalk

If you have a permanent room, then a pot of these pencils, pens and rulers can always be to hand. Always make sure that implements lent are scrupulously returned 'for the next time'. The one occasion when you are caught out and the work avoided, even for a time, will encourage the strategy to be tried again and again. It is extremely helpful if the teacher builds up a 'teacher kit' in one of the widely available plastic tool boxes. This can hold pens, rulers, pencils, glue, sticky tape, scissors, markers, paper, carbon, string, etc. This can be stored in a cupboard ready to hand and is more useful and professional than a plastic bag.

DISPLAY

Much has been written about display and the use of blackboard, whiteboard, overhead projectors and so on. It is sufficient here to state that the only way to develop a fluent blackboard/display style is to practise beforehand. It can be helpful to draw fine lines on board or paper in soft pencil which in the case of paper can be rubbed off later. Board writing can then be practised by locking the arm at the shoulder and moving across in front of the board. Two main rules need to be employed (Jarman, 1979): first, all the lines of the up and down strokes should slope in the same direction (whether print or cursive); second, all the bodies of the letters should be the same size. A third rule which might be helpful is that all the letter bodies should occupy the same amount of space.

If you use cursive or joined hand, it will speed up the rate at which you can write. It is important that infant pupils meet cursive writing in their environment as well as script particularly now that many reception class teachers are returning to the teaching of a joined hand from the outset. Even where this has not yet happened both types of writing need to be encountered in charts and displays to prepare them for this form. Visually they will find it quite easy to decipher although switching from one type of motor programme in handwriting to another is not. It is for this reason that handwriting teaching is favouring one streamlined version from infancy through to adulthood rather than learning one and having to switch to another. When teachers prepare visual displays faint pencil guidelines to write between quickly enable a clear bold style to be developed. This is especially so where large thick flat-edged felt pens can be obtained. Similar strategies apply to the use of whiteboard and flip charts where, as with the blackboard, speed of recording is often of the essence.

Overhead projection transparencies require a little more consideration – eschew typed pages printed from books, they may be easy to prepare but are usually unreadable by half the class. Clear handwritten pre-prepared transparencies with about seven words per line and the letters two or three times the size of normal handwriting prove the easiest to digest. Transparency rolls for rapid recording and pooling of responses still need to be made in larger and clearer writing than one's normal personal note-taking style if the learner is to be considered.

SOME ISOLATED CLASS CONTROL ISSUES

Truancy

Truancy has been identified as a social problem. It consists of pupils absenting themselves from school for occasional days or for gradually increasing periods of time. It is most prevalent in the fourth and fifth years of secondary schools and has been found to be as high as 80 per cent in some classrooms. These high rates, particularly at the fifth year, are concealed by averaging them over the figures for the whole school. In my opinion, one of the marks of a good secondary school would be its lack of truancy rather than its GCSE and A level grades.

To understand the causes of truancy, Rutter (1975) suggests that it is essential to ask the question 'Where is the pupil?'. The answers indicate the nature of the 'at risk' behaviour.

At home Parents condone absence or even encourage it. Parents are out at work and do not know.
At school Hiding in unoccupied areas of the school grounds or school buildings. Turns up for registration and leaves soon after.

At work Has found congenial company 'helping someone out'. Is employed by family (note, especially, local market days, harvesting times, busy selling periods).

Not at home Is hanging about local environment, (more common as weather becomes warmer) unless in shops. Need a local reporting network; high likelihood of thieving. Is fishing, sailing, swimming, sunbathing, wandering. Is at the local squat, on the fringes of drugs and theft etc. – *these are high 'at risk' factors*. Is in the local library. Is at a relative's who condones the absence. Is at peer's house, girl-friend's, boyfriend's, etc.

In each case where the pupil elects to leave school, it suggests that there is alienation from school and its purposes, a place which does not fulfil the pupil's needs for success, enjoyment and self-esteem. Schools should identify these pupils and examine their methods of teaching and working with them. It may be that the best teachers should first be mobilised to work with the least able groups and bring them back into the organisation. On a long-term basis, the whole school's teaching and learning strategies need to be reviewed and in-house programmes of staff development need to be instituted.

The first and most important factor is to identify the truants and bring them in to talk, rather than to be threatened. Here the Education Social Worker can help by visiting the parents and explaining the consequences of preventing their child from receiving education or of their duty to help and support the pupil in school. The pupil, once back in school, should be welcomed, quietly noticed and made to feel significant but not reviled or criticised. The move back in should be accomplished quietly. Often the pupil who has truanted is fearful of coming back because of the great fuss and commotion which will be made and of all the sly digs which some teachers make.

Often the pupil has been so disruptive that it has been in some teachers' interests to condone absences. These teachers need to be identified and helped to plan their lessons with such pupils. Here, an established staff development programme can be a great help and support.

Reducing large-scale truancy and alienation can radically reduce the incidence of vandalism and petty theft in the local community. Cooperation between the school and its local community can provide a reporting and safety network which can help keep pupils from being trapped in a criminal route as a result of petty misdemeanours. Through this cooperation overt criminal acts and local networks of crime can be exposed at an early stage before they become 'a way of life' for the local and vulnerable young people.

Fighting and squabbling

Most aggressive outbursts are over defence of property or defence of territory with young children. Older pupils can be provoked to fight when insults are exchanged and peers egg on the protagonists. Your arrival is often the necessary signal for the fight to stop, so utter a loud command such as 'Everybody sit down this instant!' If this does not work and the disturbance is more serious, send any pupil not involved to fetch help immediately. If this proves to have been unnecessary, nothing has been lost but it can be an essential precaution. Send all the other pupils to line up outside the classroom. This may need to be done group by group, if they do not respond immediately, because their concentration is fixed on the fight. When you are left with the two fighters, say calming things such as 'OK, it's all over now', 'Just calm down now', 'Cool off', 'Take a rest and let's see what this is all about'. Try to encourage them to sit down and take a breath. Calm the pupils and do not let them shout further insults. When the other member of staff comes, leave the class and the least hurt fighter with them and take the other one to be sponged down with some water and so on. During this period, it will be possible to find out what the disturbance was all about. Leave him/her to cool off and perhaps lie down in the medical room. Go back to the classroom and bring the other pupil along to have a cool rinse (there is a lot of perspiration generated by fighting) and a quiet talk to find out what the other point of view is. If possible, agree to meet the two pupils and sort out the dispute at the end of the lesson and then walk them quietly back to the classroom. Alternatively, take the fitter one back and allow the other one to return later when he/she feels well enough.

If the abuse is racist, sexist or of another vicious nature, pupils need to be trained to deal with it and not to inflict it. This type of issue is often tackled in social and communication skills of life skills courses but, it often comes too late at fourth and fifth year level. It is helpful if cooperative teamwork, listening and communication skills can be incorporated into each year of the pupils' programme in primary and secondary schools. For ideas on how to do this, consult the *Ways and Means* handbook (Bowers *et al.*, 1985).

It is unwise to move in between two fighting pupils unless you are confident of your abilities, or you feel you must protect one of them from further hurt. Quiet talking to the aggressor can calm him/her. Most often those fighting are relieved at being interrupted and are only too willing to stop. They are afraid to stop themselves because peers are egging them on. Report any fighting incidents to the appropriate person in your school – headteacher or head of year/pastoral care – and describe the actions which you have taken so far. They may wish to take the matter up with the pupils again later, or let it lie until another outburst occurs. It is best not to exhaust all the sanctions and sources of power too soon. It may be best to say, 'If this happens again, the headteacher has said he/she will want to see you'.

Temper tantrums

These are indulgent, attention-seeking ploys which are best ignored as far as possible. Try the ignore – distract – explain ('IDE') strategy.

Ignore
The child begins to scream and roar and beats the table or jumps up and down on the floor, going red in the face if a toy is taken away or he/she is prevented from doing something. Do not go to pacify the child, instead, move the other children away, saying nothing if possible. Turn away so that the child having the tantrum is ostensibly ignored, and continue working and talking quietly with the other children. Move any chair or table if it looks likely to be in the way. Quietly say to the other children 'When he calms down and is sensible he can join in again', so that they are not encouraged to imitate the tantrum. The tantrum may slowly, or often quickly, subside ending in sobs and sniffs.

Distract
When you turn away, be prepared for the screaming to become louder at first. Immediately the trantrum stops bring the child into any activity which is going on without mentioning the tantrum, and behaving as though nothing had happened.

Explain
If the tantrums are frequent take the opportunity, in a quiet period, of sitting beside the pupil and explaining that tantrums are not the best way of solving problems or getting one's own way and certainly that, as the teacher, you cannot be expected to pay attention to those who merely shout the loudest and make the most fuss when upset. Suggest that only 'little children have tantrums, not grown-up ones'. Ask the pupil to try to give you a warning sign if he/she feels a tantrum coming, or arrange for the child to go straight off to sit on the 'time out' chair.

Omnipotent children

Tantrums worry parents, but are a natural response to frustration in two- and three-year-olds. Worried parents give in to their children and the children learn to use tantrums as weapons to gain control, so that parents dare not do anything which might provoke one of these scenes. In school they must quickly learn that such ploys have no effect. Some children have particularly domineering personalities and soon learn to manipulate adults. One five-year-old prevented her parents from sitting or sleeping together and watching programmes on TV, until the parents learned about behaviour modification from the NSPCC officer who they beseeched to help them.

Trying to pacify or placate a child having tantrums often gives them attention and kindness at just the wrong point and thus actually encourages more tantrums and makes them last longer. Save your attention for 'good' behaviour, calmness and sociability after the tantrum is over and something constructive is being done.

Bullying

This takes place more frequently in schools, at all levels, than parents and teachers generally realise, and is suffered mostly in silence by the victims. Boys in pairs frequently harass girls, other boys and women in the streets. Both boys and girls individually and with their supporters bully others. All complaints of bullying need to be carefully and systematically investigated. Children do not generally like to tell tales, even on those who bully them, and so observation in class and playground is needed to reveal who is the aggressor. The aggression can be verbal or physical, and in either case if left, can become serious, create untold misery for months and years and, in extreme cases, prove fatal. Bullies have been known to go too far and victims have committed suicide. Confronting a bully on his/her own in an unceremonious manner with evidence of misdeeds is an important first step. It is also important to let the bully see that the victim has not told tales but that the behaviour had been independently observed. The victim needs to be accompanied in the interim period until the teacher is assured that the bullying has not resumed. If the bullying is of a more persistent or serious nature the headteacher and parents should be consulted. Bullies suffer from emotional problems and a desire to assert themselves in some way over their peers. This is often the case if there is stress at home or failure at school.

If a disruptive child cannot be calmed, the parents should be contacted and asked to come and remove their child temporarily from the school. (Consult LEA guidelines.)

Case conference
If further outbreaks occur, the parents should be invited on a separate occasion to discuss the child's behaviour and to enlist their help and support in treatment if possible. Before the meeting a full report on behaviour and attainment should be prepared and other teachers' advice obtained, especially that of the special needs coordinator.

Seek specialist advice
If the parents will not cooperate or the situation does not improve, it will be necessary for further advice to be obtained from the special needs adviser or inspector at the LEA. Assessment should include observation of the child in the classroom as well as other forms of assessment.

Temporary exclusion
On rare occasions, it may be necessary for the headteacher to seek permission from the LEA and the school governors or managers to exclude a pupil from school temporarily. LEA guidelines cover these rules and procedures.

Formal referral and 'statementing' for special educational need
If other children's learning begins to suffer and their behaviour deteriorates, it may be advisable to institute formal statementing procedures. In which case, the headteacher will need to receive a formal report in writing on the child for the 'statementing' purposes.

Organisational responses to disruption

- It may be desirable to set up a 'nurture' group for several such children or a 'withdrawal' group of about six to ten pupils for a short period.
- Special in-class support may be preferable giving help to the teacher and the child.
- A reduction in class size to twelve or fifteen could be another option.
- Review of the school's curriculum and its pedagogy.
- Transfer to another class, school or special unit may be considered as a last resort, when all the school's own resources have been exhausted.

AVOIDING CONFRONTATION WITH COLLEAGUES

When you are new and inexperienced, there are some fellow teachers and headteachers who at the least excuse march unannounced into your classroom to berate your pupils for some misdemeanour without reference to you. Registration and procedures for the collection of money can also provide opportunities for such intrusions. Make quite sure you know about school procedures and protocol on visits before term starts so that you can avoid such events by providing no opportunities for shows of power. If it does occur, take the following action:

- As the member of staff enters, move rapidly toward him/her so that you are between him/her and the class and ask what the trouble is. If he/she is clearly going to speak to the class, announce this to the children so that you are shown to be leading the situation.
- If the person starts to berate you, move towards him/her and past to the door, open it and say 'I think we should continue this discussion outside'.

You have to be observant and quick to react. Usually we miss the moves the first time and get a telling off, just like a child might. Do not be too upset, the children quickly forget even if you do not and you will be well prepared the next time. It is all a question of timing. Once deflected, the person usually does not try to continue the telling off, or repeat the intrusion.

Staffroom rules for beginners

If you are a newcomer to the staffroom, you may have a lot to learn about its rules, procedures and preferences. Assume nothing and proceed cautiously:

- On entering the staffroom, do *not* make straight for the most comfortable chair in the best position and make yourself at home. Select a hard, uncomfortable looking chair and a position which is unlikely to be favoured by 'old hands'.
- Do *not* start helping yourself to coffee or tea. Find out who is in charge and how you pay for it. Let that person or someone else talk you through. Pay promptly and be strictly honest. Tea funds are the source of great resentment if you do not behave fairly and honestly. Wash up your cup or mug and return it to its place. Large schools will have coffee machines, check the 'rules for use' and still tidy up.
- Do *not* help yourself to any coathangers, papers, tissues – they also invariably 'belong' to someone. Borrowing property without asking first can lead to grudges being harboured.

In some staffrooms, none of these cautions apply seriously. However, people are becoming more sensitive to their current powerlessness and engage in defence of symbols which they think attach to their status and importance. They can become quite aggressive in defence of status, territory and possessions. For the office secretary, territory is symbolised by his/her desk, chair and typewriter. Never sit on the desk or chair without being invited or use the typewriter without asking. As a new member of staff try:

- to listen more than you talk;
- to talk in a quiet voice;
- not to air your opinions or offer your views on teaching;
- not to interrupt other people when they are speaking;
- not to join in other people's conversation unless invited.

After the first week or so when your newness has worn off, then you can relax.

SUMMARY

In this chapter a number of factors such as the organisation of the room, the furniture, the layout and the management of resources have been shown to contribute to good teaching and effective learning, but none of them determine it. Poor organisation and poor resource management can, on the other hand, contribute to frustration in a learner who cannot see the blackboard, hear the tape, view the video, find the materials, collect the appropriate papers and read the relevant worksheets, reach the table or write without discomfort. With some pupils these irritating experiences can quickly lead to behaviour difficulties and eventual classroom disruption. It is therefore best to avoid organisational problems by arriving early, checking equipment, labelling and sorting materials and books before the lesson. Where teachers and pupils have no 'home base' and are constantly on the move having to carry their resources with them, efficient labelling, place-marking, prior sorting and a prompt start are essential – all help to show the pupils that they are important and that the teacher has enough respect for them to be well-prepared and well-resourced.

10
Task Management

INTRODUCTION

So far the role of the teacher has been considered in relation to management skills in interpersonal perception, social skills, classroom observation and behaviour management of the learner. In this chapter consideration will be given to the management of the task. Each of the three main factors, the teacher, pupil and task, can interact to create problems in the classroom.

Figure 7   *Interactions between pupil, teacher and task which can create behaviour problems*

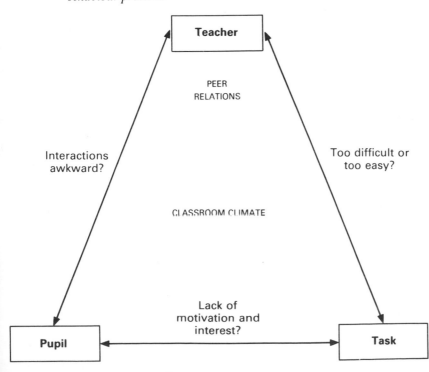

The ability to forecast lesson events and series and to plan ahead for a variety of outcomes is the mark of a successful teacher. If a teacher's mind is unprepared for a lesson and it is being given 'off the cuff', then it is more likely to lead to difficulties with awkward classes. Too much teacher-talk and too much pupil-writing can make pupils inattentive. HMI surveys of primary and secondary schools regularly criticise teachers for making writing the main means of pupil response. Lesson preparation need not consist of long, detailed notes on content. If the content is unfamiliar then only *key words* and *concepts* should be noted down for the teacher to talk around so that the 'talk' is directed at the pupils, not read to them with head bent over notes. Eye contact should be maintained at all times. Not only does this engender confidence in the pupils that the teacher 'knows the subject', but the class can be observed to see that they do not misbehave.

The style of the lesson plan chosen will also be found to be critical to class and content control. The tactical lesson plan used during our teacher appraisal research (Montgomery, 1984), has been found to be much more effective for overcoming classroom behaviour problems than the traditional form of college lesson plan.

TACTICAL LESSON PLANNING

Many teachers over the years have been trained to plan their lessons under the following general headings: objectives, introduction, method, contents, apparatus, and evaluation. Observation over the years of the results of such training, seems to lead to the rejection of this approach in favour of one which mirrors the changes in the learner's activity, which are required at different phases of the lesson – a tactical plan.

Traditional content approach

Listed below are the concepts involved in a traditional lesson plan which are best avoided:

1   A lesson topic or *objective* is defined.

2   *Introduction* – this usually takes the form of some revision or relevance to previous work and one of two presentations is given:
    (a) as a 10–25 minute talk on the subject given by the teacher, sometimes with audio/visual illustrations or demonstration; or
    (b) as a 10–25 question and answer session on the topic, delving into the pupil's knowledge, experience, attitudes and ideas.

3   *Pupil response* – the pupils are required for the next 20–40 minutes to:
    (a) write about what they have seen, heard or can invent;
    (b) carry out the instructions on the worksheet or board and produce or record results;
    (c) copy, draw, design or invent something;
    (d) follow up and complete previous work.

4   *Conclusion* – finishing off activities; checking work, packing up.

The major features of this kind of lesson are the long information sections and the long writing/practical phases during which the pupils can, and do, lose concentration and direction. This is particularly problematic in double lessons or with difficult classes, but the ineffectiveness of its design can often be concealed by short lesson periods. In primary classrooms these 'practical' activities can extend to fill half a day or more as the children take rest periods and time off task.

Other lesson plans

These are less frequently observed at secondary level and are more common in primary schools.

1 Individualised learning schemes devised by the teacher or found as published schemes. The usual problems can be observed when extended periods of individual work are engaged in, especially when there is no need for introductory activities at the outset. The pupils again take long undiscovered periods of 'rest' off task.

2 Group projects/work where the initial teaching input takes place with small groups, and then pupils proceed with individual work or sometimes with practical work in groups over a period of time. Again long undiscovered periods of time off-task can be observed.

One of the observable deficiencies of a large number of lessons stems directly from the inadequacy of the basic plan which concentrates more upon content than method. Young teachers are, of course, much concerned with getting the content of the lesson right, but this may lead to only a cursory consideration for method, or rather *tactics*. If lessons are analysed in terms of the tactics, it is possible to demonstrate the points at which the lesson will, or has deteriorated and why. When the tactics are inappropriate, this inevitably leads to behaviour problems in the pupils, which the teacher may not have enough experience to control. If the tactics are appropriate, this can act as an in-built defence against many of the common classroom problems giving the teacher time to concentrate upon the content.

The tactical plan

The plan suggested to teachers and students is as follows:

1 *Central objective* – Formulate the central objective of the lesson or lesson series as a single statement or title.

2 *Introduction* – (3–5 minutes) This occupies the first few minutes of the lesson when the teacher outlines the main purpose and/or reviews previous related work and/or revises by questioning the pupils.

3 *Phase one* – (about 10 minutes depending on age and concentration span of pupils) Presentation of the first part of the lesson content including, where possible, any visual/auditory stimulus, or *concrete* examples. Probably mainly teacher-talk with *pupils listening*. If things are going well, a dialogue can be extended to 25 minutes, and then it may be realised that slower pupils will need more help and structure for the follow-up.

4   *Phase two* – (about 10–20 minutes depending on task require-
ments) This must present an *activity change* for the pupils so
that from listening in phase one, they turn to writing, drawing, practical work or to some different activity, for example,
writing answers to questions on a worksheet with reference to
phase one and perhaps a related text (writing).

5   *Phase three* – (about 5–10 minutes depending on task require-
ments) This could be the concluding section of a single lesson
in which work written in phase two is checked for main correct
points included. This would be an activity change to *oral* work.
It could involve pupils in an extended explanation or a question
and answer session with the teacher.

If the lesson is a long one or a double period, it may be necessary
to introduce a number of activity changes. It is important to note that
it is only the *activity which needs changing, the content remains the same*.
The cue for the need for an activity change is increasing restlessness
from the pupils and an inability to settle down again when asked.
This need is frequent when the content is unstimulating or difficult
and so this aspect also needs careful appraisal during the *maintenancing*
periods when pupils are getting on with their own work. The appraisal
may result in the teacher initiating a further activity change in advance
of the original plan, introducing a further explanation or demonstration
with the pupils' aid. If, as so often happens, a large amount of writing is
required, it is helpful to provide legitimate periods of relaxation by giving
an activity change, such as hearing some pupils read aloud what they
have written; by introducing additional material; by going over the main
structure; by discussing some further ideas; by revising material already
presented; by acting out some ideas developed so far, etc.

In lessons where there is an extended period of practical work,
it is advisable to set methods and tables for recording data at the
outset so that practical work and recording on task take place in the
same period. At any point it is then possible, if the class or group
is becoming noisy and inattentive, to settle down to check the data
collected so far and reorganise the work to its conclusion.

Tactical planning thus involves activity changes based upon the
attention span of the class or its sub-groups from, for example, listening
to reading to writing to practical work to oral work to reading to practical
work to writing. For practical work in subjects such as social studies,
English, French and history one could substitute group problem solving,
role play, drama, simulation exercises, mime and so on.

If we teach, then the implicit assumption is that the pupils have
learned, whereas if we lecture or 'tell' this is not the case. We want
pupils to do more than rote learn or memorise material for examinations
and tests; we wish them to learn and understand. Tactical lesson planning
helps teachers to overcome the tendency to rely upon verbal learning
in their teaching. This is important because meaningful learning does
not take place by simply telling the potential learner what to do or
what should have been done. If learning is to take place, the learner
has to reorganise his/her constructs and implicit theories and previous
knowledge to accommodate to the new information.

Thomas and Harri-Augstein (1984) suggest that in order for individuals
to be successful learners, they need to *learn how to learn*. They suggest that
poor learning experiences cause us to acquire fixed habits or procedures

(*algorithms*) for doing things or learning new materials and strategies. These fixed habits or 'robot mode' do not work successfully at higher levels or transfer to complex tasks. Thomas and Harri-Augstein found that when approaching learning tasks some 60 per cent of people were *process blind*, for example, in spelling a difficult word, they say 'I just know it'. When they do not know the word the only strategy they can use is to consider whether it looks right, rather than a set of cognitive strategies which could help them (see Appendix 2 for a list of 12 plus 1 strategies for spelling). Pupils learn better when they can actively engage their brains with the material, learning by doing, or learning by using the skills and knowledge in new and different situations, as in problem solving and resolving. By these methods they learn more successfully and surely. Pupils who are in pre-operational (impulsive-intuitive) and concrete-operational (literal and content bound) (Piaget, 1952) stages of thinking, and this includes the vast majority of our pupils in schools, have a particular need to learn through active participation in meaningful and relevant activities, but too often they are to be seen in the passive pursuits of copying, drawing and writing.

Starting lessons

The lesson begins as the pupils draw towards the classroom. Whatever the setting, the teacher should *try to arrive before the class* especially if the room is empty, to check that it is set out and papers can be laid out in advance and so on. It is essential in primary classrooms that they are set out for the pupils so that as they arrive in the morning there are tasks or games which they can immediately take up and follow through. Start promptly.

Once in the classroom, settle the pupils down quickly, bags off the desks, and begin the lesson as soon as you have used the 3Ms (see p.101). *Do not* waste any time prevaricating; launch straight into the lesson using the tactical plan. Pupils quickly need work to do or to 'engage their brains' and capture their motivation.

Organising ways of learning content

There are two key ways to use the natural curiosity which any individual has and these are:

- To present material either as a problem or so that it can be used to solve a problem as in *Cognitive-process approaches to teaching and learning* (Montgomery, 1989).
- To present material which demands the use of study skills, not just the kind which involve searching for and copying information, but which, again, are those which have a cognitive challenge associated with them, for example, *Cognitive Study Skills* (Montgomery, 1983); Schools Council, (1981).

Study skills include, for example, sequencing, diagramming, main-pointing, flow-charting, classifying, and deletion activities. These methods are designed to allow pupils to work in pairs in collaboration and as such can satisfy much of their socio-emotional needs for self-expression. Small groups of three can sometimes be equally effective for desk jobs. In simulations, role play and drama, larger groups can be effective.

'*Talk work*' provides for extended language and will help improve oracy skills which are poorly developed in many pupils. Oral work offers more opportunities for cognitive activities and motivation. It will also to a larger extent help develop pupils' powers of understanding and thinking more than conventional product or content-based lessons. In the process approach the same amount of content is presented, but the methods of delivery are changed.

Pyramiding, – more talk work

When there are complex lists to compile or extensive information to summarise, it is useful to use the pyramid technique described in chapter 6 on page 76. We have found this technique exceptionally effective with both slow learners and able groups and also with mixed-ability groups as a teaching and learning technique. The time spent is worth the investment, particularly with important issues. The side effects are also helpful. Pupils become more involved and are prepared to tackle other tasks which are less· interesting. Centration or headlining is a variant of group work using pyramiding in which the purpose is to focus down on one main point which sums up a whole issue.

Lesson materials – readability

Many of the texts which pupils are expected to read are written in language which is too difficult for them. Check text readability and worksheet reading levels for simple clear sentences with a readability index such as that of Fry or McLauchlin's SMOG index (*Simple Measure of Gobbledygook*).

It is important that the materials are attractive, well-structured and interesting. Use original document extracts and texts as appropriate where possible to give a genuine feel of the period or the context. Pupils need *real data* to study rather than textbook summaries where this is feasible – real fish to draw rather than photographs or pictures.

Special needs

Consult your school's coordinator for special needs for further advice on readability and language skills and needs of particular pupils. Remember, all teachers should have some knowledge of special needs and how to help such pupils in their own classroom and subjects. This means your school should have a *whole school approach* worked out in relation to special needs of which you are clearly aware and to which you make your contribution. Special needs in mixed-ability settings include pupils who have lower attainments, able pupils and those with specific reading, spelling and handwriting difficulties.

'ENGAGE BRAIN' TASK MANAGEMENT

It has been suggested that while the pupils are engaged on-task, the PCI strategy should be used. In addition to this, when considering task management it is recommended that the pupils should be presented with materials and methods of teaching which 'engage brains'. Two ways in which this may be achieved are by *study skills* approaches to content which include DARTs (*Directed Activities Related to Texts*, Schools Council, 1981), and problem solving and resolivng pedagogy. Some examples follow which seek to illustrate these two approaches.

Study skills example – Main points exercise

1 The following extract is taken from Royce-Adams (1977). FIRST read for the main point of the passage:

> 'With a food surplus, the Pueblos were able to turn their attention to other activities besides locating or growing food. In one particular area – pottery making – the Pueblos developed a high degree of artistry. Potters became artists and developed individualized techniques, painting fine-lined geometric designs as well as reproductions of life forms on their vessels. Paints were improved and pottery has been found that contains three or four different colours.' (From *Columbus to Aquarius*, Dryden Press, 1975)

Write down the main point here: _____

_____

Now assign one or more of the following types a–g to it, each is a widely used writing pattern with 'a' being the most common.

(a) illustration – example   (d) sequence of events
(b) definition   (e) cause and effect
(c) comparison – contrast   (f) description
                                     (g) a mixture of a–f
                                          (state which)

The correct answer and scoring are given on the next page.

2 'Simply put, comprehension is an act of understanding or the capacity to understand. It can be divided into three levels: literal, critical, and affective. Literal comprehension is the basic level of understanding that entails the ability to identify main ideas and supporting details, to follow the sequence of events, to recognise cause-effect relationships, to interpret directions, and to perceive organisational patterns in various types or reading matter. Critical comprehension requires distinguishing opinion from fact, recognising an author's intent, attitude, and bias, and making critical judgements. Affective comprehension is your intellectual and emotional response to what you read.

Main point _____ Organisational pattern

Problem-Solving example – Mediaeval monastery

Expository method

Teacher talk with question and answer and possibly some visual stimulus.
Read chapter.
Copy the drawing of the monastery.

Cognitive-process method

You are a master mason and are invited by the Abbot of Downside to build the monks a beautiful new monastery in Portland stone. You are given a budget of £1,200 and asked to draw up plans. The monks want to retain their actual burial ground to the east and need to have their living quarters pulled down last. They want Norman windows which are three times as costly as slits and blank wall. You have to produce a three-year phased plan. They want a church, living accommodation, refectory, walled garden, pigeon lofts, well, cloisters and courtyard, and a guest house.

You are given:
Labour costs and subsistence.
Timber, stone and materials costs.
Transport costs.
Tools available: ink, no paper – quill pens.

CONFLICT RESOLUTION AS TASK MANAGEMENT ACTIVITY

Conflict resolution may be used with all pupils from the beginning of school age to adulthood whether there are problems or not. The techniques have been found to be particularly useful in schools and classrooms where there is disruptive and other behaviour problems such as withdrawal and attention seeking.

Conflict resolution techniques were developed in America in the 1960s to help leaders of student and other demonstrations prevent their crowds becoming riotous. It was realised that when large groups of people come together to demonstrate against, for example, legislation or political groups, a high level of emotion is engendered and conflict within the crowd can easily develop as well as outward hostility to those such as the police trying to control them. Trained leaders within these movements used conflict resolution strategies to keep its forces working together towards the group objective without increasing the levels of aggression.

The Quaker movement in America and the United Kingdom have been involved in preparing people for potentially violent situations since the 1960s. They do this work in schools, prisons and the community. The techniques fundamentally consist of bridge-building between people by confidence-building within the individual. Because so many pupils who are attention seeking, withdrawn or disruptive have a very low sense of self-worth and confidence in themselves, conflict resolution techniques are particularly helpful because they are directly concerned with confidence-building and building self-esteem.

Although many people naturally have the necessary conflict resolution skills, the pupil with behaviour problems does not and so can benefit from being allowed to develop them through training. The three key skills for training in conflict resolution are identified as follows:

- communication
- cooperation
- affirmation

These skills need to be developed before pupils or teachers can learn to undertake mediation activities.

Communication

The basis of communication skills is listening to the other person in order to improve the quality of the response which we make. The exercises which are undertaken in this part of the programme involve practising listening with full attention and analysing what is heard in terms of what was actually said, as distinct from what we thought we heard or what we wanted to hear. These strategies direct the learner to research the real meaning and intent of the speaker and help to develop a greater self-awareness and understanding of other people and their difficulties in the communication process. Listed below is a checklist of blocks to active listening adapted from Beer and Stief (1988) *Friends Mediation Service*, Philadelphia PA 19102:

- feeling you must give an immediate answer or decision;
- having to evaluate what is said to you;
- being in a hurry and listening on the run;
- selective listening, focusing only on what you want to hear;
- thinking out what you want to say whilst the other person is talking;
- worrying about something else;
- disagreeing with other's point of view.

The cues we then give off as we block our listening are:

- we look away from the speaker;
- we interrupt and cut across the speaker;
- we move away;
- we continue moving;
- we offer platitudes and palliatives;
- we are non-committal;
- we stare at the speaker;
- we pick on one minor aspect and avoid the real issue;
- we cut them off mid-flow;
- we introduce something different into the conversation.

Conversational rules normally require that when the speaker is speaking we look at his or her face and search eyes and mouth. When our turn is due we look away, the speaker pauses and we begin speaking.

Cooperation

Although friendly competition can encourage effort and personal fulfilment it can prove to be at the expense of one or more of the participants. The cooperation training activities and games enable pupils to realise that when people work together they can create more opportunities for fulfilment for everybody, rather than for their own selfish needs. The workshops are thus designed to foster and develop altruism amongst children which is particularly beneficial for problem pupils – both victims and victimisers.

Affirmation

This is the response to all that is positive in people. It is not a form of flattery and is not manipulative. Bowers *et al.*, (1985) express affirmation very succinctly in the following:

> ... it springs from belief in ourselves – not in the pretence that we are better than we are, but an objective awareness of our own strengths

as well as our weaknesses. Affirmation is easily discouraged. In our dislike of pretension we learn to be modest and self-effacing. Criticism is essential for growth but unless it is balanced by praise and encouragement it leads us to undervalue ourselves.

This undervaluing of self has already been noted as a characteristic of disruptive and attention-seeking children.

Affirmation is a skill than can be learnt. Building up a sense of identity is the first step, then overcoming embarrassment at saying positive things about other people and ourselves. As the ability to recognise our own personal worth increases, we can identify and respond positively to that of the people we meet. It is rewarding to see the effect that a piece of honest, spontaneous appreciation can have on someone who receives a little affirmation. Affirming a disruptive member of a group – though often difficult – is far more effective than censure.

Problem solving and problem resolution

When the three foregoing sets of skills, affirmation, cooperation and good communication are used, many difficulties simply clear up by themselves. The very process of analysing problems can suggest solutions without any further steps needing to be taken. This is where Bowers *et al.* (1985) invoke the 'iceberg principle'. They suggest that problem solving is the tip of the iceberg and that below the surface creative thinking is needed in the three areas of skill. Where problems seem insoluble then mediation processes may need to be used. Although the training materials in this field tend to be content free, it is possible to revise them and put them in curriculum contexts where decision making is required, for example, historical, geographical, environmental, scientific, religious, design, technological, aesthetic and literary contexts.

Mediation in reducing problem behaviours

This is the process of bringing about a resolution of conflict. There are schools where there is great hostility and conflict amongst pupils and between pupils and certain staff. In these schools there is a higher level of disruption and problem behaviour and it is becoming increasingly common for them to employ the services of trainers and teachers skilled in mediation techniques. In America a number of schools and colleges have their own mediation schemes, fairness committees or dispute management processes and a National Association for Mediation in Education (NAME) has been established to exchange and coordinate ideas and information. In this country similar developments are in progress. At Kingston Polytechnic members of the Kingston Friends Workshop and the Kingston Polytechnic Learning Difficulties Project have joined forces and worked to establish a National Mediation Centre under the leadership of Sue Bowers and Anne Rawlings. Modular training courses in mediation will be linked to an in-service diploma course and to the research programme being run by this expert group.

Processes in mediation (Source: Bowers *et al.*, 1985)
Defining the problem – An objective, non-judgmental description is produced, either by the mediator or all parties together if this is possible.

Expressing feelings – Each party is given the chance to describe the feelings resulting from the situation. No attempt is made to justify or blame – they are accepted with as little comment as possible.

Creating options – Consideraiton is given to anything which would alleviate these feelings. No evaluation is made at this stage of the practical implications or of whether they would be acceptable to the other party. This is meant to be a creative thinking exercise and any aids to creativity which seem appropriate are used.

Setting goals – Each of the options is considered by all parties to see whether it suggests a helpful course of action. Amendments are made and a list compiled of any acceptable actions which might ease the situation. These are finally drawn into a general plan and time schedule.

It is important that each side should be seen to be contributing and that the steps taken should not make too great a demand on either party. Each party is usually asked to sign the agreement and a date is set for an evaluation of what has been achieved.

As can be seen this provides a set of strategies and stages which could be used in developing a behaviour contract or in a counselling session between two pupils who feel they have a grievance against the other or between pupils and staff. The third person acts as the mediator and the duty performed is to bring the combatents together and help to define the problem and place it as far as possible in an unemotional context outside the relationship so that it can be considered and dealt with in an agreed manner. Mediation in the hands of trained persons can be a most useful aid in conflict resolution. Pupils, even quite young ones, can be trained to act as mediators.

PROBLEM-RESOLVING APPROACHES (Bowers *et al.*, 1985)

Negotiated agreement 1

Aim – to experience the moves and adjustments that are required in bringing about a reconciliation of conflicting views or opinions. Encourages mixing and conversation.

Equipment – a collection of objects or concepts which are ranked according to clearly described criteria. Scrap paper for participants and a flip chart or board for comparing and sharing.

At its simplest, this is the 'poster game'. Some sort of display is needed; posters, photographs, pictures, cartoons, or each member brings something. Participants are invited to select what they consider the nicest, or funniest, most interesting, etc. three items. Each person then finds a partner and together they make a joint choice of three. Each pair then joins another to form fours and the process continues. Finish either when a single group has agreed a choice or, if numbers are too large to make this practicable, the groups of 4 compare their choices and a final choice is selected by consensus.

NB. This structure can be expanded and elaborated, to include historical, environmental, scientific, linguistic, aesthetic, social and political material.

141

Negotiated agreement 2

This activity can begin with a brainstorm. We find 'What I look for in a friend' to be useful and it introduces a positive note, but any topic of interest to the groups will suffice. From all the ideas obtained, each person lists what she/he believes to be the five most important qualities, in order of priority. Then groups of five or six are formed who each draw up a list of the most important five qualities, again in order of priority. Each member should be in broad agreement with the group list. The activity can lead into discussion at this point or groups can combine again and endeavour to agree a new list acceptable to all its members.

Review and discussion
How widely did your personal list differ from your final group list?
If it was very different, were you happy with the group list?
To what extent did members of the group *really* listen to each other in the discussion and decision making?
To what extent did *everyone* participate?
Was the decision making shared or did one or more person(s) dominate?
To what extent were any conflicts resolved or were they 'swept under the carpet'?
What process did you use to come to a group decision?
  (Voting, consensus, authority of dominant member.)
  (What sort of authority – superior knowledge or louder voice!)
What are the advantages and disadvantages of:
  voting,
  consensus,
  authoritarian dominance?
Which of these methods are used in:
  your family,
  your school,
  any clubs you belong to,
  politics,
  internationally?

MORE POSITIVE COGNITIVE INTERVENTION

As soon as the pupils are busy working, move around the class and try to make positive statements about their work which will interest *them* and will make them understand why some aspect of what they are doing is good or how it will be good or better than last time.

Move around the class making a positive 'engage brain' comment to every pupil per session. You will be rewarded by finding they will concentrate and work harder for you. You may be the only bit of 'sunhsine' in their lives.

With younger pupils ask them to read their stories to you. In reading them aloud they will notice their mistakes and will learn to 'self correct'. Discuss elements of the story with pupils and offer praise and questions to extend their story skills. Leave each pupil with comments such as:

'Darren, three things to think about in your story:
(*1*) Why did the boy open the parcel?

(2) To whom was it addressed?
(3) What sort of day was it?
You might like to add these answers to your story and write it up
for the story book.'

For older pupils, use similar cognitive interventions but relate questions
to the subject content.

Peer relationships

It is wise to encourage supportiveness and to adopt a positive and
supportive style yourself. This will show the children how to behave
to each other. If you nag, are bossy and irritable, they will behave
in a similar manner. If you are calm and kindly, they will become
so, too. Encourage all peer support behaviours and discourage tale-
telling, scapegoating and unfriendly comment.

Cooperation rather than competition

Only encourage competition with self to improve on last time's work.
If you encourage competition between children, only one can win which
means that thirty-one children must fail. Failure engenders negative
feelings and low self-esteem, especially in those who are always failing
in comparison with peers. In the end, those at the bottom of the heap
give up trying and begin to evade school work or become disruptive to
gain esteem in other ways because any form of attention is better to them
than none at all. Try to find something which each child is good at and
can feel success in, even if it is only in progress being made.

SUMMARY

In this chapter a range of intervention principles and practices have
been suggested based upon action research in classrooms. The main
thrust of all the suggestions is for teachers to increase the number of
their positive and affirmatory responses to their pupils and to each other.
Until the positives substantially outweigh the negatives there will be little
change in the climate of the classroom and the pupils' behaviour. The
positive and affirmatory approaches directly address the problems of the
pupils exhibiting difficult behaviours. These behaviours are the results
of the negative self-images which pupils have and the negative attitudes
which others, especially teachers may hold towards them.

It has been suggested that effective discipline can be achieved through
providing challenging and interesting work which motivates the pupils
to want to work. Cognitive process methods using study skills and
problem-solving and resolving strategies have been advocated and briefly
illustrated. To support time on task CBG and PCI feedback have
been suggested.

When children are noisy and disruptive as a group, check through
the following list:

● *Was the task too difficult for most of them?* This will make them
noisy and frustrated so that they become irritable or clown about.

- *Was the task too easy for most of them?* Have many of them finished more quickly than you planned and are now having a good yarn – a less noisy and irritable sound?

- *Was there too much 'dead time' for the able and the slower learners?* If the range of tasks set was not sufficient, the very able (14 per cent of the class) will finish in about one-third to half the time of the average (68 per cent of the class). This gives them a large span of 'dead time' to fill or become bored in. The slower learners (14 per cent) set work for the average level will often work shallowly and finish within two or three lines and they too will have dead time on their hands to fill with mischief.

Move around the class so that you can find out these children's needs and modify the work set accordingly.

When preparing work, teachers always have to recognise that some pupils will not find it as easy as others, especially when reading and writing are involved. If the teaching is aimed towards the middle range of ability then the slower learners and lower attainers will begin to have difficulties and lose motivation. What most teachers do is to try to give these pupils more time. This is the least efficient method of dealing with a mixed-ability group because the rest of the class then receive less time, and the able pupils finish quickly and then have time when they can become disruptive.

Differentiation by content level is merely a form of streaming by ability level within the same class. This method has been widely used because it does cut down the problems which pupils have with the material and allows the teacher to spread attention fairly amongst all pupils. However, the pupils all know who is being given the lower level work and can regard this as of lower status so that this form of differentiation can be socially devisive. Much of the attitude towards it can stem from the teacher's own attitude.

Differentiation by personal contribution is where pupils are given the same task but the manner in which it is set, the pedagogical strategy, allows each individual to participate fully at his/her own level. The language-problem solving and collaborative learning approaches described and the cognitive process approaches involving study skills and problem-solving and resolving methods allow this latter form of differentiation to take place. It is this latter form of differentiation which is recommended for overcoming attention seeking and disruption in schools so that pupils of all ages can find meaning and personal identity through learning. In this way their contribution can be supported and they can gain esteem and motivation by legitimate on task activities and develop into rational autonomous human beings.

Appendix 1 – Case Studies

INTRODUCTION

The following case studies have been written by teachers following one of the courses or programmes on behaviour management discussed in this book. Each teacher, concerned about a particular pupil, adopted a procedure whereby he/she observed the pupil and presented the observations for discussion. The reports were undertaken voluntarily by teachers to help in the compilation of a data base on the management of pupils with behavioural difficulties. These brief studies will give the reader a flavour of some of the problems which many teachers face, and illustrate the tactics which they have found successful in ordinary classrooms during short up-dating courses showing that short-focused courses can effect change in teachers' behaviours toward pupils for the benefit of each.

CASE STUDY 1

Name:	Mark	**Nursery School**
Date of Birth:	10.8.79	
Family:	First born, has brother of 11 months.	
Background:	He is the youngest child in the class and had been at nursery school since September, 1982.	
CA	3 years 9 months.	

Emotional and social development

He has been very active and boisterous in much of his play during his first few weeks at school. He will frequently hit, poke and disturb children either in a play situation in which he is involved, or in a group other than this. He will throw toys around, run round the room with other children (and as yet has shown little interest in some of the messier types of activities).

He is an intelligent little boy, but appears rather tense and anxious at times. He has been ill and away this week (third week of course).

Objectives

1   I propose to try and separate him from one or two of the other very active new little boys for short spells during the morning.
2   I have altered the layout of the room to give more floor space and room for some climbing equipment which will help him.

3   I will encourage him to try some different activities, particularly the messier play with sand, paint, glue, clay, etc. which is in the other room and will give praise and encouragement when he completes an activity for whatever length of time.
4   I will try to be with him for a few moments when he is quieter and calmer to talk with him or just observe with him.

Observation on Monday morning (week 2)
9.10   Running around pointing 'strutts' (construction toy) at friend.
9.15   Did puzzle of lion beside me – did half the puzzle again – turned round to fight with child – came back to puzzle then left it to go to table with construction.
9.20   Hit Anthony then put box over his head, then threw bricks at him – ran round to hit Peter – stopped to watch someone come in classroom door.
9.25   Sat down to post shapes into box – Peter came to sit beside him. Mark hit Peter with shapes then tried to do some more – got tired and moved away.
9.30   Sat down to draw – scribbled hard – moved away to house corner.
Difficult behaviour appeared five times during this half hour.

Observation on Thursday morning (week 2)
9.05   Playing with the big bricks on the floor – went with helmet on into the house corner – looked around then came back to big bricks. Five children playing now he shouts, 'We are going to kill the sharks' – jumped off to push Peter – got back onto bricks, then pushed some bricks off and spoilt the boat.
(Five minute observation.)
On four occasions I marked difficult behaviour during that morning.

Observation on Friday morning (week 2)
He seemed quieter today and slightly apprehensive about one or two group situations. He spent nearly ten minutes quietly observing three children in the house corner. He stood back and watched most of the time without joining in the play.
    Later on when it was time to go out he hesitated about running to join a group of boys playing on coloured boxes. He went out, then came back again, but with a little encouragement he joined them for some outdoor play (it was a wet day and a few of them were outside under cover). Problem behaviour far less apparent today.

Half-term week – No observations.

Week 3 of course – Monday, Tuesday – absent.

Wednesday – First day back after half-term break and two days of illness.
9.25   He did not want to go into the climbing boxes out in classroom – said the children were being silly. I suggested he might paint. He turned round to watch children after a few brush strokes. He stopped again to watch the nursery nurse cleaning. He used several different colours on his painting.
9.30   I announced I was going outside. He said he wanted to come.
9.40   In sand pit holding spade, watching. Digs on his own, then sits in sand and watches – digs again – talks to other boy. He looked excited when some more boys arrived noisily. He stands on his own again watching with spade in hand. He turned to watch a child calling from inside a box.
9.45   Plays with Jamie – copies him by putting a bucket on Jamie's head.
9.55   Still standing in sandpit. Runs to join children on log for a few minutes. Goes on tractor. Peter arrives and tries to encourage him to play.
11.00   They both jump into standpit.

Observation on Thursday (week 3)
9.15   Played for some time beside me then went on to floor with cars beside Anthony.

9.40 Joined Peter with a construction toy on floor – went back to the cars and sat on his own chewing a car, watching children in house corner.
9.50 Wanted to go outside – he ran out and then came back again.
10.30 Outside, standing with thumb in mouth watching.
10.35 Ran after Stephen then went to Peter and made him laugh for a few moments.
10.40 Both Mark and Peter went to dig in sandpit. Mark pointed his spade at a passing child – he threw himself into the sand – used his hands to dig in the sand.
10.45 Stood watching, pointed spade at children.
10.50 Sat on edge of pit watching.

Observation on Monday (week 4)
9.10 Sat beside Christopher at table with bricks and farm animals, talked and shared animals for little enclosures Christopher had made.
9.15 They got excited and noisy with play and both went into the large climbing boxes.
9.25 Both these boys went into the house corner, one other girl and boy were there. They talked about making a space ship.
9.30 Went back into boxes, they said they were in a spaceship. It was a wet indoor day and Mark was very lively and noisy in his play but throwing things or hitting was not evident.

Observation on Tuesday (week 4)
I noticed he was easily excited. Once or twice when a child was being noisy near him or was running near him.
9.50 He sat on floor with a construction toy beside an older boy, John, and both were making car noises and other sounds while making things.
10.00 He continued to play beside this boy with some floor bricks.
He has not chosen or been willing when it was suggested, to come to the other room where the messier activities are going on.

Evaluation of intervention tactics
He has shown more relaxed behaviour and is beginning to show pleasure during play situations with his peers around him. He is beginning to say a few words to them and to smile and has not been so quick to leave them if I have got up to talk to another group. He has taken part in a little more gross motor activity.

CASE STUDY 2 by Anne Rawlings

Name:	Simon	**Infant School**
CA:	6 years	
Sex:	Boy	
Family:	Eldest of four	

During an in-service evening course on 'learning difficulties' it appeared that perhaps there were still some strategies that could be tried before Simon was actually 'excluded' from the classroom situation.
   Simon is a six-year-old boy in a class of twenty children in a 'social priority' school. On looking back through his records since he entered the nursery at three years old, part-time (but admitted full-time for 'domestic reasons) Simon has had problems. In February 1980 he was transferred to a reception class and at first settled well. Six weeks later the teacher responsible for Simon was finding him very difficult. The words she used to describe him were 'extremely stubborn, defiant, sullen, cross, rude', and she also found that his mood would swing erratically from being 'bright, helpful and eager to please, to sullen and cross'. It would appear that these mood

changes were difficult for Simon to cope with as he did not know whether to laugh or be grumpy and rude, and ended up being a combination of both. At this time it was noted that he was very pale and thin and that life at home was very unstable. Mother was on her own and a new baby was expected.

It was in September 1980 that Simon was transferred to my class. For the first two weeks he appeared to enjoy being in the classroom but the minute it was time to go home he would lie on the floor and kick and scream, hanging on to tables and chairs or anything within reach. In the mornings he would be brought to school in the same manner, i.e. kicking and screaming and generally hitting out at anyone who was near. The only way to deal with this situation was to enfold him in one's arms as much as possible and to talk quietly and comfortingly to him until he was quiet again. After a few weeks he was able to come in quietly and go home quietly so one could say that this strategy has worked but it is extremely physically wearing as one also has to cope with the other children in the class.

Simon by now had a baby brother at home. This made him the eldest of four children. During October he became withdrawn and subdued, complaining of hunger. He appeared to be fine most of the time, but his appearance was deteriorating rapidly. His hair was thin and I became very concerned about his general physical well-being. He had a medical examination and social workers visited the home to ensure he was getting enough food. It was about this time he started to take small items from the classroom. All these were indicators of extreme stress. It appeared that there must be something more that could be done to help this child. Teachers, social workers, child guidance experts and psychologists all had a case conference to decide what could be done. It was decided to have someone to help Simon's mum for a while with shopping, housework, etc. to ease the situation at home. At school Simon became much more stable in his behaviour for about one month. During this time I did some *target observation* to assess both his behaviour and his abilities. The target observations proved very interesting and enabled me to isolate one particular behaviour which I felt could be inhibited. It appeared that Simon found difficulty in handling any kind of change whether it was from one activity to another, or from inside the classroom to outside the classroom. It was this last behaviour that I thought would be a good place to start. The answer was obvious – I just made sure that I held his hand to go in and out of the classroom. In theory this sounds simple – in practice quite another matter! It is amazing how one has to have eyes everywhere at these times, especially in colder weather when some children may need help with buttons and laces, etc! However, I persevered, and it did work because eventually Simon used to anticipate me coming over to him and after a considerable number of weeks he would wander over to me when leaving the classroom. I used the target observations, looking over a period of time at specific areas. This enabled me to develop further strategies for helping him.

Physical appearance Poor appearance, thin hair, tired and listless, bow-shaped legs, pigeon-toed, pale skin and dark shadows under his eyes.

Intellect Simon has an IQ of 132 Highly Superior (mental age 7 years 6 months) on the WISC. He can predict stories and is able to point out discrepancies.

Language His language ability is good but if left to continue telling something that has happened to him in reality he goes beyond reality and into the realms of fantasy. (Simon likes talking to an adult, he likes to ensure that he has your attention.)

Emotional Simon's emotions swing from one extreme to another. He steals small items such as rubbers, etc. He can be a delightful charming child to talk to but sometimes he can be withdrawn and quiet. However, he mostly 'acts out' his inner tensions and becomes aggressive to both adults and children.

Gross motor skills Simon's gross motor movements are good but his fine motors skills are poor. His ability on large apparatus is good, but he has difficulty in skipping and could not hop on one foot.

Motivation Simon has a poor self-image which was being reinforced in activities such as music and movement as he was not able to be like his peers.

Cognitive Simon's cognitive skills are good and he practises these skills the most – he can become totally absorbed in puzzles, pattern making (Tansley, etc.). He enjoys games such as draughts and noughts and crosses.

Procedure

It appeared that there were several areas that one could try and improve. Self-image appeared to be a good starting point. A list was made of activities that Simon liked doing and was good at:

Games – draughts, snakes and ladders, etc.

Sewing

Telling stories

Number work

Listening to stories

Praise was used and a smile to reinforce: (*a*) quiet, cooperative behaviour; (*b*) success in completing small tasks. This strategy worked for all the tasks except for telling stories. Simon enjoyed standing up ostensibly to tell a story but would start to relate lurid tales using bad language. This was my fault. I should have avoided placing the child in a situation which would evoke this type of behaviour. It was much better that Simon did not have an audience for his more overt behaviour.

Results

Although Simon's general demeanour improved in the classroom, his behaviour outside at playtimes, etc. was deteriorating rapidly. He was bullying smaller children wherever there was less supervision. It became difficult during playtimes because although holding his hand would seem to be an answer for activity changes it was not possible to do this all day and in the playground. He then discovered that if he lay on the ground, this effectively kept the teacher on duty in one place which made it difficult to supervise other children effectively. He also lashed out with his feet at anyone who came near.

A second area which would 'hopefully' have a spin-off effect upon Simon's self-image was to try to improve his fine motor skills. He enjoyed using felt-tip pens, so he was given easy tasks to complete. These tasks were made as interesting as possible, because if a plain, straightforward task was given he found it boring and would refuse to do it. These tasks were also given to other children so that he did not appear to be singled out.

CASE STUDY 3 by Jan Wynne-Jones

		Junior School
Name:	Johnathan	
IQ:	95–100 (test unspecified)	
Family:	Middle child of 3 boys, was youngest child until mother recently remarried	
CA:	9 years	

I am the remedial/float teacher at a C of E Primary School. During the school week I teach children from each age range. There are five classes for the usual seven year primary age range. Sometimes I take small groups of children and at other times I take whole classes.

For about nine months, each Monday, the mother has taken Johnathan to see the psychiatrist. She says that she cannot cope with Johnathan's behaviour at home, e.g. chiselling the window frames; taking her make-up and giving it away at school; taking jewellery. After this last episode, the mother offered him £5 if he would tell her where he had hidden an antique brooch. She returned the class teacher's contact lenses which Johnathan's friend had taken from a drawer and then swapped with Johnathan.

In March, Johnathan was one of the eldest in his class. He was an exhibitionist. He enjoyed distracting others and was easily distracted. His main friend and foe was Darren. Johnathan would find any excuse to move around the room. He would call out in class and would shout out if not attracting attention.

His work was rushed and careless but he was eager to please. He worked well in the one-to-one- situation. When reprimanded he would soon 'bounce' back. After any absence his behaviour deteriorates.

The target selected from his nuisance behaviour was to stop him calling out. He was observed over the period of a week and the number of incidences of calling out recorded as the lesson subject permitted. The number of incidences depended on the nature of the lesson and on how many situations he could find. On one bad occasion it was fifteen interruptions in half an hour. On another occasion it was sixteen in an hour, at other times it was sporadic.

Intervention

The intervention I selected was IPR – inhibition and positive reinforcement and MPR. The whole class was talked to about 'manners' and calling out in particular. When Johnathan did call out he was not reprimanded but ignored, whilst some other child was praised for remembering to be quiet and wait. When Johnathan was quiet he was given praise and my attention. He did improve but soon forgot as time passed and so there had to be reminders at the start of each lesson – setting the ground rules.

Results

The results have been encouraging because of him, and the class, being praised for 'better manners' (the ripple effect). It has also helped that his friend has recently left. His visits to the psychiatrist continue. The main theme of the psychiatrist is that time should be spent talking to Johnathan and that he should not be made to feel guilty when he takes things.

Since Easter he has moved to another class and is one of the younger pupils.

CASE STUDY 4 by Margaret Rees

Name:	Stewart; older of two children	**Primary School**
Date of birth:	20.7.73	
Class:	E (mixed 2nd, 3rd year juniors)	
Family:	Sister 2 years	
CA:	9 years	

Stewart entered my class as a second-year junior in May 1982 with rather a bad record. He had been to four schools in the boroughs of Sutton and Merton. He had been given below average grades and comments such as 'rather aggressive', 'progress hindered by absences', 'noisy and disruptive', 'obvious fear of punishment' and 'cannot cope with classroom situation'. The report from his last school stated that he was unable to concentrate for more than thirty seconds, his written work was negligible, he had social problems and sought constant attention from adults and children. There was also a note saying that there was some possibility of non-accidental injury.

Stewart was obvious from the first day. While the other children were listening to a story, he was crawling from the front to the back of the class under the desks and through the children's legs. I realised very quickly that the previous reports were not an exaggeration. He displayed lack of self-control, lack of interest in most aspects of school work, belligerence and aggressiveness, attention-seeking behaviour, disregard for feelings or rights of others but also, when being spoken to by myself or another member of staff, an amazingly thoughtful and pleasant disposition.

Stewart lives with his mother and father. His father has a regular job which is well paid; his mother does not have a job. He has a sister of nearly two years. No indication of what his home background was like came from previous schools apart from the comment 'Stewart's home situation needs to be remembered'. He had also been referred to a child guidance clinic, but I do not think this was followed up as he moved to Worcester Park soon after.

His reading was quite fluent, but despite constantly telling me that he was a good reader he would only read when I was listening and not at all silently when I was hearing someone else. He has done very little in maths until recently. He was unable to add single digits together accurately using material some days. Written work was very poor – indecipherable spelling and very poor hand control – and not much of it.

Intervention

Stewart is still in my class – now as a third year. We are fortunate in having Mrs Frampton, the borough's peripatetic remedial teacher, for five hours a week. She takes Stewart for half an hour on his own three times a week. This has been possible for about two months when another child needing her help left. This teaching coincided with my decision to ignore his behaviour if it was not disrupting or harming other children and encouraging them to do so too. I encouraged Stewart and liberally gave him team points if he was actually doing what he should have been. (Reprimanding him loudly usually resulted in Stewart hitting the nearest child as soon as I had turned away – it was necessary to change the neighbouring child frequently.)

Stewart clock-watches until it is time to go to Mrs Frampton. With her he is now taking much more interest in his work and really tries to work neatly and concentrate on letter formation. He works hard, has a friendly approach but is sometimes reluctant to admit to lack of knowledge in certain areas, although he is beginning to realise that a one-to-one situation is an ideal time to sort things out. His behaviour is altogether more controlled and mature. Most of this improvement applies to his attitude in the classroom too.

I was very disappointed last week. We had had daily incidents of food disappearing from lunch boxes. All the classes were told about it but the thefts continued. When these incidents were in their second week, some of the food was discovered in Stewart's bag. He claimed it had been planted there, but then biscuit wrappers were found in his pockets. He claimed he had done it 'for fun' after he eventually confessed under pressure. Pens and pencils which belonged to other children had turned up in his desk, but as he was always losing his own other children were constantly lending him theirs and I assumed (innocently!) that he had forgotten to give them back. There had been no incidents of theft concerning Stewart since he had been at this school, but when speaking to our head about the present trouble he admitted to stealing in his last school, but he had never taken money – 'that's different' (Stewart's words and in his opinion much worse than taking food).

His mother phoned up about three weeks ago – much to my surprise because Stewart's behaviour at school was so much better – to say how dreadful he was at home and what could we do to help. I was told that she seemed to need help desperately – I didn't speak to her. She was put in touch with the welfare department and the head had a chat with Stewart during one of their lunchtime dog walks. I believe the situation has now improved.

When I have spoken to Stewart's parents in the past, I have had the impression that they have no understanding or idea of how to bring up children. Stewart's sister, nearly two, during the last parents' meeting was expected to sit still and behave for a quarter of an hour while we talked. No toys had been brought to amuse her and she exhibited all the tendencies which Stewart must have also shown at her age!

Summary

Over the last few months it has become possible and necessary to work with Stewart on several fronts IPR, MPR and CBG with PCI. The overall effects of using these techniques can be seen in his generally improved behaviour in the classroom and his thoughts expressed in his written work about a 'role' change he is working on. In relation to the learning difficulty the structured help he is being given at cognitive level and with skills, plus the opportunity to make a satisfying relationship in a one-to-one situation with an adult has greatly contributed to his general well-being at school. It seems possible that by contrast his increasing bad behaviour at home has provoked a response which has started the stealing again (a comforting offence?).

Examples of the cognitive interventions

(a) Worksheets to practise letter formation.

(b) *Springboard 2* – a simple English workbook given to get him to organise his thoughts. I insist he reads instructions carefully and, because there is a limited amount of written work, I insist on careful presentation of work and won't accept any wrongly spelled words if they are there for him to copy. He is now beginning to take more pride in his work.

(c) Simple spelling rules – one each week with follow-up material including a work-sheet and a quiz or crossword or missing wordcard, etc. Occasional spelling tests on words to which certain rules apply rather than to a list of learned words.

(d) An occasional piece of free writing.

(e) General conversation.

CASE STUDY 5 by Linda Palmer

Name:	Samantha	**Junior School**
Sex:	Girl	
CA:	9 years	
Family:	This child is a middle child of three with an older brother in secondary school, and a younger one in the infants. Her parents appear to be caring about her, and both attended open evening to discuss her progress. Several comments were made, however, by her mother despairing of her daughter, stating that in her opinion she (the daughter) will always be a 'difficult' child.	

Record

News of her behaviour preceded her into the 2nd year juniors. She has unpleasant habits – such as 'licking her nose'. This news was ignored on the basis of preconceptional images of the child. However, when the class met in the autumn term it became apparent that she alienated herself from her peers. She delighted in making them feel sick by her behaviour and they responded by 'spraying the air between her and them' and refusing to put their books next to hers.

Her behaviour towards me at the beginning of this school year (September) was solely attention seeking, apparently just to seek a new teacher's notice (as many children do with a new teacher). As time went on, attention seeking of a more deviant nature occurred. This involved cheating in her work. She could not be trusted to mark her own work on occasions as the rest of the class did. She would come up to the teacher's desk on the pretext of some other problem just to scan the desk in the hope of seeing the answers. This child is quite capable of producing the standard of work required. She (workwise) is in the top half of the class.

A sociogram undertaken by me in October 1981 revealed her to be on the extreme outer rim showing a choice towards a popular girl in her class. There was no choice towards her. On the basis of this and general observation it appeared that she works better sitting alone. Several valiant members of the class (girls) have offered to sit next to her but, on average, have only lasted one day before being moved on request.

Her behaviour culminated in an incident involving self-destruction of her coat (completely soaking it) and refusing to admit her part. She happily allowed three others to be grilled about the incident. She admitted her part after a general chat in class about why it is best to own up etc. and being a responsible 2nd year.

Interventions

Positive intervention by me around this time followed three standard procedures. The initial approach was CBG – this worked extremely well and she responded well to praise. This was followed by further CBG (such as 'I'll see how you mark your work – well done, you have done well' etc. Thirdly, PCI was implemented by means of a general survey. 'Let's see how many people, etc., remember how . . .'.

Results

I must say these three interventions worked extremely well and I felt that towards the end of the autumn term we were 'over the hill' and that we have come to terms with each other. However, since the New Year there has been severe regression. Work has declined and complaints about her behaviour have increased again. Her attention seeking to me reveals itself in a typical morning (eighteen visits to me during work time of one hour). Intervention tactics, as before, will continue with the hope of improvement as before.

I used a 'rank order' repertory grid test on her in the spring term (as per George Kelly 1955). I selected six children from the class to use as elements and various constructs to determine her place in the socio-emotional climate, and to see how she perceived herself in light of the different constructs. The constructs I chose were:

(a) wanted as a friend in class
(b) would like to sit next to in class
(c) is a nuisance in the classroom
(d) works hard in class
(e) is helpful to others in class
(f) works hard for the teacher
(g) is liked by others in class
(h) like me as a person
(i) like I'd really like to be as a person

If constructs (h) and (i) have a fairly close correspondence the individual should be fairly well adjusted. The elements (children) I chose were as follows:

1   female – well adjusted – outgoing
2   male – perceptual problems
3   male – easily top – clever
4   female – easy going – lower end of class
5   female – very quiet – some social problems
6   male – rather hasty – careless.

The results of the repertory test revealed that Samantha does *not* have a close correspondence between 'self' and 'ideal self'. She sees herself as not wanted as a friend, not wanted as a neighbour, not working hard for the teacher, not liked by the others, not helpful in class. She does, however, see herself as not being a nuisance and working moderately hard in class. Her 'ideal self' would be a much more popular child in terms of social acceptance but not working hard, and she feels she ought to be more of a nuisance.

These results, I think, show that this child has difficulties in relating her reflection of her self and her perception of her ideal self. Hence her problems. It has been useful to reveal the areas of great differences for me to work in, and it explains in a clearer light why she has such behaviour problems.

CASE STUDY 6 by S Moriarty

Name:	Mark	**Junior School**
Sex:	Male	
Date of Birth:	26.7.1972	
CA:	9 years 6 months	
Family:	One sister in infants	

General progress
Reading age: September 1981 14.25 years
Spelling age: September 1981 6.75 years
Problems identified as attention-seeking

Incapable of working as a member of the class. Seeks to gain attention especially when the class is working hard. Reads fluently and will often read rather than do what he has been told to do. As long as he reads he is quiet and is able to stay in his place, otherwise he tends to walk around seeking an opportunity to disturb another member of the class. He does this in a rather underhand way, quietly rather than aggressively. He is very much a loner and has no friends in the class or in the playground. He seeks affection and will talk to me quite openly in class, during playtime and at every available opportunity. For his age he appears to have a mature comprehension about what he reads, hears and sees and can explain himself fluently, although his manner is rather eccentric and old fashioned and this rather alienates him from his peers, e.g. reading out his work in class. I do not know whether or not he seeks to be different. He is capable of detailed, interesting stories with an excellent use of vocabulary. His work, however, is untidy and poorly spaced.

Behaviour
Behaviour problems in general are: restlessness, touching other children, picking nose, crawling under desks etc., dropping things thus providing excuses to grope around rocking on chair, laughing quietly at nothing in particular, staring at his neighbours until their attention is obtained, moving furniture about, losing worksheets or destroying them, humming, banging under desk with feet. All behaviour appears to be directed at peers to gain their attention and not mine particularly. Finally, this behaviour results in one of the group calling Mark's name out loudly which is frequently the first I hear of his behaviour although he has hummed while I have read to the class.

Intervention
Made rules explicit, ignored non-damaging behaviour, gave praise and attention when his behaviour was satisfactory, and reprimanded other children when they made undue fuss about his behaviour.

Result
I found that as well as making rules explicit to all the class I had to specifically gain Mark's attention to make sure that he had understood the rules. He is generally very slow at carrying out orders such as 'put your pencils down and face me', 'put all your books away', 'put your reading books away and get on with your maths'.

Ignoring unwanted behaviour was difficult at first because other members of his group complained about his behaviour. I explained to each child that I knew what was happening and not to worry. As well as this I made it quite plain that they often made things much worse by fussing over nothing and were often quite willing to put the blame on Mark when he was not the only one at fault.

Giving praise and attention was not really a problem because Mark has periods when he is quiet and obedient. Initially his behaviour showed a marked improvement. I moved Mark and this seemed to help as well. Suddenly Mark regressed although other members of staff commented on the improvement in his behaviour and his parents were very pleased with his progress. Towards the end of term I lost patience with him, especially during our rehearsal session for the Christmas concert. I had purposely given him a part in the play which was of significance. Previously he had been excluded from these because of bad behaviour. He learned his part well but did not really try very hard to act the part. Once off stage he disturbed the others and took advantage of the fact that I could not see him. During this period I felt that all the good had been undone. I frequently lost my temper and became exasperated. On several occasions I removed him from the stage while he was not on and on one occasion I sent him out of the hall altogether to another class. This term has started off well. Mark has moved to another house in Epsom but his parents want to keep him at our school because he appears to he settling down. I hope so.

Comment
The fact that his reading age is nearly five years above what could be predicted from his chronological age and despite his obvious spelling problem, I suggest that he should be referred for psychological assessment of ability. The profile you have recorded suggests he is an under-functioning gifted or very able child with a severe learning difficulty in relation to spelling. For the spelling problem he needs specialist remedial help on a regular tutorial basis. If he is very bright this will account for much of his difficult behaviour and suggests he also needs PCI, some work at cognitive level suited to his abstract operational level of intellectual development as this will help prevent him getting bored and disruptive.

CASE STUDY 7 by Anne Harrison

Name:	Stewart	**Middle School Remedial Work**
CA:	10 years 9 months (May, 1983)	

Mother and father separated about three years ago but seem to be together again. Stewart was very pale, thin and nervous looking when he joined us in September, 1981 after attending four other schools. He has an older brother who appears to bully him as occasionally he comes to school with bruises.

In May he said 'My father doesn't like me.' I said that all parents get harassed and ratty at times but they really love their children deep down. 'No, mine doesn't,' he replied.

Another boy chipped in with 'My dad loses his temper with me at times – all dads do – but can you blame them?' I hope that helped Stewart.

Other children have told me that Stewart's brother fights him a great deal. He appears to have stopped going to the child guidance clinic because he said 'They just upset me'. He has a persecution complex about one of the men teachers. He says he picks on him, and Stewart is always complaining about him. Could this have something to do with his feelings of rejection by father?

I would like to know how to deal with this, as it has caused some bother from time to time.

Observation
Greeting, 'Guess where my dad is going today?' . . . 'The mortuary!'
Argues about a pen.

'You ain't sittin' 'ere,' to another child who is nowhere near him.
Makes neighing noise – at mention of a horse.
Does doggy paddle.
Says – a propos of nothing. 'If you cut the L out of Douglas you would get Dougal.'
Screws up nose.
Jumps in seat.

While awaiting a TV programme he jumps up and down on bench. Turns round. Touches nose. Turns round and looks at children behind him. Touches under nose. Watches TV programme intently. At the end of programme sways to the music so violently that others are in danger of being knocked off the bench.

Late May He is much quiter when he comes for a lesson. Sits down and may chat to a neighbour until the others appear and we begin. Often asks to go outside and work on a machine.

Stewart's behaviour is considerably below the group level. When not completely absorbed, which is often, he tends to interfere with classmates, e.g. 'You ain't sittin' 'ere.' This was addressed to a boy who was seating himself quietly a few seats away. He is also a master at attention seeking, disruptive behaviour e.g. neighing noise at mere mention of a horse. These types of behaviour are repeated frequently throughout the day and happen in more than one type of situation.

Interventions (CBG and PCI)
His response to management efforts is slow. He seems to be liked by most of the children because he is always good for a laugh, although particular individuals find him aggressive and complain about him when they have been attacked. Stewart gets over any episode quickly. His response to enrichment classwork is positive only when he receives individual attention. In a group of eight his response is slightly better.

Modification of environment
Stewart responds well to work on the synchrofax with one other child – using earphones which seem to shut out distractions and aid his concentration. He enjoys taping a story and writing about autopsies and physiology. I have been able to praise him quite sincerely recently and he has responded well. The only problem is that he doesn't want to return to the classroom!

I have tried to interest his class teacher in the behaviour modification methods but she says she does praise him and support him but he just goes his own wilful way in the class group. He refuses to cooperate if he is not interested in a subject. She is a good teacher but has four other mischievous boys to contend with as well as Stewart. She did say, 'He's all right if you put your arm around him – but I can't do that all day!'

CASE STUDY 8 by Francis Hardy

Name:	Jason	**Junior School**
CA:	10 years 11 months	
RA:	9.9y. (Schonell) July 1982	
IQ:	72 (WISC FQ) October 1982	

Background
Due to very long absences from school during infant schooling, Jason had missed out on a lot of basic language development. Consequently his reading suffered and, as a seven-year-old he was a non-reader. He was then accepted by the reading centre for individual help and gradually began to improve. Now

his reading is much better, but spelling and handwriting still needs assistance. Because he was unable to take part in class lessons for so long due to his lack of reading ability, he tended to 'switch off' and not even contribute orally. He would daydream, draw, throw things or just sit during oral lessons, and wander around the room, chatter or just sit during written lesson times.

He had been segregated by necessity – poor behaviour and lack of ability – and I was anxious to try to make him more 'part of the class', and to join in with oral lessons and written work as far as possible.

Observations
Jason was already sitting by himself, at his request, so the chattering had obviously stopped – unless he got up and walked across the room. During observations he frequently did the following:

1   sat with desk lid up for ages (looking in desk, even when everything he needed was on top of it);
2   got up and wandered across to chatter to another boy;
3   scribbling;
4   deliberately breaking pencils;
5   occasionally throwing things.

During the one-minute observations, the last three actions only occurred once. Therefore I decided to concentrate on the first two actions – and to begin with number 2 – wandering across the room.

Intervention
I felt that Jason usually wandered because he needed help – and rather than ask for it he went in search of it. At least that was his excuse! Often he just wandered because he wanted company – yet he chose to sit by himself.

I decided to go to him at the beginning of every lesson to get him started on his work. I had usually done this when I felt he would have problems, but now I did it for every lesson. I also ignored him when he got up and wandered, but went to him as soon as he returned to his desk.

Results
During the three weeks Jason did wander less, but he also had his 'bad' days. I tried to ignore all his bad behaviour, but on two occasions this proved very difficult:

1   He sat tapping the edge of his desk with a pencil – loudly! This continued during a story of some length. The rest of the class kept looking at him, then at me – expecting me to do something. I could see that they were getting fed up but I was determined not to tell him off. Fortunately the bell went for playtime so I was able to ignore it.
2   He stood chatting to Mark for ages and didn't go back to his own seat for about five minutes. I didn't want to speak to him, but unfortunately Mark then began to play around so I had to tell him off, as other children were in danger. This was unfair on Mark, as Jason got away free!

The main result, though, has been a marked improvement in Jason's work. Obviously he is getting more of my time, so I expected it to improve, but his attitude is also developing along the right lines. He appears to leave his desk less than before – but is away for longer periods than before – because I'm not telling him to return. On reflection I think that things are improving but there is still a long way to go, especially as he is developing new and more annoying habits!

Comment
This is always a particularly difficult problem, he is probably seeing how far you can be pushed.

1   Try asking him to come and do something with you or for you, i.e. distract attention to something else by asking him to bring the

pencil he is tapping to you, or you moving around and taking it from him to avoid him getting up and kicking others on his way without stopping the story. Distract his attention by asking him a question about the story or to guess what will happen next in it (PCI).

2   Now you are getting some improvement, try stopping his annoying behaviour by usual means. Then go to help him soon after he has stopped. There is always the danger that other children start to imitate bad behaviour. Often one has to be unfair and stop them to change the target child's behaviour.

Look forward to hearing how you are getting on. Try a more detailed look/observational record of his off-target behaviour, for example, wandering, just prior to starting if possible. You may then find cues to intervene before he wanders. In which situations does it occur, for example, prior to writing?

Appendix 2: Analysing Handwriting Errors

Letters too small

Letters too large

Body height of letters uneven

Body spaces of the letters uneven

Erratic slant of letters

Mueformation of letters

Too large spaces between

Too small spaces between words

Inability to keep on the line
on the line

Ascenders too long or too short

Descenders too long or not long enough

Uneven spaces between letters

Appendix 3: Remediating Spelling Problems

12 PLUS 1 COGNITIVE-PROCESS APPROACHES TO REMEDIATING SPELLING PROBLEMS

Strategy SOS – Simultaneous Oral Spelling – (Stillman, 1932) to be used when all else fails. These strategies are set out as follows:

12 PLUS 1 STRATEGIES FOR SPELLING

Articulation – make sure the mis-spelled word is correctly and clearly articulated for spelling, e.g. chim(l)ey should be corrected to chimney and skel(ing)ton to skeleton. These are common errors of speech.

Over articulation – to remind the student of difficult parts of a word, e.g. parli(a)ment and gover(n)ment.

Cue articulation – say the word incorrectly to remind the student of the area of difficulty and to cue the correct spelling, e.g. necessary spoken as neckessary to remind one that the c comes before the ss's, or Wed*nes*day for We'n'sday.

Syllabification – it is easier to spell a word broken down into short syllables than spell it as a whole. Syllabifying helps avoid contractions, e.g. misdeanour – mis/de/mean/our; criticed – crit/i/cise/d. Contractions of polysyllabic words are typical of the student mis-speller. They must learn to spell a difficult polysyllabic word syllable by syllable.

Phonics – this is assigning a grapheme, a written unit, to a phoneme, a sound unit. For most words in English there is not direct sound to symbol correspondences, it only occurs in regular words in its simplest form, e.g. bed, bred, bled, pin, tram, plan. After this orthographic rules have to be applied. However, the application of these simple one to one correspondences denotes progress in spelling and can act as the framework for developing correct spelling. It provides a comprehensible skeleton and can be read correctly, e.g. marstr (master); mstry (mystery); nite time (night time). This last mis-spelling is more advanced than basic phonics incorporating orthographic knowledge beyond phoneme – grapheme correspondence. This is knowledge of the long vowel sound in a syllable denoted by the silent 'e'.

Funnies – it is sometimes not possible to apply any of the foregoing but something funny or rude can aid the memory, e.g. one subject used 'knickers' to remind her, another 'cess pit' which is also an analogy strategy to spell *necessary* correctly.

Meaning – words such as *separate* are commonly incorrectly spelled as sep(e)rate. You may know you spell it wrongly but cannot remember which is the correct version. 'Parting' or 'paring' can be used as meaning cues to correct spelling. The word's origin from 'parere' can be a second clue.

Origin – the word's roots in another language often provide the framework for correct recall, e.g. sen(c)ation was mis-spelled as well as 'sen(c)e'. The origin is SENS in both French (feeling) and Latin and helped to put the word right. For the word opportunity, commonly mis-spelled opp(u)rtunity, the origin is *port* or harbour, an effective or timely opening. This revelation clears up the mis-spelling.

Rule – e.g. 'i before e except after c'; receive, perceive; and 'when two vowels go walking the first one does the talking': breath, breathe, main, steal; there are always a few exceptions to the general rules, or another less common rule applies.

Family – this is often helpful in recalling silent letters and correct representations of the schwa (a) or 'uh' sound in some words, e.g. for Canada – Canadian, telephone – telepathic, telescope, television; for these words the *meaning/origin* clues can also be used for *tele*. Bomb, bombardment, bombardier.

Analogy – comparison with similar words or parts of words. Students should learn to say, e.g. 'it is like' braggart with two gs in braggadocio, or it is like a maze with only one z in hazard.

Orthographic or **Psycho-linguistic Structure** – affixing and syllable structure rules, e.g. effects of short and long vowel sounds in closed syllables:
short – bid (cvc)
long – bide (cvce)
When affixing short vowel syllables – double and add suffix, e.g. bid/ding.
When affixing long vowel syllables – drop 'e' and add suffix e.g. bid/ing.
When stress occurs in the second syllable, doubling occurs – reference, referral.

SOS simultaneous oral spelling – devised by Stillman (1932) is the plus 1 to be used when all else fails.
1   Identify areas of difficulty.
2   Write correctly from dictionary once, lower case.
3   *Naming* letters as you do so.
4   Fold paper to cover word.
5   Spell word aloud (naming) as you write it. Repeat 3, 4, 5 until word is spelled correctly 3 times in a row. Check each time with original.

Bibliography

ACE (1980) *Survey of Disruptive Units* (Sin bin Survey). London Advisory Centre for Education.

ACE (1981) *Suspension*, **166**, 20–6. London: ACE.

ACE (1982) *Working Together: Training Exercises for Governors, Headteachers in Primary Schools:* Joan Sallis. London: ACE.

AINSCOW, M. and TWEDDLE, D.A. (1979) *Preventing Classroom Failure an Objectives Approach* Chichester: Wiley.

AINSCOW, M. and TWEDDLE, D.A. (1984) *Early Learning Skills Analysis (ELSA)*. Chichester: Wiley.

AMMA (1986) *The Reception Class Today AMMA Report of 1984 Survey.* London: AMMA.

ARGYLE, M. (1984) *The Psychology of Interpersonal Behaviour.* Harmondsworth: Penguin.

ARGYRIS, C. (1971) in HANDY, G. *The Psychology of Organisations* (pp.319–20 and 340–1). Harmondsworth: Penguin.

AWMC (1984) *Report on Maladjustment of the Association for Workers with Maladjusted Children.* London: AWMC.

BANDURA, A. and WALTERS, R.H. (1963) *Social Learning and Personality Development.* London: Holt Rinehart and Winston.

BARKER, P. (1975) School phobia and truancy, *Practitioner*, **213**, 316–22.

BECKER W.C., BEREITER, C. and ENGLEMANN, S. (1966) *Teaching Disadvantaged Children in Pre-school.* New Jersey: Prentice Hall.

BECKER, W.C., MADSEN, C.H., ARNOLD, C.R. and THOMAS, D.R. (1967) 'The contingent use of teacher reinforcement and praise in reducing classroom behaviour problems', *Journal of Special Education* **1** 287–307.

BENNETT, N. (1976) *Teaching Styles and Pupil Performance.* London: Open Books.

BENNETT, N. (1986) Collaborative learning: Children do it in groups do they? Paper presented at DECP conference, London.

BENNETT, N. and JORDAN, A. (1975) 'A typology of teaching styles in primary schools' *British Journal of Educational Psychology*, **45**, 1, 20–8.

BERNE, E. (1957) *Games People Play.* Harmondsworth: Pelican.

BLACKHAM C.J. and SILBERMAN (1972) *Modification of Child Behaviour.* Belmont California Wadsworth.

BLAGG, N. (1988) *School Phobia and its Treatment.* Beckenham: Croom Helm.

BLAKEBROUGH, E. (1986) *No Quick Fix.* Basingstoke: Marshal Pickering.

BOOTH, A. (1982) *Special Biographies.* (OU Course E241) Milton Keynes: Open University Press.

BOOTH, A., POTTS, P. and SWANN, W. (eds) (1987) *Preventing Difficulties in Learning.* Oxford: Basil Blackwell.

BOWERS, S. and WELLS, L. (1985) *Ways and Means.* Kingston Polytechnic Learning Difficulties Project.

BOWERS, S. and WELLS, L. (1988) *Ways and Means update.* Kingston Polytechnic Learning Difficulties Project.

BRENNAN, W.K. (1979) *Curricular Needs of Slow Learners Working Paper No. 63*. London: Evans/Methuen Educational.

BROOKS, G., LATHAM, J. and REX, A. (1987) *Developing Oral Skills*. London: Heinemann.

CAMERON, R.J. and WESTMACOTT. E.V.S. (1981) *Behaviour can change*. Basingstoke: Macmillan.

CARVER, V. (1978) *Child Abuse*. Milton Keynes: Open University Press.

CHAZAN, M. (1964) 'The incidence and nature of maladjustment amongst children in schools for the educationally sub-normal' *British Journal of Educational Psychology*, **34**, 3.

CHISHOLM, B., KEARNEY, D. KNIGHT, G., LITTLE, H., MORRIS, S. and TWEDDLE, D.(1986) *Preventive Approaches to Disruption (PAD) Developing Teaching Skills*. London: Macmillan.

COHEN, A. and COHEN, L (eds) (1981) *Meeting Special Educational Needs in Ordinary Schools*. Milton Keynes: Open University Press.

COOPER, M.G. (1966) 'School Refusal An Inquiry into the Part Played by School and Home' *Educational Research*, **8**. 3, 223–9.

CRITCHLEY, M. (1970) *The Dsylexic Child*. London: Heinemann.

CROLL, P. and MOSES, D. (1985) *One in Five*. London: Routledge and Kegan Paul.

DAVIE, R. (1972) 'The behaviour and adjustment in schools of seven-year-olds: sex and social class differences' *Early Child Development and Care*, **2**, 1, 39-47.

DAVIE, R. (1988) 'Summary of NCB Report' *Times Educational Supplement*.

DAWSON, R, (ed.) (1985) *TIPs* (The Macmillan Teacher Information Pack). Basingstoke: Macmillan.

DENSCOMBE, M. (1985) *Classroom Control: A Sociological Perspective*. London: Allen and Unwin.

DEPARTMENT OF EDUCATION AND SCIENCE (1955) *Report of the Committee on Maladjusted Behaviour* (Underwood Report). London: HMSO.

DEPARTMENT OF EDUCATION AND SCIENCE (1978) *Special Educational Needs* (The Warnock Report). London: HMSO.

DEPARTMENT OF EDUCATION AND SCIENCE (1979) *Aspects of Secondary Education: A Survey of HMI*. London: HMSO.

DEPARTMENT OF EDUCATION AND SCIENCE (1981) *The School Curriculum*. London: HMSO.

DEPARTMENT OF EDUCATION AND SCIENCE (1983) *Assessment and Statements of Special Educational Needs* Circ 1/83. London: HMSO.

DEPARTMENT OF EDUCATION AND SCIENCE (1984) *CATE Criteria*. London: HMSO.

DEPARTMENT OF EDUCATION AND SCIENCE (1985) *Better Schools*. London: HMSO.

DEPARTMENT OF EDUCATION AND SCIENCE (1986) *Lower Attainers Pilot Project*. London: HMSO.

DEPARTMENT OF EDUCATION AND SCIENCE (1987) *The National Curriculum 5–16*. London: HMSO.

DOCKING, J.W. (1980) *Control and Discipline in Schools. Perspectives and approaches*. London: Harper and Row.

DONALDSON, M. (1978) *Children's Minds*. London: Fontana.

DOUGLAS, J.W.B. (1964) *The Home and the School*. London: MacGibbon and Key.

ESTES, W.K. (1964) 'Probability Learning, in MELTON. A.W. (ed.) *Categories of Human Learning*. New York: Academic Press.

GALLOWAY, D. (1981) *Teaching and Counselling: Pastoral Care in Primary Schools*. London: Longman.

GALLOWAY, D. and GOODMAN, C. (1987) *The Education of Disturbing Children*. London: Longman.

GALTON, M., SIMON, B. and CROLL, P. (1980) *Inside the Primary Classroom*. London: Routledge and Kegan Paul.

GALVIN, J.P. and ANNESLEY, F.R. (1971) 'Reading and arithmetic correlates of conduct problem and withdrawn children' *Journal of Special Education*, **5** 213–19.

GUILFORD, J.P. (1959) *Personality*. New York: McGraw Hill.

GULLIFORD, R. (1971) *Backwardness and Educational Failure*. Windsor: NFER.

HALL, R.V. (1976) *Managing Behaviour, Behaviour Modification*. Lawrence Kah H & H Enterprises Inc.

HAMBLIN, D.H. (1986) 'The failure of pastoral care' In REID, K. (ed.) *School Organisation*, **6**, 1.

HAMMERSLEY, M. (1976) 'The mobilisation of pupil attention' in HAMMERSLEY, M. and WOODS, P. (eds) *The Process of Schooling*. London: Routledge and Kegan Paul.

HARGREAVES, D. (1976) *Deviance in Classrooms*. London: Routledge and Kegan Paul.

HARGREAVES, D. (1984) *Improving Secondary Schools*. London: ILEA.

HARROP, A. (1984) *Behaviour Modification in the Classroom*. London: Unibooks.

HEMMING, J. (1988) Quality or Control in Education? WEF GB Conference Kingston Polytechnic *New Era in Education*.

HERBERT, M. (1975) *Problems of Childhood*. London: Pan.

HERSOV, L. and BERG, I. (eds) (1980) *Out of School: Modern Perspectives in Training and School Phobia*. Chichester: Wiley.

HEWITT, L.E. and JENKINS, R.L. (1946) *Fundamental Patterns of Maladjustment: The Dynamics of their Origin*. Springfield Illinois: Illinois Publications.

HMI (1986) *Lower Attaining Pupils Project*. London: HMSO.

HMI (1988) *Secondary School Survey*. London: HMSO.

HMI (1988) *The New Teacher in School*. London: HMSO

HOLT, J. (1969) *How Children Fail*. Harmondworth: Penguin, Reprinted 1984.

JARMAN, C. (1979) *The Development of Handwriting Skills*. Oxford: Basil Blackwell.

JENKINS, R.L. (1966) 'Psychiatric syndromes in children and their relation to family background' *American Journal of Orthopsychiatry*, **36**, 450–7.

JOURARD, S.M. (1966) 'An exploratory study of body accessibility' *British Journal of Social and Clinical Psychology*, **5**, 221–31.

KEMPE, H.C. and KEMPE, R. (1978) *Child Abuse*. London: Open Books.

KEMPE, R. and KEMPE, H.C. (1984) *The Common Secret: Sexual Abuse of Children and Adolescents*. New York: W.H. Freeman.

KENNEDY, W.A. (1965) School Phobia: 'A rapid treatment of 50 cases' *Journal Abnormal Psychology*, **70**, 4, 285–9.

KERRY, T.L. (1979) in WRAGG E.C. and KERRY, T.L. *op. cit.*

KERRY, T.L. (1983) *Finding and Helping the Able Child*. London: Croom Helm.

KOUNIN, J.S. (1970) *Discipline and Group Management in Classrooms*. New York: Holt Rinehart and Winston.

KRAUPL-TAYLOR, E. (1966) *Psychopathology*. London: Butterworths.

LASLETT, R. (1977) *Educating Maladjusted Children*. London: Crosby Lockwood and Staples.

LASLETT, R. (1985) A follow-up study of children leaving three residential schools for the maladjusted. *Maladjustment and Theraputic Education*, **3**, 1, 13–28.

LAWRENCE, J., STEED, D. and YOUNG, P. (1984) *Disruptive Children – Disruptive Schools*. London: Croom Helm.

LYKKEN, D. (1969) Personal communication. Also refer Ullman and Krasner (1969) p.449.

MACDONALD, E. (1978) *Women in Management*. London: E. MacDonald.

MASLOW, A.H. (1962) *Towards a Psychology of Being*. Princetown: Van Nostrand.

MCCORD, W., MCCORD, J. and ZOLA, J.K. (1959) *Origins of Crime*. New York: Columbia Press.

MCLAUGHLIN, H. (1969) Smog Grading – a new readability formula (Simple Measure of Gobbledygook (SMOG)) *Journal of Reading*, **22**, 639–46.

MILES, T.R. (1983) *Dyslexia – The pattern of difficulties*. London: Granada.

MITCHELL, S. and ROSA, P. (1981) 'Boyhood behaviour problems as precursors of criminality: a 15 year follow-up study' *Journal of Child Psychology and Psychiatry*, **22**, 1, 19–33.

MONGON, D. (1985) 'Patterns of delivery and its implications for training' in SAYER, J. and JONES, N. (eds) *Teacher Training and Special Educational Needs*. Beckenham: Croom Helm.

MONGON, D. and HART, S. (1988) *Making a Diference*. London: Cassell.

MONTGOMERY, D. (1983) *Study Skills; Learning and Teaching Strategies:* Kingston Polytechnic Learning Difficulties Project.

MONTGOMERY, D. (1984) *Managing Behaviour Problems:* Kingston Polytechnic Learning Difficulties Project.

MONTGOMERY, D. (1985) *Helping Able Pupils in the Ordinary Classroom:* Kingston Polytechnic Learning Difficulties Project.

MONTGOMERY, D. (1988) 'Teacher Appraisal' *The New Era in Education*, **68**, 3, 85–90.

MONTGOMERY, D. (1989) *Children with Learning Difficulties*. London: Cassell.

MONTGOMERY, D., RAWLINGS, A. and HADFIELD, N. (1987) *Lifesavers*. Leamington Spa: Scholastic.

MORSE, P. (1986) *The Handwriting Copy Book:* Kingston Polytechnic Learning Difficulties Project.

MOSES, D. (1982) in CROLL, P. and MOSES, D. *op. cit.*

O'LEARY, K.D. and O'LEARY, S.C. (eds) (1973) *Classroom Management: The Successful Use of Behaviour Management*. New York: Pergamon.

OPPÉ, T.E. (1979) *Child Abuse: Identification Issues and Problems:* Year of the Child Multidisciplinary Conference, Kingston Polytechnic.

ORACLE (1978) Report in GALTON *et al. op. cit.*

ORNSTEIN, R. (1977) *The Psychology of Consciousness* (2nd Edition). New York: Harcourt Brace Jovanovitch.

OSGOOD, C.E., SUCI, G.J. and TANNENBAUM, P.H. (1957) *The Measurement of Meaning*. London: University Illinois Press.

PECK, R.F. and HAVIGHURST, R.J. (1960) *The Psychology of Character Development*. London: John Wiley.

PETERS, M. and SMITH, B. (1986) 'The Productive Process: An approach to literacy for children with difficulties' in ROOT, B. (ed.) *Resources for Reading*. Reading: UKRA.

PIAGET, J. (1952) *The Origins of Intelligence in Children*. New York: International University Press.

PRINGLE, K.M. (1973) *Able Misfits*. London: Longmans/NCB.

PRINGLE, K.M. (1980) *The Needs of Children* (2nd Edition). London: Hutchinson.

PURKEY, W.W. (1970) *Self Concept and School Achievement* New York: Prentice Hall.

REID, K. (1986) *Disaffection from School*. London: Methuen.

RICH, J. (1956) 'Types of stealing' *Lancet* **496**.

ROBINS, L. (1966) *Deviant Children Grow Up* 1922–66. Baltimore: Williams and Williams.

ROBINSON, M. (1981) *Schools and Social Work* London: Routledge and Kegan Paul.

RUTTER, M. (1975) *Helping Troubled Children*. Harmondsworth: Penguin.

RUTTER, M.L. and MADGE, N. (1976) *Cycles of Disadvantage*. London: Heinemann.

RUTTER, M.L., MAUGHAN, M., MORTIMORE, P. and OUSTON, J. (1979) *Fifteen Thousand Hours*. London: Open Books.

RUTTER, M., TIZARD, J. and WHITMORE, K. (eds) (1970) *Educational Health and Behaviour*. London: Longman.

SCOTT MCDONALD, W. (1971) *Battle in the Classroom*. Brighton: Intext.

SCOTTISH EDUCATION DEPARTMENT (SED) (1978) *The Education of Pupils with Learning Difficulties in Primary and Secondary Schools: A Progress Report by HMI*. Edinburgh: HMSO.

SHEPHERD, M., OPPENHEIM, B. and MITCHELL, S. (1971) *Childhood Behaviour and Mental Health*. London: London University Press.

SKINNER, B.F. (1953) *Science and Human Behaviour*. New York: Macmillan.

SOLITY, J. and BULL, S. (1987) *Special Needs: Bridging the Curriculum Gap* Milton Keynes: Open University Press.

STENHOUSE, L.A. (1975) *An Introduction to Curriculum Research and Development*. London: Heinemann.

STILLMAN, B. (1932) Quoted in GILLINGHAM, A. and STILLMAN, B. (1940, 1956 and 1970) *Remedial Training for Children with Specific Disability in Reading, Spelling and Penmanship'*. New York: Sackett and Williams.

STORMER, D. (1970) 'Disruptive behaviour', *Therapeutic Education*, **2**, 32–8.

SCOTT, D.H. (1981) 'Behaviour disturbance and failure to learn: A study of cause and effect', *Educational Research* **23**, 3.

THOMAS, L. and HARRI-AUGSTEIN, S. (1984) *Learning Conversations: Self-organised Learning*. Kingston Polytechnic: SCEDSIP/COPOL Conference.

THORNDIKE, E.L. (1931) *Human Learning*. New York: Prentice Hall.

ULLMAN, L.P. and KRASNER (1969) *A Psychological Approach to Abnormal Behaviour* (2nd Edition 1975). London: Prentice Hall.

WAGNER, R.F. (1971) *Dyslexia and Your Child* New York: Harper and Row (Revised 1979).

WEST, D.J. (1967) *The Young Offender*. Harmondsworth: Penguin.

WEST, D.J. (1982) *Delinquency*. London: Heinemann.

WHELDALL, K. (1988) 'Noisiest lads are likeliest to succeed' *Times Educational Supplement*, September.

WHELDALL, K. and MERRITT, F. (1984) *Positive Teaching; The Behavioural Approach*. London: Unwin Educational.

WHELDALL, K. and MERRITT, F. (1985) *BATPACK Positive Products*. Birmingham: Birmingham University.

WHELDALL, K. and MERRITT, F. (1986) 'Looking for a positive route out of poor class behaviour' *Special Children*, **2**, 22–7.

WHELDALL, K., MORRIS, M. and VAUGHAN, D. (1981) 'Rows versus tables: an example of the use of behavioural ecology in two classes of eleven-year-old children', *Educational Psychology* **1**, 171–84.

WHELDALL, K. and RIDING, R. (eds) (1983) *Psychological Aspects of Teaching and Learning*. Beckenham: Croom Helm.

WILSON, M. and EVANS, M. (1980) *Education of Disturbed Children*. London: Schools Council/Methuen.

WOOD, J. (1984) *Adapting Instruction for the Mainstream*. Columbus Ohio: Charles E. Merrill.

WOOD, S. and SHEARS, B. (1986) *Teaching Children with Severe Learning Difficulties: A Radical Reappraisal*. London: Croom Helm.

WRAGG, E.C. (ed) (1984) *Classroom Teaching Skills*. Beckenham: Croom Helm.

WRAGG, E.C. and KERRY, T.L. (1979) *Classroom Interaction Research*. Nottingham: Nottingham University.

WRIGHT, D. (1960) In MUSSEN, P.H. *Handbook of Research Methods in Child Development*.

Index

abuse
  child   48–50
  drug   10, 27, 37–8
ACE   7, 11
acting out   43
administrative routines   116
affirmation   139
aggression   29, 125
agoraphobia   44
ambience   123
anxiety   42–3
arrivals   115
assessment through teaching   91
Association of Workers with
  Maladjusted Children (AWMC)   6,
  8
attention
  gaining   29
  seeking   29, 40, 43–4
austere parents   30
authoritarian style   22

BATPAK   57, 89
Becker *et al.*   67–9
behaviour
  contract (BC)   97–8
  disturbance   5–12
  management scheme   76–7
  problems   9, 13, 80
behavioural
  aspects of emotion   45
  objectives   90
  strategies   93
Bennett, N.   35, 37
bias, observer   82
Booth, A.   3
boredom   10, 38
Brennan, W.K.   11
bullying   127–8

calming strategies   108
case conference   128
'catch them being good' (CBG)   61–2,
  75, 96, 99–100
cognitive
  exhilaration   38
  intervention strategies   96–99, 101

comforting offences   52
coming in and going out   114
compensating parents   31
cone zone   121
confidants   42
conflict resolution   138–40
confrontation with colleagues   129–
  30
construct systems   80
contingent reinforcement   67–8
control statements   112
cooperation   139, 143
critical incident analysis   17
Croll, P. and Moses, D.   10, 11, 104
cueing   18, 19, 20, 107–8, 110, 139
curriculum   10

Dawson, R.   51
delinquency   5, 6
depression   46, 47
DES aims   74–5
desist behaviours   63
deviant family approaches   32–3
deviant personality approaches   34
diary description   80
differentiation   144
direct instruction   91–2
discipline   113, 121
dismissing   115
display   123–4
disruption   3, 4, 5, 8–9, 10
dominance   120
dominance checklist   120
drug abuse   10, 27, 37–8

Education Act 1981   7, 91
EDY project   89
ego states   23, 29, 33
emotional
  behavioural difficulties   7, 42–3
  health   43, 44–6
  illness   43, 46
  problems   42, 44
'engage brain'   136–43
equipment routines   116, 118
exclusions   128

failure
  to cope   20, 27
  to learn   13
fear of failure   56
fighting   125–6
furniture   123

gaining
  attention   107
  quiet   114–15
Galloway, D. and Goodwin, C.   5, 11, 26
galvanic skin response (GSR)   34–5
'game', the   34
good managers   21
group work   121–2
Gulliford, J.P.   6

handwriting   106, 159
Hargreaves, D.   9, 35, 39
Hegarty *et al.*   104
Herbert, M.   42
HMI   8, 9, 12, 14, 35
Holt, J.   11
hysteria   46

ignoring bad behaviour   126–7
immature parents   30, 31
inadequacy   33
inconsistent disciplining   30
independence   117
individual instruction   89–91
indulgent parents   31
inference   81
inferiority feelings   33
inhibition and positive reinforcement (IPR)   93
integration   10

Jenkins, R.L.   29–33

Kingston Friends Workshop Group   138–42
Kingston Polytechnic Learning Difficulties Research Project   1, 9, 13

Laslett, R.   11
Lawrence *et al.*   30–1
leading into the hall   116
learning difficulties   11, 13, 94, 106
lesson phases   132–5
liaison   25–6
lining up   113–14
locus of control   43
lowest likely level of intervention   105
Lykken, D.   34

MacDonald, E.   21
maintenancing behaviour   37, 103
management skills   37, 101–4
Maslow, A.H.   65
mediation   140–1
meeting and greeting   20
'meeting of friends' smile   19
metacognition   90
modelling and positive reinforcement (MPR)   93, 94
Mongon, D.   40
monitoring   36, 102–3, 107

naming   103
national curriculum   11, 27, 91
neglect by parents   30, 48
negotiation   141–2
nervous
  health   43
  illness   43
neurosis   42–4
neurotic behaviour problems   33
'not sure if I can cope' smile   19

observation recording system   79–88
observing behaviour   43, 80, 81, 83–8, 107
obsessional compulsions   46
OK boss   23
omnipotence   127
ORACLE   104
organisation of setting   121–4
organisational responses to disruption   128
over-indulgent parents   31

preventive approaches to disruption (PAD)   89
paradigm   81–2
parents crushes   109–10
parents' role   66
pastoral care   26–7
peer relationships   143
person perception   16
personality theory   28
phobias   46, 50–2
physical contact   108
physiological aspects of emotion   44
policing   36–7
positive attitude to learning (PAL)   75, 76
positive cognitive intervention (PCI)   62, 75, 100–1, 142–3
positive incentives   59, 66
probationary teachers   8
problem-resolving strategies   140, 141–2

problem solving   137–8, 140
prosocial behaviour   89
pseudo-social behaviour
    problems   32, 33
punishment   58, 59, 60, 61, 66, 68
pyramiding   76, 136

questions   94
queues   121–2

readability   136
reading difficulties   14
record sheets   83–7
recording   79–88
referral   128
Reid, K.   9, 26
reinforcements   58, 60, 65, 66, 68, 69
rejection by parents   31
reprimands   107
rewards   59
ripple effect   64, 107
risk   33, 38–40, 125
role shift and positive reinforcement
    (RSPR)   94–5
Rutter et al.   13

school
    aims   74
    ethos   35, 36
    phobia   46, 52–4
    refusal   50–2
    uniform   20–1
Scott Macdonald, W.   61–5
Scottish Education Department
    (SED)   12
self-esteem   54–7
sending out   96
shouting   113
smiles   19–20
social
    agenda   112
    skills   16–24
socially disapproved behaviours   5
socialised behaviour problems   29, 32
socio-emotional theory   28–41
sociopath   34
Solity, J. and Bull, S.   91, 92
special needs   136
special needs action programme
    (SNAP)   89

specific learning difficulties   14, 106
spelling difficulties   14, 106
squabbling   125–6
staffroom rules   129–30
starting lessons   135
stealing   30, 52–4
Stenhouse, L.A.   91
'stink look'   105, 112
stress   42, 44
study skills   117
supportive positive attitude
    (SPA)   63, 75

tables   117, 121
tactical lesson plan   132–5
targeting   80
task
    analysis   89–90
    directed arrangements   122
    management   131, 136–8
teacher information packs (TIPs)   51,
    89
Teachers Action Collective (TAC)   26
teacher's kit   123
telling and asking   20
temper tantrums   125, 126–7
temporary exclusions   128
theft   52–4
theories of behaviour
    disturbance   28–9
time out (TO)   30, 95
time sampling   80
token economies   30, 96
transactional analysis   22, 23
truancies   9, 124–5
trusties   117

Underwood Report   6
unsocialised behaviour problems   29,
    30, 31

victimiser   34

Warnock Report   7, 10, 91
West, D.J.   6, 9, 10, 39
Wheldall et al.   44, 57, 58, 108
Wilson, M. and Evans, M.   11, 40
withdrawal   10, 42
Wood, S, Shears, B.   91
working groups   74